English
Transformational
Grammar

RODERICK A. JACOBS

University of California at San Diego

PETER S. ROSENBAUM

Teachers College, Columbia University

With an Epilogue by
Paul M. Postal

Thomas J. Watson Research Center, IBM Corporation

Xerox College Publishing

Lexington, Massachusetts | *Toronto*

To Joan and Suzie

Preface

When we speak of studying transformational grammar, we refer to a framework within which a number of questions about human intellectual capacity, questions concerning the knowledge involved in "speaking" a language, have been answered and currently are being answered. This framework is a set of principles, called linguistic universals, which allow us to describe what we, as native speakers of English, know about our language intuitively. Without such guiding principles, it would be very difficult, if not impossible, to obtain a correct description of English. Before we can describe what we know, we must know *how* to describe it; we must know, in other words, how to classify the facts which we observe.

These linguistic facts cannot be classified by any random method; they must be classified so they represent all that we know about our language and only that information. After investigating some of these facts in the chapters of this book, you will be able to appreciate that it is no simple matter to discover a classification scheme which meets this requirement. If such a classification scheme, in the form of a set of principles, existed right now, the description of our language would not be the enormously difficult task that it is at present. Unfortunately, only the barest outline of this set of principles is visible. This means that we can acquire at the moment only the most general understanding of our own competence to speak and comprehend the sentences of English. Not only will our understanding necessarily be incomplete; it will often, when we overextend our speculations and make unjustified assumptions about how to organize the facts, be incorrect. There are a great many observations to be made about English which the following chapters completely ignore. In part, this neglect is the result of simply not understanding how these various observations are related and how they should be classified. Under such circumstances it is possible to do no more than state the data, the raw facts, which are scarcely of interest in themselves. Furthermore, the text proposes a number of descriptions, for example those of aspect and the auxiliary, which have not been universally accepted and which compete with alternative descriptions proposed by other grammarians studying these topics. Thus, exclusive correctness for these analyses cannot be claimed. We must be satisfied, at present, that such analyses are, at the very least, consistent with the more or less established linguistic principles and are, furthermore, adequate with respect to the facts they purport to describe. The crux of these matters is that not enough is known about how linguistic facts are to be organized correctly.

These seemingly bleak observations about the current state of scientific knowledge of linguistic phenomena are not intended either as a disparaging evaluation or as a gloomy prognosis. Quite the contrary, these remarks constitute a challenge to the inquiring intellect. More has been learned in the past fifteen years about the organization of human linguistic knowledge than at any time since the seventeenth century, when similar questions were addressed by French philosophers and grammarians under the intellectual leadership of Descartes. Furthermore, during the same fifteen-year period, the scientific understanding of the grammar of English, the set of defining rules which represents linguistic knowledge, has grown enormously. The meaning of these developments is clear and impressive. Linguistic research has produced, and is currently producing, results which constitute something of a breakthrough in the study of the operations and behavior of the human mind.

Since linguistic universals determine the form of a complete and accurate representation of what human beings know when they know a language (or would, in any case, if we knew them all), these concepts tell us exactly what makes human intelligence so human, what makes it unique. They tell us of the innate propensities of the human organism to acquire behavioral and intellectual characteristics which set it apart from other animal organisms. Taken together with a complete and accurate description of a particular language, constructed in accordance with them, these universals would provide the information necessary to answer questions about the strategy by means of which human beings acquire a language in the first place.

As you can see, the search for linguistic universals and the construction of a correct description of a speaker's linguistic knowledge must go hand in hand. Without justifiable universals, it is impossible to know whether a proposed description is correct. Without grammatical descriptions which make empirical claims about the speaker's knowledge, it is impossible to test the correctness of the proposed universals. The consequence of this is that it is not particularly illuminating to speak in the abstract of either the grammatical description of a language or the universals which constitute a theory of grammars. Each must be discussed in the context of the other. To a certain extent these two dimensions have been integrated in this book. The discussion of the existence of deep and surface structures, of transformational rules composed of elementary transformational processes (substitution, deletion, and adjunction), of the fact that transformations are partially ordered, of the recursive character of the phrase structure rules allowing the embedding of sentences within sentences, and so forth, is a treatment of linguistic universals, of properties which all human languages will share. On the other hand, other parts of the presentation deal with the particular deep structures and transformations contained in English—in other words, with the general topic of how English as a system of knowledge makes use of the kinds of constructs given by the linguistic universals.

To speak, then, of transformational grammar is to speak of a point of view concerning what questions about human language are important to ask and to answer. These questions invariably center upon the nature of the abilities displayed by human beings in acquiring and using a language. Partial answers to a number of questions of this sort have already been provided; certain of these are implicit in the analyses of the various syntactic constructions proposed in the chapters which follow. Others, because of their complexity, are not presented. Despite the progress made so far, attempts to develop a comprehensive theory of grammars and precise descriptions of actual human languages in terms of such a theory are in their preliminary stages. The theoretical proposals set forth in this volume are already being questioned and modified. Correspondingly, the syntactic descriptions currently ascribed to most of the constructions in English studied in the early days of transformational research are, wherever possible, being revamped so as to accord with newer and more insightful formulations of linguistic universals. In this way, the science of transformational grammar progresses, rarely in an atmosphere of certainty and security, always in an atmosphere of challenge and curiosity.

Three people were of fundamental importance to the creation of this book (although, it goes without saying, they are in no way responsible for the correctness of the linguistic formulations). The first is John Ross of M.I.T., who spent many hours dissecting the original manuscript on linguistic and stylistic grounds and supplying the authors with invaluable comments. The second person is Cay Dietrich of IBM, Thomas J.

Watson Research Center, who gave the authors extensive editorial assistance. If this presentation is comprehensible, it is largely the result of Miss Dietrich's ability to detect and express the essential components of complex ideas. The third person is Noam Chomsky of M.I.T., who was kind enough to review the manuscript in detail, after the final draft had been prepared. Professor Chomsky offered a great many helpful suggestions which, wherever feasible, were incorporated into the copy-edited manuscript. To these three people the authors offer their thanks.

R.A.J.
P.S.R.

Contents

SECTION ONE | *The Study of Language*

1. Language As a Scientific Subject Matter   3
2. Constituent Structure   10
3. Deep Structures, Surface Structures, and Transformations   17
4. Transformations and Elementary Transformational Processes   23
5. Linguistic Explanation and Ordered Rules   30

SECTION TWO | *Constituents and Features*

6. Determining the Constituents of a Sentence   37
7. Noun Phrase Constituents   44
8. Verb Phrase Constituents   52
9. Features, Lexical Items, and Deep Structures   59
10. Constituent Functions   70

SECTION THREE | *Segment Transformations and Syntactic Processes*

11. Articles, Suffixes, and Segment Transformations   81
12. Pronouns and Articles   92
13. Verbals and Particles   100
14. Aspect—Perfect and Progressive   108

15. The Auxiliary   120

16. Agreement   130

17. Prepositions   136

18. Prepositions, Indirect Objects, and the Cross-Over Principle   143

19. Questions   150

SECTION FOUR | *Sentence Embedding*

20. Noun Phrase Complements and Complementizers   163

21. Extraposition and "It" Deletion   171

22. Indirect (or Embedded) Questions   179

23. "It" Replacement, Reflexives, and Synonymy   184

24. Verb Phrase Complements   192

25. Relative Clauses   199

SECTION FIVE | *Simplicity and Linguistic Explanation*

26. Pronouns and Case   217

27. Simplicity and the Search for Deep Structures   224

28. The Cyclic Principle   235

SECTION SIX | *Conjunction*

29. Conjunction and Non-Restrictive Clauses   253

Epilogue   267

Index   290

SECTION ONE

The Study of Language

CHAPTER 1

Language as a Scientific Subject Matter

The most puzzling scientific mysteries are often uncovered when scientists investigate natural phenomena that are taken for granted. Until this century the color change of metal during heating was known to every blacksmith, but was not explainable by classical physics. Max Planck, the German physicist, studied this phenomenon and derived a rule that became the basis of modern quantum physics. The primary purpose of this book is to call attention to the mysteries of a natural phenomenon common to the experience of every normal human being —the knowledge and use of language—and to present some partial explanations of these mysteries. Most of the major discoveries in this field have yet to be made.

The mysteries about language that will be discussed here seem trivial and obvious at first sight. For example: Every normal human being is capable of distinguishing the sentences of his language from all other objects in the universe. Yet, how can this fact be explained? A sentence is a *string* of words, but not every string of words is a sentence. The following strings are English sentences:

1. the trains are most crowded during the holidays } *normal*
2. aren't you thinking of a perambulator?
3. wash that car before breakfast!

Suppose the word order of these strings was reversed:

4. * holidays the during crowded most are trains the } *crazy*
5. * perambulator a of thinking you aren't
6. * breakfast before car that wash.

[handwritten margin notes: "either" " = syntactically" "or" "semantically deviant" "or both"]*

Every speaker of English knows, without a moment's hesitation, that these strings are not English sentences, even though they contain English words. (An asterisk is always placed before a string which is syntactically or semantically deviant.) What is it that you know when you distinguish between strings of words which are sentences of your language and strings which are not sentences of your language? And where did you get this knowledge?

One possible answer to the latter question is that you memorized the possible sentences of your language while learning it in your infancy, much as you memorized the faces or names of classmates and friends. But this is not the way a human being learns his language. It is impossible to memorize *all* sentences possible in your language, and you frequently utter or hear sentences that do not duplicate any of your past experience. (In fact, the sentence you are reading now has probably not occurred previously in your experience.) Nonetheless, you have been able to distinguish between the grammatical strings and those strings made ungrammatical by reversal of word order. Obviously, you have not learned your language by memorizing its sentences. This, then, is one important human ability that needs to be investigated: How is a normal human being capable of deciding whether a string of words is a sentence in his language, and how is he able to do this for any of a potentially infinite number of strings he has never seen nor heard before?

But this is far from all that needs to be explained. For example, a speaker of a language can almost always tell whether a string is peculiar because of its meaning (i.e., its semantic interpretation) or because of its form (its "syntax"). In his first book on transformational grammar, Noam Chomsky pointed out that the following string is grammatical:[1] *[handwritten: syntactica]*

*colorless green ideas sleep furiously.

[handwritten: semantically]
However, it is nonsensical. It could be described as well-formed grammatically but ill-formed semantically.

Finally, the meaning of a string may be quite clear, but the string may be ungrammatical: *[handwritten: ie sensical]* *[handwritten right margin: seman OK / synt bad]*

* John and I jumps over wall and we shoots he
* you don't can putting your feet on the table in here
* is reading your father this book.

Thus we are often able to understand foreigners and others who do not correctly use the rules of English.

Furthermore, what is left unsaid may also be very important in a normal sentence of English. You would not be able to explain the full

---

[1] *Syntactic Structures* (Gravenhage, 1957), p. 15.

meaning of the following ungrammatical string:

* so was Norbert Wiener

but you would understand and be able to explain this string if it appeared as part of a grammatical string:

Yehudi Menuhin was a child prodigy and so was Norbert Wiener.

You understand the last four words to mean that Norbert Wiener was a child prodigy, although this is not stated in so many words. A speaker of a particular human language can often understand the full meaning of a sentence in his language without explicit statements in the words of the sentence. Such sentences are characterized by a very important kind of grammatical rule which will be presented later. Compare the following sentences:

1. Dr. Johnson asked someone to behave himself
2. Dr. Johnson promised someone to behave himself.

When you read the first of these superficially similar sentences, you understood the person who was to behave to be "someone." But when you read the second sentence, you understood the person who was to behave to be "Dr. Johnson." In these two sentences, the items which you understood to refer to the person who was to behave were in different positions, although the sentences were identical on the surface except for one word. What is it that you know about English that enables you to understand the sentences correctly? How is it that you understand

finding the revolver in that drawer worried us

as meaning that *we* are the ones who found the revolver in that drawer? Your knowledge of your language includes the ability to reconstruct the full meaning of a sentence from a string of words which may not contain all the words necessary for an accurate interpretation if you were, say, a Thai learning English.

Frequently, a native speaker of English will understand a sentence as having more than one meaning, as being *ambiguous*. Sometimes just one word is ambiguous, as the word "bank" in

the police station was right by the bank.

Here "bank" could be either the bank where money may be deposited or the bank of a river. Sometimes, however, the ambiguity has to do with the grammatical structure of the sentence:

the lamb is too hot to eat.

This sentence means either that the lamb is so hot that it cannot eat anything or that the lamb is so hot that no one can eat it. Can you see the ambiguity in the following sentence:

> visiting relatives can be a nuisance.

Sentences may be multiply ambiguous. Six possible interpretations of the following sentence are given below:

> the seniors were told to stop demonstrating on campus.

1. The seniors were demonstrating on campus and were asked to desist.
2. The seniors were demonstrating and were asked, on campus, to desist.
3. The seniors were demonstrating and were asked to desist on campus (although they could demonstrate elsewhere). told
4. People were demonstrating on campus, and seniors were asked to stop them. told
5. People were demonstrating and seniors were asked, on campus, to stop them.
6. People were demonstrating and seniors were asked to stop them from doing this on the campus (although they could do it elsewhere).

This ability that you have to extract more than one meaning from some sentences of your language is matched by one other skill. You can usually tell when two or more sentences have the same meaning—when they are *synonymous*. Sometimes this synonymity arises from the existence of more than one word for a meaning, as in the joke translation of "Twinkle, twinkle, little star," which begins:

> Scintillate, scintillate, diminutive asteroid,
> How I speculate as to your identity.

Frequently the synonymy is a result of the way the sentences are structured, as demonstrated by the following sentences:

1. six out of seven salesmen agree that walruses have buckteeth
2. that walruses have buckteeth is agreed by six out of seven salesmen
3. it is agreed by six out of seven salesmen that walruses have buckteeth.

You have never seen nor heard these sentences before; yet you need little or no conscious thought to decide that all three of them have a common meaning—a meaning distinct from that of

> six out of seven walruses believe that salesmen have buckteeth.

(The simplest type of synonymy is word synonymy.) As you saw in
the alternative version of "Twinkle, twinkle, little star," different words
may have the same meaning, though sometimes some alternatives may
carry slightly differing connotations.   Word synonymy is obviously
responsible for the synonymy of the following pair of sentences:

> oculists are expected to be well trained
> eye doctors are expected to be well trained.

Anyone who speaks English as his native language understands these
sentences to be synonymous because he has memorized the meanings of
"oculist" and "eye doctor."   Since these meanings are the same, he
knows that the otherwise identical sentences must have the same
meaning.

It is not as simple, however, to explain the native speaker's ability to
detect synonymy in such sentences as:

1. the chicken crossed the expressway
   the expressway was crossed by the chicken
2. it is believed that the framers of the Constitution met in
   Philadelphia
   the framers of the Constitution are believed to have met in
   Philadelphia
3. economists claim that a recession is not inevitable, and economists
   are not noted for optimism
   economists, who are not noted for optimism, claim that a recession
   is not inevitable.

SUMMARY

grammaticality is comprised of both syntactic correctness & semantic

When you use skills such as the four discussed in this chapter:

1. the ability to distinguish between the grammatical and ungrammatical strings of a potentially infinite set of utterances,
2. the ability to interpret certain grammatical strings even though
   elements of the interpretation may not be physically present in the
   string,
3. the ability to perceive ambiguity in a grammatical string,
4. the ability to perceive when two or more strings are synonymous,

you are making use of a kind of knowledge that can best be described
as knowledge of the grammar of your language.   This provides you
with the grammatical information you need to understand and produce
(or generate) the sentences of English.   Although these four skills seem

too obvious to bother with, they have never been satisfactorily explained. As remarked earlier, science often progresses by trying to explain well-known, everyday phenomena.   Planck's investigation of the color change in heated metal revealed unexpected complexities, and you will see that the same is true in the case of these four skills.

Language is a specifically human characteristic.   Descartes noted in Part V of his *Discourse on Method:*

> It is a very remarkable fact that there are none so depraved and stupid, without even excepting idiots, that they cannot arrange different words together forming of them a statement by which they make known their thoughts; while, on the other hand, there is no other animal, however perfect and fortunately circumstanced it may be, which can do the same.[2]

The particular skills that human beings use when they speak and understand their own language are quite remarkable, especially when you realize that a language is basically an infinite set of sentences.

In a very real sense, then, the study of what a grammar must be like if it is to account for the sentences of our language is more than the study of the structure of English sentences and the processes which operate on these structures.   The various linguistic skills reflect aspects of the intellectual abilities we possess by virtue of being human.   When we attempt to explain these skills, we are really seeking to explain an important part of what makes us human.

EXERCISE ONE

1. Using these statements as starting-off points, explain the different uses to which the word "grammar" is put:

   a. His grammar is excellent.   He rarely makes errors either in speech or writing.
   b. His grammar is excellent.   It reveals very interesting insights into the structure of English.
   c. Human beings possess a grammar which makes it possible for them to use, produce, and understand a human language.

2. In your grammar classes in high school, you probably learned to divide a sentence into two parts.   Thus you would probably divide the following sentence

   A grammar specifies a speaker's intuitive knowledge.

   in this way:

---

[2] Quoted in N. Chomsky, *Cartesian Linguistics* (New York, 1966), p. 4.

a. A grammar specifies a speaker's intuitive knowledge.

How could you justify dividing the sentence as it is done above rather than as it is done in *b* below?

b. A grammar specifies a speaker's intuitive knowledge.

3. Discuss the difference in the relationship between the italicized words in *a*, those in *b*, and those in *c* with respect to the phrase "to paint in Paris."

   a. *Whistler* persuaded *his mother* to paint in Paris.
   b. *Whistler* promised *his mother* to paint in Paris.
   c. *Whistler* left *his mother* to paint in Paris.

Note the ambiguity of *c*.

4. Explain the ambiguity in the sentences below:

   a. Eating apples can be enjoyable.
   b. She told me to leave at five o'clock.
   c. Could this be the invisible man's hair tonic?
   d. The old matron fed her dog biscuits.
   e. Every citizen may vote.

5. Describe the difference in the relationship of "Eberhart" to "please" in *a* and *b*:

   a. Eberhart is eager to please.
   b. Eberhart is easy to please.

6. What does Descartes have to say about the relationship of human intelligence to human linguistic ability?

7. Show how the sentence below may be reorganized so that the new version

   a. is synonymous with the original version.
   b. has a different meaning from that of the original sentence:

   The cheese was purchased by Aunt Tillie.

8. Certain material has been deleted from the sentences below. Show what this deleted material must have been:

   a. She adopted forty-two cats simply because she wanted to.
   b. John likes Mary, Bill, and Sally.
   c. Oaks are taller than maples.
   d. Discovering the truth pleases scientists.
   e. Ladies wearing high heels are not welcome on tennis courts.

9. The following pairs of sentences are synonymous, but in a different way. Can you describe and explain the differences?

   a. My attorney specializes in copyright law.
      My lawyer specializes in copyright law.
   b. A proposal was made which bothered me.
      A proposal which bothered me was made.

CHAPTER 2

Constituent Structure

If you are to explain the speaker's knowledge of the sentences in his language, you must start by asking a question about something that is seemingly obvious. *What exactly is a sentence?* In a certain sense, everyone who speaks English knows what a sentence is; but if you try to give a definition of a sentence which is not circular, you will find that the task is not so easy. Traditionally, sentences are spoken of as expressing complete thoughts. This answer does nothing more than raise a second question: *What exactly is a complete thought?* Clearly, if this question is answered by saying "a sentence," nothing has been achieved. So, the problem is clear. Speakers know the sentences of their language. But what exactly are these objects, these sentences, that speakers know? This chapter begins to sketch an answer to this question.

At first glance, you would naturally consider a sentence to be a string of words. When sentences are written, they are written as strings of words; when sentences are read, they are read as strings of words. Sentences are, indeed, strings of words, but strings with very unusual properties. For example, a consideration of the two strings below reveals the most characteristic property of sentences. *Sentences are structured strings of words.*

   1. This human language reveals a systematic property.

   2.   4   1   3   7   6   5   2

This structure is not apparent in the string itself; it is invisible. But it is there nonetheless, and speakers of English can readily demonstrate this structure. The words in sentences fall into groups or clusters, and speakers of English have little difficulty recognizing these clusters. Suppose someone asked you to divide string 1 into two parts, the two parts which seemed most natural to you. What would your answer be:

       this   human language reveals a systematic property

or

       this human language reveals a systematic   property

or

       this human   language reveals a systematic property?

You would probably pick none of these, but divide the string instead into

       this human language   reveals a systematic property.

On the other hand, if you were asked to divide string 2 into the two parts which seemed most natural to you, you probably would not know where to begin. Your answer would almost certainly differ from someone else's answer. What is going on here? The answer is that string 1 is structured; string 2 is not.

A convenient way to show how words are grouped in sentences is to use a diagram which resembles those often used to depict family trees. For example, the two groups of words which compose string 1 can be presented in the following fashion:

SENTENCE

this human language   reveals a systematic property

Going a few steps further, suppose you were asked to break the string

       reveals a systematic property

into two parts. It is likely that the two parts would be "reveals" and "a systematic property." This division can be shown in a "tree" diagram as follows:

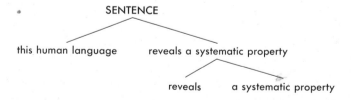

SENTENCE

this human language   reveals a systematic property

reveals   a systematic property

The clusters of words into which a sentence can be subdivided in this manner are called *constituents* of a sentence. Our example can be further subdivided by breaking "this human language" into "this" and "human language," and by breaking "a systematic property" into "a" and "systematic property." Another division yields "human" and "language" from the cluster "human language," and "systematic" and "property" from "systematic." Following is a tree diagram which gives the full set of constituents of our sentence,

this human language reveals a systematic property.

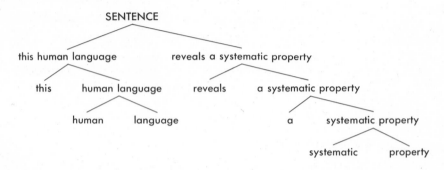

Often sentences may contain two or more constituents of the same type. This can be seen by examining the list of constituents below:

1. this human language reveals a systematic property
2. this human language
3. reveals a systematic property
4. this
5. human language
6. human
7. language
8. reveals
9. a systematic property
10. a
11. systematic property
12. systematic
13. property

Comparing constituents, you encounter many which, intuitively, do not seem to have anything in common. For example, the constituent "property" does not seem to be the same kind of constituent as the constituent "a." The constituent "reveals" does not seem to be the same kind of constituent as the constituent "reveals a systematic property." On the other hand, "this human language" does seem to be the same kind of constituent as "a systematic property." The constituent "this" does seem to be similar to the constituent "a."

[handwritten annotation: similar constituents may be grouped into types prove by substitution]

If two or more constituents appear to be of one general type, their similarity can be checked by a simple process which we shall call the *substitution test*. For this, replace one constituent in a tree diagram with another constituent from the diagram. If a grammatical string results, the similarity is proven; if the string is ungrammatical, the constituents are not of the same type. We will apply the substitution test to our sentence,

> this human language reveals a systematic property.

Would you consider the constituent "human" to be of the same type as the constituent "a systematic property"? Intuitively, you would be inclined to say "no." Your intuition is justified since the substitution test would produce nonsense in one instance,

> * this human language reveals human

and an ungrammatical string in another,

> * this a systematic property language reveals a systematic property.

On the other hand, what about "human language" and "systematic property"? Substitution here would result in a grammatical string:

> this systematic property reveals a human language.

In view of this fact, you could conclude, if no other contrary evidence existed, that "human language" and "systematic property" are constituents of the same type.

Analyzing the sentence in this fashion, one discovers that

> this human language reveals a systematic property

contains eight different kinds of constituents. If you perform the substitution test systematically, you should find the following constituent types:

1. this human language reveals a systematic property
2. this human language, a systematic property
3. this, a
4. human language, systematic property
5. human, systematic
6. language, property
7. reveals a systematic property
8. reveals

In the tree diagram below, the same types of constituents are given with the corresponding numbers.

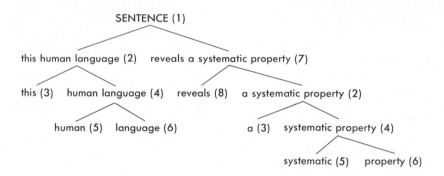

Returning to the original question about the speaker's knowledge of the sentences of his language, you may see an answer emerging. Consider the following sentences, all of which have the same *constituent structure* as the sentence

this human language reveals a systematic property

and none of which, in all likelihood, you have seen before:

the snowbound platypus gobbled a mentholated cigarette
this electric typewriter makes bilious carbon copies
my twelve cockroaches chase his testy snails

How do you know these sentences are grammatical? One answer is that you can accept these sentences as having correct English constituent structure. For example, although you will accept the constituent "the snowbound platypus" when it precedes the constituent "gobbled a mentholated cigarette," you will reject a string where the positions are reversed:

* gobbled a mentholated cigarette the snowbound platypus.

The knowledge of constituent structure is critical to knowledge of sentences. Thus, you can take the constituents of the three sentences above and make new grammatical sentences, providing you adhere to the constituent structure of English:

the snowbound platypus makes bilious carbon copies
the snowbound platypus chases his testy snails
my twelve cockroaches make bilious carbon copies
my twelve cockroaches gobbled a mentholated cigarette.

In short, speakers of English know the constituent structure of English. When a speaker is confronted with a string of English words which violates the rules of English constituent structure, he immediately recognizes this string to be ungrammatical.

[handwritten marginal notes: By this phrase new verb phrase syntax overcomes nominative for declarative sentence]

SUMMARY

The discussion in this chapter has dealt with the question: What exactly is a sentence in the English language?   Sentences are something more than just strings. A sentence is a structured string whose words fall into natural groups. These groups are called constituents. Furthermore, constituents can often be classified through use of the substitution test.   This test is not very sophisticated, however, and will be replaced by more precise tests in later chapters.

EXERCISE TWO

1. What elements are understood but not physically present in the following sentences?
    a. Some people climb mountains just because they want to.
    b. Tell me the truth!
    c. What worried Septimus was being considered egotistical. (Contrast: What worried Septimus was Virginia's being considered egotistical.)

2. Explain, using your own examples, the two types of synonymy discussed so far.

3. What is meant by the word "structure" as it is used in this chapter?

4. Draw a tree diagram showing the constituents of

    The fiery conservationist denounced the industrial lobbies.

5. Eight kinds of constituents should have been shown on the tree above. List the examples of each kind together.

6. What do the following sentences suggest about the reliability of the substitution test?

    a. Falstaff drank hot buttered rum.
    b. Falstaff drank incessantly.

7. What inferences could be drawn from the following sentences:

    a. 1. Alexander regrets that unfortunate investment.
       2. Alexander is sorry about that unfortunate investment.
    b. 1. He always liked Alfred.
       2. He was always fond of Alfred.

  c. 1. The news about Lara appalled him.
   2. The news about Lara was appalling to him.
  d. 1. Fitzgibbon amuses Amanda.
   2. Fitzgibbon is amusing to Amanda.
  e. 1. Squire Allgood's letter surprises me.
   2. Squire Allgood's letter is surprising to me.
  f. 1. I must always consider Mrs. Tannhauser's feelings.
   2. I must always be considerate of Mrs. Tannhauser's feelings.

8. Find three definitions of a sentence, quoting your sources, and briefly describe how adequate they would be in explaining to a foreigner how to write an English sentence rather than an English sentence fragment.

9. Suppose that the following sentence is treated as a full definition:

 A sentence is a structured string whose words fall into natural groups.

Now write down three structured strings which are not sentences although their words fall into natural groups.

[handwritten: particular structure which is syntax]

CHAPTER 3

Deep Structures, Surface Structures, and Transformations

Constituent structure in itself provides little help in accounting for a native speaker's ability to understand those grammatical sentences which might seem incomplete to someone less well acquainted with the language. For example, you understand the sentence

1. the papers refused to report the trial because they were afraid to

as if it were really

2. the papers refused to report the trial because they were afraid to report the trial.

How did you know that the meaning of the first sentence was exactly the same as the meaning of the second sentence? You knew because, even though the *surface structures* of the two sentences were different—even though, in other words, the sentences had different shapes—both sentences have exactly the same *deep structure*. Perhaps the most important fact about the sentences of human languages is that *all sentences have both a deep structure and a surface structure.*

The central role of deep and surface structures can readily be understood if you imagine a situation in which an English-speaking person listens to someone else speaking in English. Suppose you are listening to a news broadcast on the radio. How would you respond if asked: What do you hear coming out of the radio? There are several answers you might give: the news, English sentences, John Doe (if John Doe is the newscaster), and other answers of this sort. These answers are in some sense true, of course. But what if the question were put to a person who understood no English? He would be able to say that some human being was speaking, but he would not be able to identify the speech as anything but a continuous stream of acoustic signals or noise. For, in a very real and important sense, what comes out of the radio is nothing but noise. The question to be answered is: What does the hearer need to do in order to understand the message carried by the noise—to know, in other words, that the noise he hears is, in fact, a newscast? He must do this: He must somehow connect this continuous stream of noise with a meaning. He must somehow relate the sound to meaning. The fact that human beings perform this feat all the time when they communicate with one another suggests that they are equipped with some sort of neural interpreter which processes the noise impinging on the ears, converting these sensations into a coherent meaning.

Thus the general problem of understanding a language is finding a meaning in sound. This is exactly what an English-speaking person does when he hears English sentences spoken. This fact is crucial to the notions of deep and surface sentence structure. More specifically, *the meaning of a sentence is conveyed by its deep structure; the form of a sentence is given by its surface structure.*

Several examples illustrate this point. Consider

a new idea is often valuable.

What is the meaning of the constituent "a new idea"? Unquestionably, part of the meaning is that the idea is, in fact, new. In some fashion the constituent "a new idea" contains the sentence "The idea is new." This claim is substantiated by the relative clause version: "the idea which is new." What is the status of "which is new"? It is actually a modified form of "The idea is new." Thus, in the deep structure of the constituent "a new idea," there exists the sentence "The idea is new." Such constructions will be investigated in more detail later. For now, it is important simply to recognize that the deep structure of a sentence or constituent provides an explicit account of the meaning of the sentence or constituent, a meaning which is often not contained in any *explicit* way in the surface structure. We know that "The idea is new" when we hear "a new idea," but the surface structure does not explicitly contain the sentence "The idea is new."

Consider now a second example. In particular, think about the sentences:

stepping in puddles is what little girls try to do
not being able to sleep worried Lady Macbeth
watching television late is fun for Cynthia.

You know more about the meaning of these sentences than is actually contained in their words. For instance, if you are asked the questions:

Who is doing the stepping? Who is not able to sleep? Who does the watching? Your respective answers will invariably be: "little girls," "Lady Macbeth," "Cynthia." This is because you have unconsciously plugged the following sentences into those given above:

> little girls step in puddles
> Lady Macbeth is not able to sleep
> Cynthia watches television late.

Thus we can say that the deep structure of a sentence gives its meaning because the deep structure contains all of the information required to determine the meaning of a sentence.

The most important question of all is: *How* is the deep structure of a sentence related to its surface structure? A deep structure becomes a surface structure via *transformations.*

| DEEP STRUCTURE | Transformations | SURFACE STRUCTURE |
| meaning | | form used in communication |

The notion "transformation" may seem strange at first, but you really know more about it than you realize. Compare the two sentences below, the first of which is a so-called *declarative sentence,* the second an *interrogative sentence:*

> anyone can solve this problem
> can anyone solve this problem?

As you can see, these sentences are very similar syntactically. In fact, the first differs from the second only in respect to the change in position of their first two words. This kind of rearrangement illustrates a process of transformation. This particular instance is the *interrogative transformation.* Despite their similarity, however, these two sentences do not have the same deep structure. In fact, they could not have the same deep structure because they are different in meaning.

The deep structure of the second sentence, in a much oversimplified form, is:

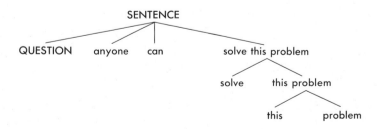

Notice that this deep structure contains a hypothetical constituent QUESTION, which does two things. First, it specifies that the sentence is a question semantically. Second, it provides a structure upon which the *interrogative transformation* is defined and can apply. By requiring that the *interrogative transformation* apply only if the QUESTION constituent is present, the grammar prevents the application of the transformation to deep structures which are not semantically interpreted as questions. The *interrogative transformation* is the process which changes the word order of the deep structure, given above, so as to *generate* the surface structure diagrammed below:

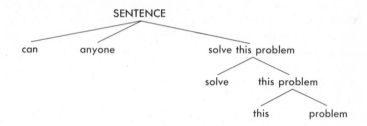

You can question assertions or you can deny them. For example, you can affirm or deny the desirability of the study of Plato by undergraduates, with the following sentences:

> undergraduates should study Plato
> undergraduates should not study Plato.

These two sentences are identical except that the second is the negation of the first. Since these sentences are not synonymous, they have different deep structures. One way to represent this difference is with the hypothetical constituent NEGATIVE (NEG), as in the following tree diagram:

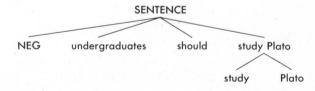

The addition of NEG represents the information that, although the remainder of the structure is identical to that of the first sentence, this sentence has a negative interpretation.

The negation transformation converts the NEG constituent into "not" and introduces this word to the right of "should," generating the surface structure below:

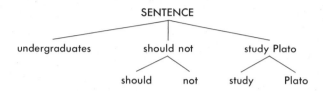

It is rare for a single transformation to change a deep structure into a surface structure. When a number of transformations are required, the constituent structures formed between the deep structure and the surface structure are called *intermediate structures*. In this sense, the surface structure given above for "Undergraduates should not study Plato" would become an intermediate structure if the final surface structure were to be "Undergraduates shouldn't study Plato." The transformation which may (optionally) apply to a structure such as that above is the *contraction transformation*. The conversion of "not" into "n't" and its attachment to the preceding word is reflected in the following surface structure:

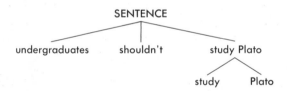

SUMMARY

Sentences of all languages have both a deep structure, which gives the meaning of the sentence, and a surface structure, which gives the form of the sentence as it is used in communication. Thus, a deep structure is an *abstract* object; it is a structure one assumes on the basis of the meaning of a sentence and its syntax. A surface structure is closer to physical reality in that it concretely specifies the syntactic structure necessary for spoken or written communication.

Transformations relate deep structures and surface structures, or, more specifically, they transform one constituent structure into another. If more than one transformation is necessary, intermediate structures will be generated by each transformation until the surface structure is formed.

EXERCISE THREE

1. What is the function of the deep structure of a sentence?

2. Draw tree diagrams (like the ones in the chapter) showing the deep structure of

   a. Can Armbruster discuss the earthquake?
   b. McLuhan couldn't operate this computer.

3. Explain the effects of the interrogative, negative, and contraction transformations in the sentences above.

4. What is the function of the surface structure of a sentence?

5. What conclusions can you draw from the following:

   a. 1. Franklin is acquainted with the lady *who* snubbed you last Friday.
      2. * the idea *who* occurred to me was that you could refuse to participate

   b. 1. The lamp *which* Davy invented saved many lives.
      2. * the officer *which* met Clarissa escorted her into the ballroom

   c. 1. Franklin is acquainted with the lady *that* snubbed you last Friday.
      2. The idea *that* occurred to me was that you could refuse to participate.

   d. 1. The boy *whose* mother had abandoned him in the Urals finally arrived in Murmansk.
      2. A sentence is a structured string, the words *of which* fall into natural groups.
      3. A sentence is a structured string *whose* words fall into natural groups.

6. What is a transformation and how does it affect meaning?

7. Explain the ambiguity of

   Hotchkiss was imprisoned by the bank.

8. Write unambiguous sentences for each meaning of the sentence in 7. You may, if necessary, change word order and also add or omit words.

CHAPTER 4

Transformations and Elementary Transformational Processes

Transformations have been defined as those processes which convert deep structures into intermediate and/or surface structures. This chapter describes the processes themselves and discusses the "building blocks" from which transformations in every language are constructed.

Consider the following examples:

1. a. Smerdyakov distrusted Karamazov
   b. Karamazov was distrusted by Smerdyakov
2. a. Daisy puzzled Winterbourne
   b. Winterbourne was puzzled by Daisy.

Although 1a is an *active* sentence in which the subject is "Smerdyakov," and 1b is a *passive* sentence in which the subject is "Karamazov," you know that the two sentences are synonymous. The same statement may be made about 2a and 2b. The explanation for this is that, in each pair, the a and b sentences have virtually identical deep structures, and, for present purposes, we shall assume that they are identical. Using sentence 2, we can diagram a rough deep structure for a and b as:

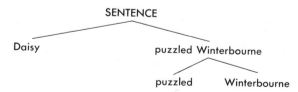

If the passive transformation is not applied to it, the above structure is equivalent to the surface structure of sentence 2a. If the passive transformation is applied, then a surface structure of the following form is generated, giving sentence 2*b*:

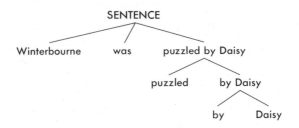

If you compare the deep and surface structures above, you will see that the following changes have been made by the passive transformation: First, the constituents "Daisy" and "Winterbourne" have been inter-changed. Second, "was," a form of "be," has been introduced. Finally, the preposition "by" has been inserted before the constituent "Daisy."

The passive transformation can be described roughly as the process which interchanges the constituents "Daisy" and "Winterbourne." But, obviously, this is not enough, for it only defines what occurs in a specific sentence. (The passive transformation, of course, not only interchanges the two constituents, but also introduces a form of "be" and adds the preposition "by." When we speak of the interchange of constituents by the passive transformation, we assume the other alterations of the phrase structure.) What is needed is a definition that characterizes any and all passive sentences, such as those below:

> the spook was stung by a bee
> that mighty oak was toppled by Mickey Mouse
> each of us was mentioned by the local newspaper.

In Chapter 2 you saw that constituents like "Daisy," "Winterbourne," "this human language," "a systematic property," "the spook," and "a bee" could usually be substituted for each other without making the sentence ungrammatical. You have now seen that they have another property in common. They may be interchanged by the passive trans-formation. Constituents having the two properties discussed above will be called *noun phrases*, abbreviated as NP on tree diagrams. The passive transformation thus interchanges noun phrases, and the deep and surface structures for

Winterbourne was puzzled by Daisy

should now be redrawn as:

Deep Structure

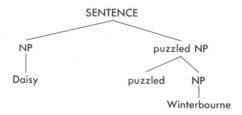

Surface Structure

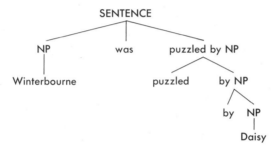

This definition of the passive transformation—or the part considered here—is true for every application of this transformation. Under this definition, "the fact that Hannibal intended to avenge the Carthaginian defeat in the First Punic War" is a noun phrase despite its length and complexity, and it is included as such in the following deep structure:

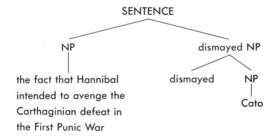

The application of the passive transformation generates the following surface structure:

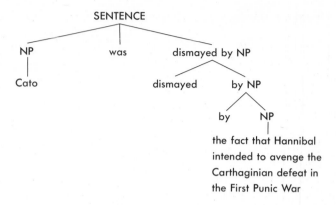

The interchanged constituents must be noun phrases. The passive transformation can interchange noun phrases regardless of the number or kinds of words that each includes. This property of the passive transformation is, in fact, an example of a general property of all transformations: the ability to operate on constituents such as noun phrases without being affected by the words which make up the constituent. All languages contain transformations which transform deep structures into surface structures. However, the specific transformations of languages other than English, say Eskimo or Navajo or Finnish, are almost always different from the specific transformations of English. What is most important is the fact that transformations of all languages seem to involve basically the same kinds of operations on constituent structures. The operations, called *elementary transformations*, may be used differently in different languages, but the operations remain the same.

There seem to be at least three different kinds of elementary transformations which can be used in the formulation of a particular transformation:

1. adjunction
2. substitution
3. deletion

Within these transformation types there are probably subtypes, but discussion of these will be postponed for now.

A simple transformation in English which makes use of the adjunction operation is the *contraction transformation*, which can be demonstrated quite easily without presenting a tree diagram. By this transformation, the structure for

the shepherd must not leave us

is converted into the structure for

the shepherd mustn't leave us.

Here the constituent "not" is contracted and adjoined to the constituent "must," thereby generating the new single constituent "mustn't."

The substitution elementary operation is most clearly illustrated by the transformation which relates the following sentences:

it is difficult for me to concentrate on calculus
calculus is difficult for me to concentrate on.

One does not need to construct tree diagrams to show that in the second sentence the noun phrase containing "calculus" is substituted for the noun phrase containing "it."

A transformation hardly discussed yet will serve as an illustration of the elementary transformational process of deletion. It is an important transformation known as *identical noun phrase deletion*. In the following sentences:

1. a. Miriam wanted Paul to leave home
   b. Miriam wanted to leave home

it is obvious that Paul is the one to leave home in 1*a*, but Miriam is the one to leave home in 1*b*, even though Miriam is not explicitly mentioned after the verb "wanted." This suggests that the deep structure of 1*b* contains "Miriam" as the subject of "leave home"

* Miriam wanted Miriam to leave home

and that there is a transformation deleting "Miriam," since "Miriam" has occurred as the subject of "wanted."

Actually this identity condition applies not only to the deletion of noun phrases but also to such constituents as "report the trial" and "play the violin." These constituents will be called *verb phrases* (abbreviated VP). The following pairs of sentences illustrate this kind of deletion—*identical verb phrase deletion*.

2. a. the papers refused to report the trial because they were afraid to report the trial
   b. the papers refused to report the trial because they were afraid to
3. a. Igor can play the violin, and that cat can play the violin too
   b. Igor can play the violin, and that cat can too.

These elementary transformational processes are an important clue for the answer to the question: How do people the world over learn to speak their native language? Very early in life, a normal child acquires the language of his family and community.   Normal infants are born fully equipped to learn any human language spoken anywhere in the world, and all normal children go through more or less the same stages of learning language, with no language appearing to be more difficult to learn than any other.   For example, if an American child were adopted as a baby by an Arab family in Saudi Arabia and were raised by them in their homeland, he would come to speak their Arab language as fluently as he would have learned American English if he had remained in the United States.

There are two approaches to an explanation of this phenomenon, approaches which should complement each other.   The first is a neurological investigation of the speech and brain mechanisms—mechanisms common to every normal child.   The second is a linguistic investigation into what all languages have in common—linguistic universals.   The fact that transformations in all languages studied to date seem to make use of the same elementary transformational processes—adjunction, substitution, and deletion—provides a partial answer.   Precisely because he is human, a child comes into the world knowing, quite unconsciously, what to look for in a language.   He is equipped to recognize which of the elementary transformational processes are used in the transformations of his language.   He uses his innate knowledge to construct the particular transformations of his language, to piece together in a remarkably short time the grammar of the language to which he is exposed.   This explains in part how a human child can learn any native language at all.   Once the child has discovered the particular transformations of his language, the transformations that convert deep structures into the surface structures of the language, he is able to distinguish, with relatively few errors, the grammatical utterances of his language, to interpret certain grammatical structures, even though elements of his interpretation may not be physically present in the utterance, and to perceive ambiguity and synonymy.

This is very far from the whole answer to the mystery of language acquisition.   No one yet knows just how the child goes about using his knowledge of elementary transformational processes in the acquisition of a language.   The discovery of these processes and of the way they work in particular languages is only a first step, important as it is.

SUMMARY

Transformations convert one sentence structure into another sentence structure by performing various operations on the constituents making up these structures.

Any language makes use of three elementary transformational processes: adjunction, substitution, and deletion.

EXERCISE FOUR

1. Draw deep structure trees for

   a. The town was besieged by the English.
   b. Can the town survive?
   c. The mayor shouldn't surrender.

2. Now explain how each of these deep structures became the surface structures (i.e., by what transformations) for the sentences shown above.

3. In an earlier exercise you were asked to describe the difference in the relationship of "Eberhart" to "please" in *a* and *b* below. Do this again.

   a. Eberhart is eager to please.
   b. Eberhart is easy to please.

   The relationship in one of these sentences may be at least partially explained if it is assumed that the sentence has come from a structure to which a particular transformation has been applied, the one described as relating

   > It is difficult for me to concentrate on calculus.

   to

   > Calculus is difficult for me to concentrate on.

   Now look at sentences *a* and *b*. Which one is like this example? In what way?

4. Explain what is meant by linguistic universals.

5. The reflexive transformation often converts a second identical noun phrase into a reflexive pronoun. Thus the structure for

   > * Charles deceived Charles

   becomes

   > Charles deceived himself.

   What fact can you infer about the passive transformation from the string following?

   > * himself was deceived by Charles

6. What general property of all transformations is discussed in this chapter?

7. What is an "intermediate structure"?

8. How might the passive transformation be useful in finding out whether a particular constituent was a noun phrase or not? Give an example.

9. When would the passive transformation be useless for finding noun phrases? Give an example.

CHAPTER 5

Linguistic Explanation and Ordered Rules

Deep structures, it will be remembered, are converted into surface structures by transformations which are meaning-preserving, which refer not to words but to particular constituent types, and which consist of one or more of the elementary transformational processes of adjunction, substitution, and deletion. The concepts of deep structure, surface structure, and transformations provide, as seen in Chapter 4, a tool which explains many of the peculiarities of English syntax and yields insights into the linguistic capabilities of the native speaker of a language. In this chapter, we examine two problems in English syntax from the point of view of transformational analysis. The solutions offered, which are revealing in their own right, introduce another important property of transformations—there are ordering relations among transformations. There will be more on that later.

First, look at the following sentences, often called *reflexive* sentences:

1. a. I shot *myself*
    b. you shot *yourself*
    c. Cesario shot *himself*
    d. Ophelia shot *herself*
    e. we shot *ourselves*
    f. they shot *themselves*

The italicized words are known as *reflexive pronouns*. What is the interpretation of reflexive pronouns? They are always understood as referring to a noun phrase previously mentioned in the sentence. This intuition is confirmed by the ungrammaticality of the following string:

* Marilyn shot themselves.

This intuition is accounted for if it is assumed that the deep structures of the six reflexive sentences contain object noun phrases identical to the subject noun phrases. These structures, abbreviated below as strings of words, provide exact interpretations of the surface structures for the sentences:

2. a. * I shot I
    b. * you shot you
    c. * Cesario shot Cesario
    d. * Ophelia shot Ophelia
    e. * we shot we
    f. * they shot they

These deep structures have yet to be transformed by the *reflexive transformation*, which applies whenever two noun phrases appearing in the same simple sentence are identical. When it is applied, the second of the identical noun phrases is converted into the corresponding reflexive pronoun.

This approach to reflexive sentences will also help to solve one minor mystery in English—the "*you* understood." When you studied imperative or common sentences in English, you probably learned that the subject of sentences like "Go home!" was "*you* understood." Some grammarians have either ignored the existence of the understood element or claimed that there is no such element. In fact, you normally *do* understand sentences like the following as if they began with the subject noun phrase "you":

3. a. wash the car!
    b. wash the windows!

If you compare these with

4. a. Jonathan washed the car
    b. those girls washed the windows

you see that the imperative sentences do not have an explicit subject as the others do. What evidence is there, apart from your own native-speaker intuition, that the subject is "you" and not "he" or some other noun phrase in the deep structure of such imperative sentences?

There are sentences which are both reflexive and imperative. What you have already found out about reflexive sentences will be relevant in establishing "you," and only "you," as the deep subject of both these sentences:

5. a. wash yourself!
    b. wash yourselves!

Earlier we showed that noun phrases were converted into reflexive pronouns only when the deep structure contained an earlier identical noun phrase. Thus, the sentences above must originally have contained subject noun phrases containing "you." At least two transformations had to be applied to convert the deep structures into surface structures containing reflexive pronouns. The first, the reflexive transformation, was needed to change the second occurrence of the noun phrase "you" into the reflexive pronouns "yourself" and "yourselves." The results are:

> you wash yourself!
> you wash yourselves!

However, in order to generate 5a and 5b, it was necessary to apply the *imperative transformation,* an important process which deletes the subject "you" of the reflexive sentences to generate:

> wash yourself!
> wash yourselves!

The ungrammaticality of the following strings demonstrates that the subject of an imperative sentence could not be anything except "you":

6. a. * wash myself
   b. * wash himself
   c. * wash herself
   d. * wash itself
   e. * wash ourselves
   f. * wash themselves

Since the reflexive transformation has been applied in the generation of these strings (6a–f), the subjects of these sentences must have been something other than "you." The ungrammaticality of these strings suggests that "you" is the only possible subject for imperative sentences. Thus, the notion of "*you* understood" for imperative sentences, interpreted in transformational terms, makes a great deal of sense. (It is worth noting that there are certain imperative constructions like

is not imperative?   let's shoot ourselves   ?

which are not analyzed as having a "you" subject understood, an observation which is borne out by the ungrammaticality of such strings as

> * let's wash yourselves.)

This analysis illustrates the important property mentioned at the beginning of the chapter: *There are ordering relations among transfor-*

of deep structures

mations. Certain transformations must be applied before other transformations, just as the reflexive and imperative transformations had to be applied in a particular order to generate a grammatical sentence.

If we were to reverse the order of application and apply the imperative transformation first, for example, to the deep structure

* you wash you

the resulting string would be the intermediate structure

* wash you.

But the reflexive transformation cannot be applied to this string, since it contains only one noun phrase, and two identical noun phrases are necessary for its application. Thus, these transformations must be applied in this order:

1. reflexive transformation
2. imperative transformation.

Applying the reflexive transformation first to the deep structure

* you wash you

will generate the intermediate string (presuming a singular subject "you")

you wash yourself.

The imperative transformation then generates

wash yourself!

SUMMARY

The reflexive and imperative transformations account for the grammaticality of certain strings of English and the ungrammaticality of others. Furthermore, they illustrate yet another important property of transformations in any language: *Transformations may be ordered.*

EXERCISE FIVE

1. The reflexive transformation converts into a reflexive pronoun the second of two identical noun phrases *within the same simple sentence.* Construct an explanation based upon this assumption which would explain the ungrammaticality of the sentences below:

a. * Joan thought that herself would go
b. * the man's disliking herself worried the nurse
c. * I hate people who criticize myself

2. Draw deep structures for

    a. Polish the limousine!
    b. Samson can't accept those terms.
    c. The general was summoned by the President.
    d. Shouldn't the general refuse him?

3. Explain how the deep structures for the sentences in 2 become surface structures.

4. The analysis of the reflexive and imperative transformations illustrates that transformations may be ordered. What do your answers in question 3 for sentences *b* and *d* above indicate about the ordering of other transformations?

5. The sentence

    The workmen tore up the street.

    is ambiguous. Use paraphrases to explain the ambiguity.

6. Change the word order of

    The workmen tore up the street.

    so that only one interpretation is possible. Do not omit or add any words.

7. Explain the conditions under which the sentence below could be a grammatical English sentence. Also explain the conditions under which it would be ungrammatical.

    Jones admires Jones.

8. Virtually all human languages exhibit the phenomenon of reflexivization, although the form of the reflexive naturally varies considerably from language to language. Speculate as to why reflexivization should be so universal a phenomenon.

SECTION TWO

Constituents and Features

CHAPTER 6

Determining the Constituents
of a Sentence

An intuitive feeling for constituent structure often emerges upon the consideration of surface structures. When you think about a sentence like

the boy surprised himself

you might well conclude that "the boy" is a constituent, a natural unit, and that "surprised himself" is also a constituent. Intuitions concerning surface structure constituents are, unfortunately, not very reliable. A more satisfactory procedure for the isolation and identification of constituents involves the use of certain syntactic tests based upon the fact that transformations delete constituents and move them around in sentences. Thus, observation of the effects of certain transformations often helps in the identification of a constituent.

Syntactic tests notwithstanding, evidence for the constituent status of most strings is very scanty indeed. Moreover, the constituents which are consistently isolated by syntactic tests are, in many cases, constituents of the surface structure. Thus, at least for the present, it is not possible to specify the constituents of deep structures with certainty.

For heuristic purposes, it will be assumed that the deep structure of sentences consists of three basic constituents: noun phrases (NP's), auxiliaries (AUX's), and verb phrases (VP's). Syntactic evidence for the existence of noun phrases is the most conclusive. Less compelling, perhaps, are the facts which suggest the existence of auxiliaries and verb phrases. Still, such constituent classifications of the strings which make up sentences are of considerable value in discussing and analyzing a number of syntactic phenomena, even though these classifications cannot claim undoubted correctness. Thus, the present discussion will be devoted to a consideration of the various transformational effects which suggest such classifications.

THE NOUN PHRASE

One of the most important tests for the string types referred to as noun phrases is the *passive* test. Compare the following active and passive sentences:

> the roar of the jets drove the alderman crazy
> the alderman was driven crazy by the roar of the jets.

The constituents inverted by the passive transformation are noun phrases. The passive test may also be used to demonstrate that a group of words is not a noun phrase. For example, "the alderman crazy" is not a noun phrase in the first sentence above. If it were, the passive transformation would produce the following sentence:

> * the alderman crazy was driven by the roar of the jets.

Since this string is not grammatical, it follows that "the alderman crazy" is not a noun phrase.

The passive test, however, cannot be used to show that "the boy" in

> the boy can sleep late

is a noun phrase. There is no grammatical passive sentence corresponding to this sentence. In this case the interrogative transformation, which shifts the auxiliary around the subject noun phrase to the front of the string, may be used as a test. Since application of this transformation generates the following grammatical utterance:

> can the boy sleep late?

you can assume that the constituent "the boy," around which the auxiliary "can" was moved, is a noun phrase. The same test can be used to show that "afterwards the boy" in the sentence

> afterwards the boy can sleep late

is not a noun phrase, for application of the interrogative transformation generates the following ungrammatical string:

> * can afterwards the boy sleep late?

Yet another test of the noun phrase is the *reflexive*, which makes use of the fact that the reflexive transformation applies only to noun phrases.

For example, the string "the philosopher" is a noun phrase in the sentence below, since the reflexive transformation normally applies where a noun phrase is identical to another one, in this case "the philosopher."

> The philosopher contradicted himself.

The last test to be discussed here involves the *cleft sentence transformation,* a rather complex transformation. All that will be done at this point is to note the effect of it.

> Coughs cause diseases

has two synonymous cleft sentences:

> what coughs cause are diseases
> what causes diseases are coughs.

The constituent appearing immediately to the right of any form of "be" in a cleft sentence is always a noun phrase. For present purposes the transformational process can be simulated by the following three steps:

1. place "what" at the beginning of the string
2. place the appropriate form of "be" at the end of the string
3. select the word or group of words to be tested and transpose to the end of the string.

If the result is a grammatical sentence, then the word or group of words is likely to be a noun phrase.

Suppose you wanted to apply this test, to

> the frog jumped into the soup.

The first step changes it to

> * what the frog jumped into the soup

the second, to

> * what the frog jumped into the soup was.

For the third step, tests of "the frog," "into the soup," and "the soup" would generate, respectively:

> what jumped into the soup was *the frog*
> * what the frog jumped was *into the soup*
> what the frog jumped into was *the soup.*

You can see that "the frog" and "the soup" are noun phrases, whereas "into the soup" is not.

One important situation in which this test does not work occurs when the noun phrase contains a noun like "John," "someone," "the red-faced general," or "he," which all refer to *humans*. If you try to apply the cleft sentence test to

John ignored Sidney

you get the ungrammatical strings

* what John ignored was Sidney
* what ignored Sidney was John.

Thus, the cleft sentence test is not productive in all cases, but it can be extremely useful, and further use of this test will be made.[3]

THE AUXILIARY

Many surface structures contain a constituent which behaves in an extremely consistent manner when certain transformations are applied. This constituent, called an auxiliary, is contained in the following surface structures:

the Undersecretary *can* deny all knowledge of it
the union *will* defy the court order
the miscreant *must* answer for this outrage.

The obvious test for identifying auxiliaries in the surface structure is the interrogative transformation, since it shifts the auxiliary around the subject noun phrase. Applied to the three sentences above, the interrogative transformation would generate the following:

Can the Undersecretary deny all knowledge of it?
Will the union defy the court order?
Must the miscreant answer for this outrage?

The following sentences do not have auxiliaries in their surface structures:

the Governor denied the rumors of his resignation
the Ghanaian government offers its services in arbitrating
Nigerian disputes.

---

[3] The cleft sentence test should, wherever possible, be used in conjunction with other tests since there are known cases where the cleft sentence test is unreliable. For example, in the sentence

what John certainly is not is *honest*

the word "honest" does not seem to be a noun phrase, but simply an adjective in an adjective phrase. Thus, the cleft sentence test may not be a pure noun phrase test and should, therefore, be used with care.

Such sentences raise a very important question: Is the existence of a constituent which is permuted under the interrogative transformation a surface structure phenomenon or a deep structure phenomenon? In other words, are there auxiliaries in the deep structure? This question is currently being disputed by grammarians, and no definitive answer can be given. However, it is important to note certain facts—in particular, what happens when the interrogative transformation is applied to the sentences above.

did the Governor deny the rumors of his resignation?
did the Ghanaian government offer its services in arbitrating
    Nigerian disputes?

The word "did" in these sentences appears exactly where an auxiliary such as "will" or "can" would be expected. This suggests the possibility that an auxiliary does exist in the deep structure for all sentences. The auxiliary appears in declarative as well as in interrogative sentences if it is a so-called *modal*, like "will" or "can." If the auxiliary is not a modal, it will be deleted in declarative sentences and will appear only in interrogative sentences. If this hypothesis is true, then all sentences contain auxiliaries in their deep structures.

The existence of auxiliaries in deep structures is anything but conclusively confirmed. However, this assumption does lead to a partial explanation of some salient syntactic facts, and, for the present at least, we lose little of descriptive importance if we accept this hypothesis as true.

THE VERB PHRASE

The third major constituent of a sentence is the verb phrase, which contains the main verb of a sentence. In the sentence

the queen plays the piano

the string "plays the piano" is a verb phrase. The notion of verb phrase is illusive, and, indeed, there are few syntactic facts which suggest its existence. In the present analysis, this constituent plays a heuristic role in that it will allow the discussion of various syntactic phenomena in terms of a reasonable phrase structure classification.

In any case, there are certain transformational phenomena which indicate that strings such as "plays the piano" in the sentence above function as constituents. One of the tests involves what will be called *identical verb phrase deletion transformation.*

This transformation deletes the second verb phrase in each of the following sentences, since the verb phrases are identical (the tense suffixes are not important here).

> Stefan argues because his parents expect him to *argue.*
> Tino plays the harp because his family forces him to *play the harp.*

The results?

> Stefan argues because his parents expect him to.
> Tino plays the harp because his family forces him to.

A suspected verb phrase may be put in a string in which it can be deleted by the identical verb phrase deletion transformation. For example, if you think that "slew a Gorgon" may be a verb phrase, put it in a sentence from which it may be deleted:

> Stefan slew a Gorgon because his parents expected him to
> (slay a Gorgon).

The parentheses denote optionality of occurrence. In other words, "slew a Gorgon" is a verb phrase.

One of the factors which limits the value of the identical verb phrase deletion test is that it isolates surface structure constituents. For example, the identical verb phrase deletion test will show that "left at dawn" is a verb phrase in the sentence

> the magicians left at dawn.

However, it is not obvious that "left at dawn" is a constituent in the deep structure. In fact, one could reasonably argue that the deep structure of this sentence far more closely resembles that of the sentence

> it was at dawn that the magicians left.

SUMMARY

Noun phrases, auxiliaries, and verb phrases have been postulated as the basic constituents of sentences. Various transformational tests have been shown to isolate, more or less definitely, these constituents in surface structures and, in certain cases, in deep structures. The tests which are apparently relevant to the discovery of deep structure noun phrases are the passive, the reflexive, and the cleft sentence tests. The interrogative test reveals surface structure noun phrases and can also isolate auxiliaries. Finally, certain verb phrases are often discovered through use of the identical verb deletion test.

EXERCISE SIX

1. Draw deep structures for the following sentences:

   a. Was the Congressman influenced by that letter?
   b. Daisy should not reproach herself.

2. Explain how the deep structures of the sentences above become surface structures.

3. Find out whether the following are verb phrases by means of the verb phrase deletion test.

   a. caught the jewel thief
   b. become an artist
   c. buy worthless souvenirs

4. Explain how the interrogative test isolates auxiliaries.

5. As you have seen, "do" and its forms "did" and "does" function as auxiliaries in English.   How, then, can you explain the peculiar behavior of "did" in the sentences below?

   a. John did something.
   b. * did John something
   c. * John didn't something

   Is "do" perhaps not an auxiliary or is it the case that it can have more than one function?   Decide between these two alternatives and give evidence for your conclusion.

6. Are there other auxiliaries which have the same properties as "do"?   If so, state them, and show the properties in illustrative examples.

7. Explain in your own words how the existence of forms of "do" in negative and interrogative sentences suggests that auxiliaries exist in the deep structures of all sentences.

CHAPTER 7

Noun Phrase Constituents

We have assumed that every sentence consists of three major constituents. If we formulate a rule which represents this fact, this rule would be a kind of model for the unconscious psychological rule followed by every human being speaking a human language. The deep structure arrangement of the major constituents—noun phrase, auxiliary, and verb phrase—may be shown as a tree:

A rule representing this tree would state the following:

A sentence consists of a noun phrase followed by an auxiliary and a verb phrase. This rule can be abbreviated by convention as

$$S \rightarrow NP \ AUX \ VP$$

Such rules are called *phrase structure rules*. In this chapter, the phrase structure rule format will be used to show some of the constituents of noun phrases.

Look at the italicized noun phrases in the sentences following:

1. *the poet* intoned *the sonnet*
2. linguists are frequently unsure of *these intuitions*
3. *a minstrel* is said to have rescued Richard.

The words appearing in front of the nouns are called ARTICLES, with *the* designated as "definite," *a* as "indefinite," and *these*, as well as *this*, *that*, and *those*, as "demonstrative." (Traditionally, what we are

44

⟶ = CONSISTS OF

calling *demonstrative articles* have been called *demonstrative adjectives*. Here, the traditional terminology is misleading and incorrect. These words simply do not function in the same way that adjectives do, except that they can precede nouns, but so, for that matter, can the regular articles. Thus, there is little reason to call them adjectives. On the other hand, in a great many respects which are intuitively apparent, these words function in very much the same way as the articles "the" and "a." Thus, it is natural to call them articles.)

Two rules describe noun phrases. One says that a noun phrase need only consist of a noun:

$$NP \rightarrow N$$

The other says that a noun phrase consists of an article and a noun:

$$NP \rightarrow ART\ N$$

The two rules may be combined into one indicating both possibilities:

$$NP \rightarrow (ART)\ N$$

with the parentheses indicating that the enclosed constituent does not have to appear in every noun phrase.

Noun phrases may contain not only articles but sentences as well. Each italicized noun phrase in the sentences below contains an *embedded sentence:*

4. *The fact that the author was present* pleased the publishers
5. Rawlings rejected *the idea that we could sell the stadium.*

Since the passive transformation can be applied to the structures of these sentences, as shown below, the italicized strings are confirmed as noun phrases:

the publishers were pleased by *the fact that the author was present*
the idea that we could sell the stadium was rejected by Rawlings.

If the word "that" is excluded, the italicized noun phrases in 4 and 5 are seen to contain the sentences:

the author was present
we could sell the stadium.

The sole function of "that" here seems to be to indicate that the following string is an embedded sentence.

Since noun phrases can optionally contain sentences, the phrase structure rule above must now be amended to show the possibility of a sentence following a noun.

3 $NP \rightarrow (ART)\ N\ (S)$

Therefore the sentence

Rawlings rejected the idea that we could sell the stadium

will have this surface structure:

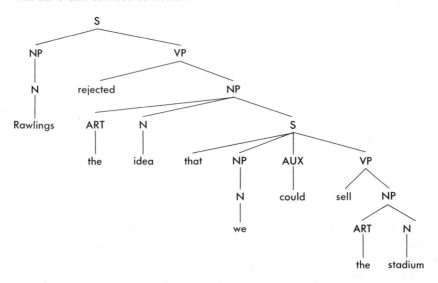

From Chapter 1 of this book you will recall that the number of English sentences known to the native speaker of English is infinite. For, if sentences contain noun phrases and if noun phrases may contain sentences, then sentences may be constructed which are indefinitely "deep." A sentence structure like the one below is possible:

> Epstein had mentioned the fact that Kant believed the rumor that Descartes rejected the hypothesis that matter had originated . . . .

Sentences like this are extremely uncommon in English, not because they are ungrammatical but because it is too easy to lose one's way in such a sentence.

English contains a *recursive* sequence of rules—the rule which expands S, and the rule which expands NP.

$$S \rightarrow NP\ AUX\ VP$$
$$NP \rightarrow ART\ N\ (S)$$

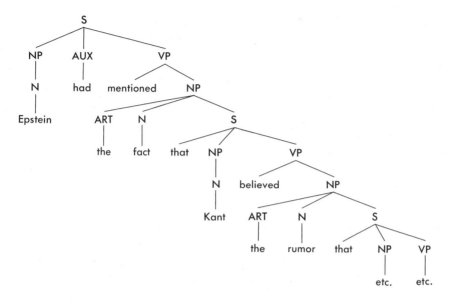

These rules can be applied one after the other, to each other's output, in a derivation which can be made as long as is desired.

There is one other very important noun phrase constituent configuration which requires discussion. In such a configuration, the noun phrase contains another noun phrase followed by a sentence. This construction, known as the *relative clause* construction, would appear in the following tree form:

Noun phrases containing relative clauses are italicized below:

6. *sentences which linguists should discuss* may perplex students
7. *the poem which won the award* amused the committee.

(You can show these are noun phrases by applying the passive test.) Assuming, in accordance with your intuitive understanding of these sentences, that the word "which" is nothing more than an altered form of "sentences" in 6 and "the poem" in 7, you can see that these noun phrases contain the two sentences below:

Linguists should discuss sentences
the poem won the award.

Consider now the rough deep structure for sentence 7 in which constituents such as "won" and "amused" are called *verbals*, abbreviated VB.

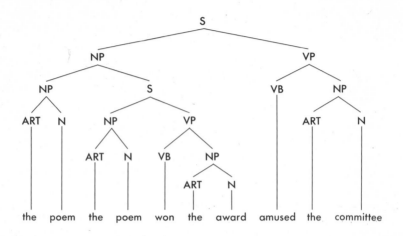

(The auxiliary is excluded from this structure in order to simplify the illustration. Whenever the auxiliary is irrelevant to the topic under discussion, it will be omitted.)

Two distinct phrase structures have now been given for sentences embedded inside noun phrases:

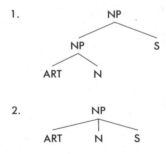

Corresponding to structure 1 are noun phrases such as:

> 1'   the boy whom I saw.

Corresponding to structure 2 are noun phrases of the form:

> 2'   the fact that Ricky came late.

Two distinct deep structures are posited in order to account for a very important difference between noun phrase 1' and noun phrase 2'. Noun phrase 1' contains a *relativized* noun phrase, i.e., "the boy." The embedded sentence in this noun phrase originated as "I saw the boy." In the generation of the surface structure for 1', "the boy" has, in effect, been replaced by "whom" and moved to the front of the embedded sentence. However, no such operation has been performed in noun phrase 2'. The word "that" is not a relative pronoun; it has not replaced a noun phrase in the embedded sentence; it simply marks the existence of an embedded sentence. If the two noun phrases had the same structure, then it would be impossible to state when the relative clause transformations, which will be studied in detail later, apply and when they do not. If the deep structures of relative clauses, i.e., 1', are distinct from *noun phrase complements* (as they are called), i.e., 2', then a unique phrase structure is provided to which the relative clause transformations can apply.

A more positive argument for postulating a distinct structure for relative clauses is that the relativization process seems to involve the identity of a noun phrase in the embedded sentence with a noun phrase outside of the embedded sentence to its left. If this is true, then structure 2 would have to fail as a plausible candidate for the deep structure of a relative clause, since to the left of the embedded sentence is not a noun phrase but a noun. Structure 1, on the other hand, succeeds, since a noun phrase does appear to the left of the embedded sentence and the identity requirement can be given in terms of this noun phrase and the identical noun phrase in the embedded sentence. It will be assumed, therefore, that relative clauses are analyzed as noun phrases which themselves contain a noun phrase followed by a sentence. This may be shown by the phrase structure rule:

noun phrase consist. of noun phrase & sentence

$$NP \rightarrow NP\ S$$

PHRASE STRUCTURE RULE

Actually, these arguments are far from conclusive. All that they really show is that relative clauses and noun phrase complements constructions have distinctly different properties. But they do not prove that these constructions have the phrase structures, attributed to them in the preceding pages. In particular the phrase structure 1 on page 48 is suspect since there is no known sense in which "the boy" inside of "the boy whom I saw" behaves like an NP. The structure proposed, then, for relative clauses is only tentative. Most probably it is not correct. Still, it is all that can be offered at the present time as at least a partial explanation for a number of facts. The inquiring student may well want to investigate this particular problem further.

SUMMARY

The phrase structure possibilities for noun phrases discussed in this chapter are summarized by the following rule, which uses braces to indicate alternatives:

$$NP \rightarrow \begin{Bmatrix} NP & S & \\ (ART) & N & (S) \end{Bmatrix} \textit{alternatively}$$

This rule now indicates several phrase structure possibilities. If the upper line of the two is taken, the structure is that of a noun phrase which contains a relative clause:

a scientist who studies compounds.

If the lower line of the rule is taken, four possibilities are open:

1. a noun only: Samson
2. an article and a noun: these principles
3. an article, a noun, and a sentence: the fact that light is matter
4. (on rare occasions) a noun followed by a sentence:

    I saw to *it that you were out of town.*

The last possibility is rare because the noun—which is usually the pronoun "it" if there is no article—is usually deleted by a transformation you will study later.

EXERCISE SEVEN

1. The following sentence is ambiguous:

    Washing machines will be unnecessary within two decades.

Explain the ambiguity in two ways:

  a. Write a paraphrase for each interpretation.
  b. Use terms like "subject," "verb," and "object" to characterize the relationships of "washing" to "machines."

2. The cleft sentence transformation cannot be used to identify certain types of noun phrase. The relative pronoun "who" cannot be substituted for "which" or vice versa. These facts suggest that in English, noun phrases may need to be described as possessing or not possessing a certain characteristic. Determine what this characteristic might be and how the two facts above support your conclusion.

3. Draw deep structures for

  a. The doctor who condemned the bill horrified the community.
  b. The fact that the doctor condemned the bill horrified the community.

4. Differences in deep structure should reveal differences in meaning. Explain the difference in meaning, if there is one, between 3*a* and 3*b*.

5. What facts justify the assumption that the italicized words in

   a. The idea that *Grimes exploited children* shocked Tom.
   b. The employer *who exploited children* left the country.

   are sentences embedded in noun phrases in deep structures?

6. What facts in addition to semantic ones justify the assumption that the italicized noun phrases in

   a. *The idea that Grimes exploited children* shocked Tom.
   b. *The employer who exploited children* left the country.

   have different deep structures?

7. In the sentence

   David defeated *Goliath.*

   the italicized words are nouns. However, they also must be analyzed as noun phrases. What arguments can you think of which support this assertion? (Hint: The passive transformation applies to the structure of the sentence above.)

8. Explain the differences in meaning, as far as you can detect them, among the following sentences:

   a. A book would be very useful now.
   b. The book would be very useful now.
   c. This book would be very useful now.
   d. That book would be very useful now.

9. Explain the differences in meaning among the following sentences:

   a. Some books would be very useful now.
   b. Books would be very useful now.
   c. The books would be very useful now.

CHAPTER **8**

Verb Phrase Constituents

Noun phrases and verb phrases may often contain some of the same kinds of constituents. But, just as every noun phrase has to contain at least one constituent, a noun, every verb phrase has to contain at least one constituent, a *verbal,* abbreviated VB. The verbals are italicized in the sentences below:

1. Annamaria can *clean* the manse
2. too much time *elapsed*
3. the doctor *condescended to* review my manuscript
4. a dispatcher *handed* the engineer a message
5. the instructor *fainted.*

A verbal is thus the primary constituent of a verb phrase (and is invariably the first constituent of a verb phrase in the deep structure). Some verb phrases contain only a verbal, as shown by sentence 5, which has the following tree representation:

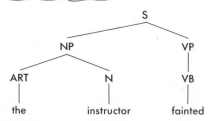

This can be described in a phrase structure rule:

$$VP \rightarrow VB$$

A verbal which is the only constituent of a verb phrase is known as an *intransitive* verbal.

Verb phrases may contain both a verbal and a noun phrase:

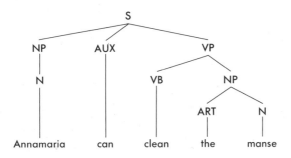

The phrase structure rule for this verb phrase is:

$$VP \rightarrow VB \ NP$$

Verbals which may be followed by a noun phrase are called *transitive* verbals. Some verbals do not immediately appear to be transitive because the noun phrase following the verbal contains a preposition:

6. the physicists worried about the radioactivity
7. Chicagoans approve of subways.

The noun phrases underlined contain the prepositions "about" and "of." Noun phrases without prepositions are not as different from these as they might seem, because before the sentences in which they occur become surface structures, all noun phrases contain prepositions.

The evidence for this is the process, called *nominalization,* which transforms whole sentences into noun phrases. Nominalization transforms a deep structure containing a sentence like

the old man collapsed

into the noun phrase

the old man's collapse

which could be the subject noun phrase of a sentence like

the old man's collapse horrified us.

The following sentences contain noun phrases without prepositions:

a. Annamaria cleans the manse
b. the doctor mentioned the fact that Joseph was late
c. the dispatcher hated the engineer
d. they destroyed the handbooks.

not clear

Compare these with the nominalized forms appearing below:

a. Annamaria's cleaning *of* the manse
b. the doctor's mention *of* the fact that Joseph was late
c. the dispatcher's hatred *of* (or *for*) the engineer
d. their destruction *of* the handbooks.

In each case, a preposition has appeared before the noun phrase which was the object in the original sentence above. The prepositions are in the constituent structure of the original four sentences, but have to be deleted *unless* the sentences are nominalized. Sometime during the generation of the sentences above, a preposition transformation deleted the prepositions. This will be discussed in more detail later. The point here is that the verb phrases in

the dispatcher hated the engineer

and

the physicists worried about the radioactivity

both contain transitive verbals. The presence or absence of the preposition does not affect the transitivity of the verbal.

The two verb phrase rules discussed earlier,

VP → VB
VP → VB NP

may be combined:

VP → VB (NP)

Such a rule, however, does not account for the presence of *two* noun phrases in some verb phrases:

a dispatcher handed *the engineer a message*
Balzac sent *Hugo a journal*
the citizens gave *DeGaulle their votes.*

These sentences contain what are called indirect object constructions. The indirect object noun phrases, "the engineer," "Hugo," and "DeGaulle," also had prepositions at an earlier stage in their generation. Again a preposition deletion transformation removed them. They would not have been deleted, however, if an *indirect object inversion transformation* had been applied. The resulting sentences would have been:

a dispatcher handed a message *to the engineer*
Balzac sent a journal *to Hugo*
the citizens gave their votes *to DeGaulle.*

The phrase structure rule for the verb phrase must be amended to show the possibility of two noun phrases in the verb phrase:

$$VP \rightarrow VB \ (NP) \ (NP)$$

Yet even this rule still excludes another possibility—verb phrases, like noun phrases, may contain an embedded sentence as a constituent. For example,

> the doctor condescended *to review my manuscript*
> the children refuse *to eat.*

At first glance, the italicized constituents bear only a partial resemblance to embedded sentences. In fact, they are what remains of embedded sentences after certain transformations have been applied. The subject noun phrase of each of the embedded sentences has been deleted by the identical noun phrase deletion transformation mentioned earlier, and another transformation, which will be studied later, has inserted "to" in front of the verb phrase of the embedded sentence. Undoing the effects of these two transformations on the constituents

> to review my manuscript
> to eat

will yield the sentences

> the doctor reviewed my manuscript
> the children eat.

The deep structure of a sentence may thus differ considerably from its surface structure, as demonstrated by the tree diagrams below for the sentence

> the children refuse to eat.

(Here, as elsewhere, the auxiliary and certain other details have been omitted for clarity.)

Deep Structure

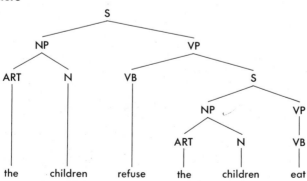

Surface Structure

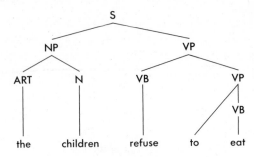

By application of noun phrase tests, it can be shown that the above sentences are embedded in verb phrases. Applying, for example, the most reliable of these, the cleft sentence test, we generate

> * what the doctor condescended was to review my manuscript
> * what the children refuse is to eat.

Had the sentences been embedded in noun phrases, however, the test would have yielded a positive result.

The phrase structure rule for verb phrases is now seen to be

$$VP \rightarrow VB \begin{Bmatrix} (NP)\ (NP) \\ (S) \end{Bmatrix}$$

This rule allows:

1) a verb phrase containing only a verbal,
2) a verb phrase containing a verbal followed by a single noun phrase,
3) a verb phrase containing a verbal followed by two noun phrases, and
4) a verb phrase containing a verbal followed by a sentence.

Actually, there is one further possibility which allows a verb phrase to be followed by a noun phrase followed itself by a sentence, as in

> the professor admonished Adams to proofread the paper
> we defy you to stay home.

This requires updating the phrase structure once more:

$$VP \rightarrow VB\ (NP) \begin{Bmatrix} (NP) \\ (S) \end{Bmatrix}$$

SUMMARY

This chapter has dealt with the constituents of verb phrases and has developed a phrase structure rule which characterizes possible verb phrase constituent structures.   The three phrase structure rules given thus far for the possible deep structures of English sentences are:

(1)   S → NP AUX VP

(2)   NP → $\begin{Bmatrix} \text{NP S} \\ \text{(ART) N (S)} \end{Bmatrix}$

(3)   VP → VB (NP) $\begin{Bmatrix} \text{(NP)} \\ \text{(S)} \end{Bmatrix}$

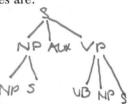

EXERCISE EIGHT

1. What inferences can you draw from the following data about the properties of verbs, adjectives, and nouns?

    a. 1. *Leavis* knew that a clique dominated book reviewing.
       2. * *the lamp* knew that a clique dominated book reviewing

    b. 1. *Leavis* was aware that a clique dominated book reviewing.
       2. * *the lamp* was aware that a clique dominated book reviewing

    c. 1. The scandal irritated Boswell exceedingly.
       2. * the scandal irritated *cheese* exceedingly

    d. 1. The scandal was exceedingly irritating *to Boswell*.
       2. * the scandal was exceedingly irritating *to cheese*

2. The rule for the verb phrase

    VP → VB (NP) $\begin{Bmatrix} \text{(NP)} \\ \text{(S)} \end{Bmatrix}$

    accounts for the verb phrase in sentences like

    >Bloom liked Stephen Daedalus.

    Does it also account for the verb phrase in

    >Bloom was fond of Stephen Daedalus.

    TENSE
    AUX?

    If it does, explain how.   If it doesn't, amend the rule so that it does, and explain how your rule accounts for the sentence.

3. Draw deep structures for:

    a. Balzac sent a journal to Hugo.
    b. A lady condescended to introduce Alice.
    c. The story I chose was written by Joyce.
    d. Joan was dismayed by the fact that the French would not attack the city.

4. Describe in as much detail as you can how each of the deep structures for the sentences in 3 is converted into surface structures.

5. What are the various meanings of the following sentence?

> The auditor said that he had married Antoinette.

6. Apply the cleft transformation to

> Joyce wrote the story that I chose.

7. Define the following terms:

   a. constituent
   b. transformation
   c. noun phrase
   d. relative clause
   e. deletion

8. Utilizing the phrase structure rules you have studied thus far, construct five deep structures which make use of recursion, the embedding of S's within other S's, and state the sentences to which these deep structures correspond.

9. Justify the following ordering of transformations by showing how ungrammatical surface structures would be generated if the ordering were different:

   a. Passive
   b. Negative
   c. Contraction
   d. Interrogative

CHAPTER 9

Features, Lexical Items, and Deep Structures

Obviously much of what you know about English is learned rather than innate. The particular words of a language have individual properties that are not an inevitable consequence of the fact that the language is a human one. You should not expect that the word for "trousers," for example, is plural in Finnish simply because it is plural in English. Many of the properties of particular words in a particular language may be peculiar to that language or perhaps to one group of closely-related languages. Other properties might well be expected to be the same in all languages. For example, it is highly improbable that a string meaning

* the schedule admired meat

would be a normal sentence in any human language.

Your knowledge of the idiosyncratic properties of words may be represented as a kind of internalized dictionary, which is here called a lexicon. Although you have never explicitly been told that certain verbals may not have certain types of subject nouns when occurring in the deep structures of sentences, you nevertheless do know, for example, that "schedule" is not the type of noun that may occur as the subject of a verbal like "admire," that verbals like "see" must have a subject noun with the property of *animateness* ("woman," "butcher," "dog," "Charles"), and that a verbal like "skate" almost always has a noun subject with the property *human* ("John," "the boys"). Cats normally skate only in works of fantasy, where both the linguistic and physical rules may be very different.

These lexical restrictions on the kinds of nouns that may serve as the

59

subject (or object, for that matter) of particular verbals are called *selectional restrictions*. Any account intended to explain your knowledge of your language must be able to explain why it is that a string like

The doctor smiled ingratiatingly

is a normal sentence of English, while

* the schedule admired meat

is not.

Grammarians treat a lexicon as an inventory of pairs of elements, with each pair called a *lexical entry*. The first element is a representation of the sound of a word, or of a part of a word in the cases of prefixes and suffixes. For our purposes, this element will be represented by the normal spelled version of the word. The second element is a representation of the meaning of the word, prefix, or suffix, except in those cases where no meaning is possessed. The properties of this element will be represented as a set of features. The presence of a feature is indicated by a plus (+) sign and its absence, by a minus (−) sign. In the discussion to follow, only the most salient features, e.g., ⟨+human⟩ or ⟨−human⟩, will be represented in lexical entries. To give a simple account of the word "doctor," it will suffice to list the word "doctor" and the features which indicate that it is a noun and human.

first element of lexical entry	doctor
second element	⟨+N⟩
	⟨+human⟩

Although it may seem that ⟨+animate⟩ belongs in the second element of the lexical entry, this feature is covered by a rule which says that all nouns with the feature ⟨+human⟩ are to be interpreted as containing the feature ⟨+animate⟩.

In a noun like "walrus," ⟨+animate⟩ would have to be included as this noun is ⟨−human⟩:

walrus
$$\begin{bmatrix} \text{walrus} \\ \langle +N \rangle \\ \langle +\text{animate} \rangle \\ \langle -\text{human} \rangle \end{bmatrix}$$

Nouns are either concrete, ⟨+concrete⟩, like "pipe," "diaper," or "anteater," or abstract, ⟨−concrete⟩, like "truth," "justice," or "politics"; they may be common, ⟨+common⟩, like "door," "linguist," or "loyalty," or proper, ⟨−common⟩, like "Chicago" or "George"; they are either count nouns, ⟨+count⟩, like "eraser," or "guitar," or mass nouns,

⟨−count⟩, like "sugar," "water," or "money."   Mass nouns normally take "much" rather than "many,"

> Is there much sugar in the sack?
> * Are there many sugars in the sack?

and are not normally counted, although this may occur in some specialized disciplines:

> Our analysis reveals thirteen different sugars in this compound.

Nouns have many other features, more than can be adequately dealt with here.   Those which have been discussed here provide a good illustration of how nouns are represented in the lexicon.   Some other important features are presented later in this chapter.   Following is a sample lexicon for eight nouns.[4]

bakery
$$\begin{bmatrix} \text{bakery} \\ \langle +N \rangle \\ \langle +\text{common} \rangle \\ \langle +\text{concrete} \rangle \\ \langle -\text{animate} \rangle \\ \langle +\text{count} \rangle \end{bmatrix}$$

honesty
$$\begin{bmatrix} \text{honesty} \\ \langle +N \rangle \\ \langle +\text{common} \rangle \\ \langle -\text{concrete} \rangle \\ \langle -\text{count} \rangle \end{bmatrix}$$

psychiatrist
$$\begin{bmatrix} \text{psychiatrist} \\ \langle +N \rangle \\ \langle +\text{common} \rangle \\ \langle +\text{concrete} \rangle \\ \langle +\text{human} \rangle \\ \langle +\text{count} \rangle \end{bmatrix}$$

Rome
$$\begin{bmatrix} \text{Rome} \\ \langle +N \rangle \\ \langle -\text{common} \rangle \\ \langle +\text{concrete} \rangle \\ \langle -\text{animate} \rangle \\ \langle +\text{count} \rangle \end{bmatrix}$$

---

[4] The order in which features are listed in a lexical entry such as the above is not consequential.

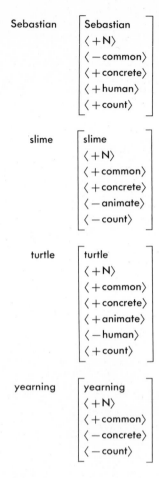

Sebastian
$$\begin{bmatrix} \text{Sebastian} \\ \langle +N \rangle \\ \langle -\text{common} \rangle \\ \langle +\text{concrete} \rangle \\ \langle +\text{human} \rangle \\ \langle +\text{count} \rangle \end{bmatrix}$$

slime
$$\begin{bmatrix} \text{slime} \\ \langle +N \rangle \\ \langle +\text{common} \rangle \\ \langle +\text{concrete} \rangle \\ \langle -\text{animate} \rangle \\ \langle -\text{count} \rangle \end{bmatrix}$$

turtle
$$\begin{bmatrix} \text{turtle} \\ \langle +N \rangle \\ \langle +\text{common} \rangle \\ \langle +\text{concrete} \rangle \\ \langle +\text{animate} \rangle \\ \langle -\text{human} \rangle \\ \langle +\text{count} \rangle \end{bmatrix}$$

yearning
$$\begin{bmatrix} \text{yearning} \\ \langle +N \rangle \\ \langle +\text{common} \rangle \\ \langle -\text{concrete} \rangle \\ \langle -\text{count} \rangle \end{bmatrix}$$

These features may influence in important ways the choice of words and the arrangement of words in a surface structure. In the following strings, for example, the distinction between $\langle +\text{human} \rangle$ and $\langle -\text{human} \rangle$ is essential to the explanation of the ungrammaticality of strings 3 and 4:

1. the ideas which influenced me most were highly abstract
2. the philosopher who claimed that matter is indivisible was a schizophrenic
3. * the ideas who influenced me most were highly abstract
4. * the philosopher which claimed that matter is indivisible was a schizophrenic.

In English and in some other languages, relative pronouns are differentiated according to whether they have replaced human or nonhuman nouns. While "that" can be used for either in English, "who" is used only with human nouns, and "which" only with non-human nouns.

A similar effect is observable for the masculine, ⟨+masculine⟩, and feminine, ⟨+feminine⟩, features when applying transformations like the reflexive. In order to apply the reflexive transformation correctly to the following strings, one needs to know whether the subject noun is masculine or feminine:

> the boy hurt the boy
> the ewe hurt the ewe.

The presence of ⟨+masculine⟩ or ⟨+feminine⟩ determines the conversion of the object noun phrases into the correct reflexive pronouns:

> the boy hurt himself
> the ewe hurt herself.

In the event that the subject noun is a third person neuter, the correct reflexive pronoun, "itself," is generated in the absence of the features ⟨+masculine⟩ or ⟨+feminine⟩.

Quite recently, several grammarians have found some reason to believe that verbs and adjectives are not distinct constituents in deep structures. Rather, it is supposed, both are verbals, and their differences are represented in the lexicon in terms of the feature ⟨+V⟩ for verbs, and ⟨−V⟩ for adjectives. Thus, the verb "kick" would basically carry the features ⟨+VB⟩, indicating the word is a verbal, and ⟨+V⟩, indicating that the verbal is a verb. The adjective "honest," on the other hand, would carry the features ⟨+VB⟩ and ⟨−V⟩.

One of the reasons underlying this conclusion is that verbs and adjectives seem to share many properties. For instance, just as there are non-action verbs, like "own" and "resemble," and action verbs, like "kick" and "persuade," there are nonaction adjectives, like "short" and "tipsy," and action adjectives, like "honest" and "patient." The differences between action and non-action verbals show up in a number of interesting ways, one of which is the fact that action verbals can appear in imperative sentences but non-action verbals cannot:

> kick the ball!
> persuade him to leave!
> be honest!
> be patient!
>
> * own the house
> * resemble your father
> * be short
> * be tipsy.

Secondly, action verbals may take the so-called *progressive aspect;* non-action verbals cannot:

> the girl is kicking the ball
> the girl is persuading him to leave
> I am being honest
> the conductor is being patient

> * the patron is owning the house
> * the girl is resembling her father
> * they are being short
> * the men were being tipsy.

Finally, action verbals can appear in a number of embedded sentences in which non-action verbals cannot. This is apparently determined by the verb in the main sentence, and the restriction holds, for example, for the verb "told":

> I told the girl to kick the ball
> I told the girl to persuade him to leave
> I told the girl to be honest
> I told the girl to be patient

> * I told the girl to own the house
> * I told the girl to resemble her father
> * I told the girl to be short
> * I told the girl to be tipsy.

The common characteristics of verbs and adjectives are at least partially explained on the assumption that both are instances of the same kind of constituent. Thus, lexical entries for four verbals would appear as follows:

$$
\text{kick} \quad
\begin{bmatrix}
\text{kick} \\
\langle +\text{VB} \rangle \\
\langle +\text{V} \rangle \\
\langle +\text{action} \rangle
\end{bmatrix}
$$

$$
\text{own} \quad
\begin{bmatrix}
\text{own} \\
\langle +\text{VB} \rangle \\
\langle +\text{V} \rangle \\
\langle -\text{action} \rangle
\end{bmatrix}
$$

$$
\text{honest} \quad
\begin{bmatrix}
\text{honest} \\
\langle +\text{VB} \rangle \\
\langle -\text{V} \rangle \\
\langle +\text{action} \rangle
\end{bmatrix}
$$

$$
\text{tipsy} \quad \begin{bmatrix} \text{tipsy} \\ \langle +VB \rangle \\ \langle -V \rangle \\ \langle -\text{action} \rangle \end{bmatrix}
$$

This assumption also allows one to speak of such things as transitive and intransitive adjectives. For example, the adjectives "dead" and "tall" in the following sentences can be thought of as intransitive:

> the king is dead
> the warrior is tall,

while the adjectives "fond" and "alien" in the sentences below are in this sense transitive:

> the boy is fond of his dog
> that chant is alien to our culture.

One can even find cases of verb phrases containing an adjective and an embedded sentence:

> this boy is competent to run a laboratory
> the machine is able to produce a million envelopes an hour.

These sentences exhaust three cases of the phrase structure rule for verb phrases:

$$
\text{VP} \rightarrow \text{VB (NP)} \begin{Bmatrix} \text{(NP)} \\ \text{(S)} \end{Bmatrix}
$$

Of current interest in grammatical research is the fact that no instances have yet been found of the phrase structure configurations

$$
\text{VB NP NP}
$$

or

$$
\text{VB NP S}
$$

when the verbal is an adjective.

Many grammarians do not accept the view that verbs and adjectives are the same kind of constituent. They point out that, by the same logic used to reach this conclusion, one could reach an equally plausible conclusion that adjectives and nouns are the same kind of constituent in deep structures. The results of these ongoing deliberations are still too fragmentary to warrant detailed study. The point to keep in mind is simply this: The view that adjectives and verbs are the same kind of constituent in the deep structure, the view adopted in this presentation, explains many phenomena, but it cannot at present be accepted as proven or as being the final word on how seemingly different surface structure constituents are linked in deep structures.

To return to the discussion of noun features, there are other features which a particular noun may or may not have. Such a feature is the one which represents singularity, ⟨+singular⟩, and plurality, ⟨−singular⟩. Most nouns, with the exception of ⟨−count⟩ nouns, can be either singular or plural, e.g., "book," "books." This raises an important question: Is it necessary to list both the singular and plural forms of a noun in the lexicon, thus creating two lexical entries? This is possible, of course, but to do so would obscure the information that, except for the *number* differences, these nouns are identical. The problem is to indicate in the deep structure that a noun is either singular or plural without having to represent this distinction with two separate lexical items in the lexicon.

One of the ways in which grammarians resolve this problem is to assume the existence of rules which subcategorize constituents such as nouns and verbals. These rules apply before lexical items are introduced into deep structures. An example of these rules is given below:

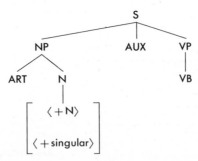

This rule asserts that a noun dominates a *segment* (a cluster of features) which is a noun segment, indicated by the feature ⟨+N⟩, and is either singular (if the ⟨+singular⟩ option is chosen) or plural (if the ⟨−singular⟩ option is chosen). Rules such as the one above are called *segment structure rules*.

All the phrase structure rules studied so far have been applied to the following constituent structure. Note in particular the part affected by the segment structure rule:

This shows that the subject noun phrase contains a noun which has the features ⟨+N⟩ and ⟨+singular⟩—or, a singular noun. As we stated above, segment structure rules must be applied before items from the lexicon are introduced into the deep structure. For example, the item "book" does not have a singular or plural feature in the lexicon, but takes on the feature, in this case ⟨+singular⟩, which has already been specified for the subject noun position in the deep structure by the segment structure rule. Thus, the lexical entry

$$
\text{book} \quad
\begin{bmatrix}
\text{book} \\
\langle +\text{N} \rangle \\
\langle +\text{common} \rangle \\
\langle +\text{concrete} \rangle \\
\langle -\text{animate} \rangle \\
\langle +\text{count} \rangle
\end{bmatrix}
$$

would appear in the deep structure as follows:

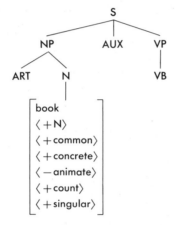

The assumption of segment structure rules makes it unnecessary to mark lexical items with respect to singularity and plurality. Now it is not necessary for the lexical item to contain any indication as to number, since this information is supplied by the segment structure rule before lexical items are placed into the deep structure.

whereby # becomes a grammatical not lexical notion

SUMMARY

Features which are idiosyncratic for particular words are represented in the lexicon. For each word there is a lexical entry element containing all particular features of the word, except those which are predictable from other features—e.g., ⟨+human⟩ predicts ⟨+animate⟩, ⟨+animate⟩ predicts ⟨+concrete⟩.

This allows us to revise certain of the lexical entries previously given, for example, the entry for "turtle" on page 62. As is now seen, this entry need not contain the features ⟨+concrete⟩ and ⟨+animate⟩ since both of these features are predicted implicitly by the feature ⟨−human⟩.

Going one step further, one can understand why the feature ⟨−animate⟩ has been left out of the lexical entry for "honesty" (p. 61) and "yearning" (p. 62). Since these nouns are ⟨−concrete⟩, they are necessarily inanimate, i.e., ⟨−animate⟩.

Certain features are also introduced into deep structures by segment structure rules, which subcategorize nouns and verbals. Such rules, for example, make it unnecessary to have the singular and plural forms of a noun listed separately in the lexicon. When a lexical item is introduced into a deep structure, its features are combined with those in the segment generated by the segment structure rules. Thus, the segment now possesses the generated features and those which accompanied the lexical item in the lexicon.

EXERCISE NINE

1. a. List the embedded sentences below.
   b. Identify each as either embedded in an NP or in a VP.
   c. Apply the cleft sentence transformation to show whether each embedded sentence is or is not embedded in an NP.

   The first sentence is done for you.

   1. I wanted to file a protest.
   2. Caesar refused to submit to the senate.
   3. Voltaire denied that the world was like a clock.
   4. De Stogumber continued to protest vociferously.
   5. Melissa hated leaving the house untidy.

   Sample Answer:

   1. a. to file a protest
      b. embedded in a noun phrase
      c. What I wanted was to file a protest.

2. Explain the terms

   a. selectional restrictions
   b. subcategorization
   c. segment

3. Make up lexical entries for the following nouns:

   a. materialism   f. Wyatt
   b. porter   g. mud
   c. panda   h. gender
   d. caution   i. song
   e. allergy   j. Cleveland

4. Why is gender a syntactically important feature of nouns as well as of pronouns?

5. Draw deep structures for

   a. The announcement that the allies refused to release the prisoners was released by the commander.
   b. Ira thinks that Mary likes to dance.

6. What is the difference in meaning between sentence *a* and sentence *b*?

   a. The committee, which hopes to provide the best available medical care for the children, consists mainly of doctors.
   b. The committee which hopes to provide the best available medical care for the children consists mainly of doctors.

7. Write two examples of sentences to which the identical verb phrase deletion transformation has been applied. Then rewrite the sentences, putting back the deleted verb phrase.

8. What are the elementary transformations? Give examples of transformations in English that make use of these processes.

CHAPTER 10

Constituent Functions

In the chapters preceding this, the terms "subject" and "object" have been used quite loosely without any attempt at definition. You were expected to fill the gap with the residual knowledge of English grammar that most readers of this book have acquired. This omission does not mean that these concepts are either too obvious or too trivial to require discussion. Rather, these notions raise a number of important questions which could not be tackled without a prior understanding of the differences between deep and surface structures but which, unfortunately, are not fully elucidated even by these concepts.

If a grammar is to explain the linguistic abilities of the speaker of English, it should be able to account for the difference in meaning between two sentences which contain exactly the same words:

1. ambassadors should ignore generals
2. generals should ignore ambassadors.

First, look at the deep structures for these two sentences. Details such as the complete segment structure have been omitted, since they are not germane here. Instead, actual lexical items have been inserted:

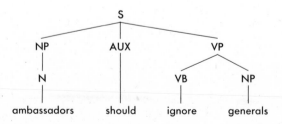

70

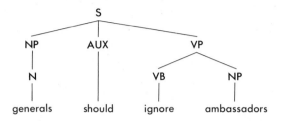

It is easily seen that, although both deep structures contain the same words, the positioning of those words in the two trees is quite different structurally. Your understanding of English sentences involves considerably more than a knowledge of words. A major part of the meaning of any sentence is associated with the structure within which words are arranged. Your interpretation of the constituents may vary according to their position in the deep structure. For instance, although the noun phrase "ambassadors" seems to be the same in both structures, you understand in the first that the "ambassadors" should be doing the "ignoring," whereas in the second, "ambassadors" are the ones who should be ignored.

This kind of information, vital for the semantic interpretation of sentences, is often called *functional information*. Functional information is obtained not from the lexical meaning of the individual constituents but from the way constituents are organized in deep structures. A constituent A which is a "descendant" of a constituent B is said to be *dominated* by B. A constituent A which is a "descendant" of a constituent B is said to be *immediately dominated* by B if no other constituents intervene between A and B.

Look again at the first deep structure. The constituent S immediately dominates three constituents, only one of which is a noun phrase. In the simple tree diagram below,

the noun phrase is immediately dominated by S. A noun phrase immediately dominated by S will be called the deep structure subject of a sentence. In this example, the deep subject noun phrase tells who or what is doing the ignoring.

The notion "doer of an action," of being an "agent," is not generally explained by the notion "deep subject of a sentence," however, and this is one of the primary facts which grammarians are currently trying to

explain.   For example, in the sentence

> John underwent surgery at the hands of Dr. Jones

it is clear that the doer of the action is not John but Dr. Jones.   The action done is not "undergoing" but what is included in "surgery." Yet, as far as is known, Dr. Jones is not the deep structure subject of the sentence above.   Still, the concept of deep structure subject does allow an explanation of the semantic distinction between sentences 1 and 2 above, and a vast number of other similar pairs.   When a verb has an agent at all, the deep subject is invariably the agent.

Keep in mind that the deep subject of a sentence is not a constituent, as is an NP, an AUX, or a VP.   It would be wrong to assume that a subject is a constituent rather than a function played by a constituent in a particular configuration.   If, for example, one assumed a deep structure which contained a subject constituent as well as a noun phrase, as in the following structure,

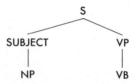

one would be missing the generalization that the notion of subject is completely characterized in terms of a noun phrase being immediately dominated by S.   Thus, the constituent SUBJECT is redundant.   Subject is a particular position in a sentence that may be occupied by a noun phrase; it is not the content of the constituent which is important here, but its position.

A noun phrase immediately dominated by the verb phrase of a deep structure is the *object of that verb phrase:*

Thus, in deep structure 1, the object of the verb phrase is "generals," and in deep structure 2, it is "ambassadors."   The notion of "object of a verb phrase" partially represents the kind of knowledge which a native speaker utilizes when he identifies "generals" in deep structure 1 and "ambassadors" in deep structure 2 as what are traditionally called the "recipients of the action."

Once again, however, semantic intuitions do not seem to be entirely reflected in the notion "object of the verb phrase." Such objects seem to receive many kinds of interpretations, depending upon the verbal in the verb phrase. Consider the following sentences:

they built a house
they destroyed a house.

Only in the second sentence could the object be thought of as receiving some action, in traditional terms. In the first sentence, the object "a house" is interpreted as an object of result, something which does not receive building, but which is the result of building. The same kind of observation can be made for subjects. In the first sentence below, the subject seems to be acting as some kind of agent. In the second, the subject is the recipient of something:

the boy slammed the door
the boy suffered a blow.

In the sentence following, the subject is in some sense a participant, but neither an agent nor a recipient:

the cat died from pneumonia.

The meaning of a sentence depends to a certain extent on the functional role of the constituents of the sentence. Still, it should be kept in mind that the functional relations between constituents in deep structures do not characterize all that a speaker knows about the relations between noun phrases and verbals. The characterization of this knowledge is currently one of the central issues in grammatical research.

The following sentences suggest that it is necessary to make a distinction between the subject of the deep structure and the subject of the surface structure:

1. ambassadors should ignore generals
3. generals should be ignored by ambassadors.

The two sentences have exactly the same meaning. They are synonymous because they have identical deep structures. The difference in form is due to the fact that in the generation of sentence 3, the passive transformation was applied to produce the passive version of sentence 1. Despite the application of this transformation, the deep structure functions of the noun phrases remain unchanged. The noun phrase containing "ambassadors" is still the deep subject of the sentence because, even though its position has been changed, the noun phrase is still traceable to a deep structure in which this noun phrase is immediately dominated by S.   This is borne out by the native speaker's recognition of "ambassadors" as the "doer" of the ignoring in both sentences.   And the noun phrase containing "generals" is still the object of the verb phrase in the sense that it remains the recipient of the action.   Transformations are, you should remember, meaning-preserving.   This implies that the deep structure is not lost, that it is still traceable, or as it is sometimes worded, that the deep structure is *recoverable*.   Thus the noun phrase containing "generals" in sentence 3 may still be traced to a deep structure in which it was immediately dominated by VP.

The noun phrase containing the word "generals" is the object of the verb phrase in the deep structure of sentence 3, and it is also the *surface subject of the sentence*.   The term "surface subject of the sentence" refers to the *subject of the surface structure of the sentence*, never the deep structure.   The subject relation remains the same,

$$S$$
$$NP$$

but the relationship is in the surface structure, not the deep structure.

It is the surface structure subject which is relevant to *agreement*.   For example, in the following strings:

> the omens are auspicious
> * the omens is auspicious

the second string is ungrammatical; the singular form of "be" has been used rather than the plural form.   The surface subject of the sentence determines whether the singular or plural form of "be" is required. The claim that the subject used to determine agreement is the surface subject is substantiated by the following examples:

4. Lucifer was being denounced by the archangels
5. the archangels were denouncing Lucifer.

In sentence 4, the form of "be" is singular because the subject noun phrase "Lucifer" is singular.   However, "Lucifer" is not the deep subject of the sentence, only the surface subject.   In the deep structure, "Lucifer" is the object of the verb phrase, as it is in sentence 5. If agreement were determined by the deep structure functions of constituents, instead of the surface structure functions, the following string would have been generated:

* Lucifer were being denounced by the archangels.

Sentences, then, have two subjects: deep subjects and surface subjects. Deep subjects give limited but important information about the meaning of a sentence; surface subjects determine agreement. However, they are not always different. For example, the deep subject of sentence 5 is "the archangels." And the surface subject is also "the archangels," since no transformation has moved this noun phrase to some other position.

Many sentences contain no surface subjects because the noun phrases which would have fulfilled this function have been deleted. Examples of this are imperative sentences:

> help yourself!
> fire the cannon!

and many kinds of embedded sentences, like those italicized below:

> Siegfried wants *to find the ring*
> the opportunity *to study in London* appealed to Cabot.

Subjects and objects are not the only syntactic functions, and noun phrases are not the only constituents which have functions. The constituent *sentence,* for example, carries out a particular function in the sentence

> knowledge which is implicit interests Michael Polanyi.

To see what this function is, look more closely at the noun phrase subject of the sentence:

> knowledge which is implicit.

This noun phrase has roughly the following deep structure:

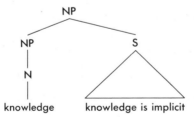

(The triangle is the customary abbreviation for constituent structures when full details are not required.)

Here the noun phrase consists of a noun phrase followed by an embedded sentence. The name given to the function performed by the embedded sentence is *relative clause.* Note that relative clauses are not constituents but functions performed by embedded sentences. Although only the constituent S may function as a relative clause, this constituent has other functions as well. The following diagram

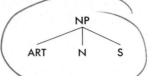

is the approximate structure of noun phrases like

> the fact that unemployment rose
> an opportunity for Cabot to study in London.

In this tree the S immediately follows a noun, *not* a noun phrase. When a sentence is embedded in a noun phrase and follows a noun, it is said to be functioning as a *noun phrase complement*. (Embedded sentence structures are discussed in greater detail in subsequent chapters.)

Finally, you have already met with sentences embedded in verb phrases, as shown in this diagram:

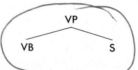

This is roughly the deep structure of verb phrases like

> refused to sign the petition
> condescended to review the manuscript.

When a sentence is embedded in a verb phrase and is immediately dominated by a verb phrase, it is said to be functioning as a *verb phrase complement*.

SUMMARY

In this chapter you have seen that constituents of a sentence may function in various ways. Noun phrases were described as performing three basic functions:

1. deep subjects of sentences
2. surface subjects of sentences
3. objects of verb phrases.

The deep subject and the object provide certain semantic information about a sentence; the surface subject determines agreement.

Sentences, too, were described as performing three basic syntactic functions:

1. relative clauses

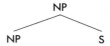

2. noun phrase complements

3. verb phrase complements

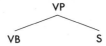

When a sentence is not embedded at all, it is called a *main sentence.* Remember that all sentences, embedded or main, contain deep subjects, although the noun phrase which might have been the surface subject is deleted under certain circumstances.

EXERCISE TEN

1. The recursive mechanism in language, which allows sentences to be embedded inside of other sentences, permits the generation of sentences of infinite length. But none of the sentences which you ever use is infinite. Write a brief paragraph offering an explanation for the fact that the full resources of English are not made use of by speakers of English.

2. Draw deep structure trees for

   a. The chairman proposed a solution which someone didn't like.
   b. Was the story that Herbert refused to pay taxes invented by malicious neighbors?
   c. John hurt himself.

3. State five syntactic functions in the deep structure.

4. What justifications can you find for treating sentences *a* and *b* as different grammatically from sentences *c* and *d*?

   a. Souza sent Mahalia an orchid.
   b. The college gave Steerforth a scholarship.

  c. The Bishop called Julian a fool.

  d. The association elected Russell president.

5. What are segment structure rules?

6. What inferences can you draw from the following?

  a. An intruder is in the garden.

  b. There is an intruder in the garden.

  c. The intruder is in the garden.

  d. * there is the intruder in the garden (This string is ungrammatical with respect to use of the expletive "there.")

More specifically, what transformation would you propose to explain these facts, and what is the limitation on its application?

7. As you shall see in a later chapter, the agreement transformation makes use of the number (i.e., singular or plural) and person (i.e., first, second, or third) information contained in the subject noun in the surface structure. What is the ordering of the agreement transformation with respect to the transformation which you formulated in 6? The following data will help:

  a. There are three boys in the room.

  b. There is a boy in the room.

  c. * there is three boys in the room

  d. * there are a boy in the room

What conclusions can you draw about "there"? Is it a surface subject? In fact, do sentences *a* and *b* have surface subjects? If not, what has become of them?

8. What differences in meaning can you perceive between the *a* and *b* sentence in each set, and how would this difference be represented in the deep structure?

  1. a. All of the workers will wear carnations.
     b. All workers will wear carnations.

  2. a. Many of the poets won't teach for a living.
     b. Many poets won't teach for a living.

  3. a. None of the smokers has ever had lung cancer.
     b. No smokers have ever had lung cancer.

  4. a. Few of the doctors approve of our remedy.
     b. Few doctors approve of our remedy.

  5. a. Several of the women dived into the pool.
     b. Several women dived into the pool.

  6. a. Six of the characters searched for an author.
     b. Six characters searched for an author.

SECTION THREE

Segment Transformations and Syntactic Processes

Articles, Suffixes, and Segment Transformations

One of the most important conclusions reached in the preceding chapters is that the deep structure of a sentence provides a specification of the meaning of a sentence. The meaning is given by the constituent structure of the deep structure and by the features of the segments.

Segments appear in deep structures as the result of two processes. First, they are created by the segment structure rules. Second, their feature content is further specified by the introduction from the lexicon of lexical items whose features are added to those generated earlier by the segment structure rules.

It is an interesting and important fact about English and other languages that certain characteristics of nouns and verbals are reflected in the surface structure while others are not. For example, the features ⟨ +animate⟩ and ⟨ −animate⟩ have no surface structure characteristics. It is generally the case for such features that nouns cannot be marked + for them on one occasion and − on another.[5] Thus, the noun "pen" never has the feature ⟨ −concrete⟩, and the noun "truth" never has the feature ⟨ +concrete⟩. Presumably, because these features are unchanging in a noun from one use to the next, there is no reason why they should be indicated in the surface structure.

---

[5] These restrictions are often violated in literature, especially in fantasies such as *Alice in Wonderland*. These violations assist in the general otherworldly effect of such works. Generally the violations accompany violations of the natural physical order. For interesting comments on this, see D. Rackin's fine article, "Alice's Journey to the End of Night," *PMLA*, 81 (1966). Note also that some words have more than one meaning ("stroller," "speaker," etc.). This would be shown in the lexicon, of course.

Consider the following words with respect to singularity and plurality:

> engineer
> typists
> floor
> hopes
> wolverines

You know that two of the words are singular, ⟨+singular⟩, and three are plural, ⟨−singular⟩. This is because the plural nouns have the suffix "s." (Certain nouns, of course, have the variant spelling "es," or use somewhat different forms. In Chapter 9 you saw that a noun *could* have the feature ⟨+singular⟩ on one occasion and ⟨−singular⟩ on another. In other words, number is not normally part of the meaning of most nouns. It is hardly surprising, then, that number normally has to be signaled in the surface structure form of nouns by the presence or absence of the suffix "s."

Such syntactic phenomena as number on nouns raise a very important question, one to which a definitive answer cannot be given at the present time: How can number be represented in deep structures? First, it could be represented in terms of the features ⟨+singular⟩ and ⟨−singular⟩ generated on noun segments by the segment structure rules, in the fashion discussed earlier.

Second, number can be thought of in terms of constituent structure. Here, one might suppose the existence of two constituents, SG (for singular) and PL (for plural), generated by the phrase structure rule for noun phrases. The noun phrase "the books" would appear roughly as follows in the two systems.

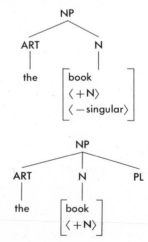

In the first system, a transformation is required to generate a plural suffix, i.e., "s." In the second, the constituent PL ultimately becomes "s."

Most grammarians currently believe the feature analysis to be more sound than the constituent analysis for rather complex reasons. Generally, it can be said that there is absolutely no evidence for the existence of constituents such as SG (singular) and PL (plural) in deep structures. Furthermore, if it is assumed that singular and plural are represented as features, the grammar becomes that much more general. The reason is that it is necessary to employ these features on nouns even where singular and plural are represented as constituents. For example, nouns such as "pants" must always be plural. There are two ways to represent this fact. First, one might propose some sort of special feature on "pants" in the lexicon which would require it to appear just before the PL constituent and not before the SG constituent. Second, one might simply add the feature ⟨ −singular⟩ to the noun "pants" in the lexicon. This latter proposal eliminates the need for both the PL or SG constituent and the special lexical feature required by nouns such as "pants." Thus the lexicon would only contain inherent features which indicate not position but characteristics of the words.

In the deep structure, the noun "poets" would look something like this:

$$
\begin{array}{c}
\text{NP} \\
| \\
\text{N} \\
| \\
\begin{bmatrix}
\text{poet} \\
\langle +\text{N}\rangle \\
\langle +\text{human}\rangle \\
\langle -\text{singular}\rangle
\end{bmatrix}
\end{array}
$$

What happens next is that the *noun suffix transformation* introduces a segment which will eventually become the noun suffix "s." This transformation can only be applied to nouns which carry the feature ⟨ −singular⟩ and form their plurals in the regular way. (A noun like "foot" is not regular, as its plural is "feet." In such cases the noun suffix transformation is blocked. The form "feet" is introduced when the segment structure rule has generated the feature ⟨ −singular⟩.) The introduced segment, which contains the feature ⟨ −singular⟩, is usually called the *affix* segment and is labeled ⟨ +affix⟩. The diagram that follows on page 84 shows the effect of the noun suffix transformation.

It is important to notice that transformations can introduce segments but not words into structures. The question that remains concerns how

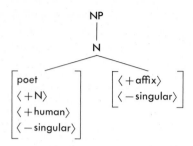

segments introduced by transformations become actual words or affixes. The answer is that after all transformations have been applied, words are introduced from the lexicon for a second time.   At this time, during what is called *second lexical pass,* words or affixes replace the segments generated by transformations.   The first lexical pass occurs when lexical items are introduced into deep structures before the application of the transformations.   It is particularly interesting that lexical items introduced in the first lexical pass can be replaced, although not too often, during the second lexical pass.   This is what happens in the case of reflexive sentences.   You will recall that the sentence

John hurt himself

originates roughly as the structure of the following string:

* John hurt John.

When the object noun phrase acquires the feature ⟨ +reflexive⟩ by the reflexive transformation, it is replaced in the second lexical pass by the appropriate form of the reflexive pronoun.
    The effect of the second lexical pass on the NP diagrammed below is:

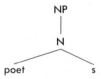

Both "poet" and "s" are immediately dominated by N.   This shows that, taken together, they constitute a single noun, the noun "poets."
    The noun suffix transformation is just one of the family of segment transformations which introduce segments into constituent structures, provided the deep structure contains certain specified features.   A particularly important one is the *article transformation.*
    Until now, articles have been represented in deep structures by the constituent ART.   For reasons which will become clearer in the

chapter on pronouns, it will be assumed here that articles are represented in deep structures not as constituents, but as features of nouns. Look now at these articles:

the
a, an
this
that
these
those

Since these articles are different in meaning, they must be represented by different features in the deep structures. First, notice that the article "a" and its variant differ syntactically from other articles. For example, from

a book is on the table

a transformation produces the variant sentence

there is a book on the table.

However, if the article is not "a" or "an," this transformation cannot apply. Thus, the sentence

the mare is running at Hialeah

does not allow the variant

* there is the mare running at Hialeah

except in the totally different sense of the location interpretation of "there." But this is something quite different from the *existential* interpretation of "there" in sentences like

there is truth in what you say.

Thus, the transformation which produces the existential "there" sentences can apply just in cases where the subject noun of the deep structure has the article "a" (or "an"), as in

a book

or no article, as in

books.

The articles "a" and "an" are generally called *indefinite articles* and may be shown in the deep structure as the noun feature ⟨ −definite⟩.

They appear only before singular nouns:

> a poet wrote this
> * a poets wrote this.

When plural nouns are not preceded by an article, they are interpreted as indefinite:

> poets wrote this.

The deep structure of the noun phrase "a poet" should therefore look something like this:

NP
|
N
|

$$
\begin{bmatrix}
\text{poet} \\
\langle +N \rangle \\
\langle +\text{human} \rangle \\
\langle -\text{DEF} \rangle \\
\langle +\text{singular} \rangle
\end{bmatrix}
$$

The article transformation must be applied. It adjoins to the N a segment labeled ⟨ +article⟩, or simply ⟨ +ART⟩, with all of the features contained in the noun except ⟨ +N⟩. This generates the following structure:

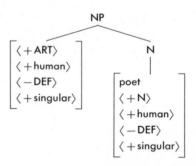

When all the transformations are completed, the article segment is replaced in the second lexical pass by "a," thus yielding "a poet."

The remaining articles in the list are called *definite* articles and are marked ⟨ +definite⟩, or simply ⟨ +DEF⟩. Within this group there are still important distinctions to make. In particular, certain properties of "the," on the one hand, and "this," "that," "these," and "those," on the other, are distinct. For example, if the noun is the pronoun "one," it can be preceded by any one of the latter group of articles:

> this one pleased John
> that one pleased John
> these ones pleased John
> those ones pleased John.

(In the plural, "ones" is often deleted, giving "These pleased John" and "Those pleased John.") Unless "one" is followed by a relative clause, the article "the" cannot precede this noun:

> * the one pleased John
> the one who pleased John.

The four articles which can precede "one" are normally called *demonstrative* articles and carry the feature ⟨+demonstrative⟩, or simply ⟨+DEM⟩. The article "the" is not demonstrative and is marked ⟨−DEM⟩.

The demonstrative articles "this" and "that" differ from "these" and "those" in that the former are singular, ⟨+singular⟩, and the latter are plural, ⟨−singular⟩:

> this desk   not * this desks
> that desk   not * that desks
> these desks   not * these desk
> those desks   not * those desk

Finally, there is a difference between "this" and "these" on the one hand, and "that" and "those" on the other. Notice, for example the grammaticality of the sentences

> this book here is a good one
> these books here are good ones

and the ungrammaticality of

> * that book here is a good one
> * those books here are good ones.

Similarly, notice the grammaticality of

> that book there is a good one
> those books there are good ones

and the ungrammaticality of the following strings:

> * this book there is a good one
> * these books there are good ones.

"This" and "these" are given the feature ⟨+near⟩, and "that" and "those," the feature ⟨−near⟩. The demonstrative articles would thus look like this in the lexicon:

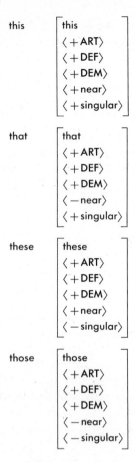

It should be helpful to follow the derivation of the noun phrase "these desks," which has the deep structure

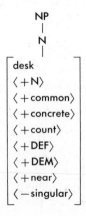

The first transformation to apply to this structure is the article transformation, which creates an article segment:

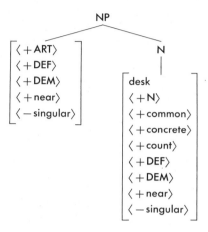

(The article actually acquires all of the features of the noun segment, but in the diagram above, and elsewhere, many of those features which are irrelevant to the present discussion are omitted for the sake of brevity.)

Another transformation to apply is the noun suffix transformation, which introduces an affix segment following the noun segment. (The ordering of the two transformations is apparently not crucial here.)

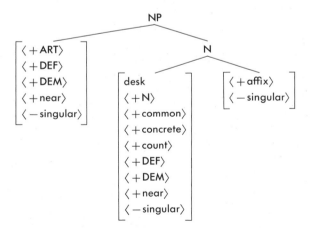

Once all transformations have been applied, the article segment is replaced by "these," the noun segment remains "desk," and the affix segment is replaced by "s" to give the final structure:

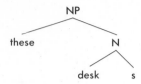

As we have mentioned before, it is of some interest to observe that nouns which are plural and indefinite do not have an article in the surface structure. Thus,

elephants trampled the hut

is grammatical, but

* an elephants trampled the hut

is not. Two explanations can be considered. First, the article transformation simply fails to apply under these circumstances. Second, the transformation does apply, but since no lexical item exists which corresponds to the segment created by the article transformation, the segment is deleted by convention. Which of these solutions is correct is not known at the present time.

SUMMARY

Transformations which introduce segments into deep structures are called *segment transformations*. The two segment transformations studied in this chapter are the *noun suffix transformation,* which introduces the plural ending on nouns, and the *article transformation,* which, in effect, introduces articles. As you will see in the next chapter, the article transformation plays a larger role than this in English syntax.

Segments introduced by transformations are replaced by words or affixes from the lexicon during the second lexical pass, which follows the application of all transformations.

EXERCISE ELEVEN

1. The lexicon may be drawn upon twice in the generation of a sentence. Explain.
2. What is the article transformation, and how is it similar to other segment transformations?
3. Define the following:
   a. function of a constituent
   b. noun phrase complement

c. lexicon
d. constituent structure
e. surface subject

4. Why is it often impossible to determine the lexical classification of a word if it is not in a sentence context?

5. Show how the following items are represented in the lexicon:

a. we
b. apple
c. politics
d. ugly
e. know

f. feet
g. she
h. therapist
i. lizard

6. What are the critical differences between a feature and a constituent? What are the kinds of information that each provides?

7. For which of the following pairs of transformations is the ordering important? In the cases where the ordering is important, what is the order?

a. passive transformation, article transformation
b. imperative transformation, reflexive transformation
c. passive transformation, imperative transformation
d. noun suffix transformation, article transformation
e. passive transformation, agreement transformation
f. article transformation, agreement transformation

8. Give your reasons for proposing certain ordering requirements in 7.

CHAPTER 12

Pronouns and Articles

You have learned that a word is not a particular part of speech in itself. It has to be in a context, in a particular sentence. What is particularly interesting is that it does not really make sense simply to say that such and such a form is a noun in some sentence, for the assertion has no meaning unless one specifies whether he is referring to the deep or surface structure. This is a difficult point to grasp at first, but a very important one. Perhaps the most clear-cut example of this involves the class of words traditionally identified as *personal* pronouns.

In deep structures, pronouns are represented as special types of noun segments having the feature $\langle +\text{PRO} \rangle$. All other noun segments have the feature $\langle -\text{PRO} \rangle$. Differentiation of pronouns is accomplished by the addition of other features. For instance, personal pronouns have a number feature:

$\langle +\text{singular} \rangle$	$\langle -\text{singular} \rangle$
I	we
you	you
he	they
she	
it	

Furthermore, personal pronouns possess features of *person*. Traditionally referred to as *first person,* and marked by the feature $\langle +\text{I} \rangle$, are

$$\text{I} \qquad \text{we}$$

The *second person,* both singular and plural, is the pronoun

$$\text{you}$$

and is marked $\langle +\text{II} \rangle$. Finally, the *third person* pronouns, $\langle +\text{III} \rangle$, are

he	they
she	
it	

The last distinction involves the third person singular pronouns: "He" has the feature ⟨+masculine⟩; "she" has the feature ⟨+feminine⟩; and "it" is marked ⟨−masculine⟩ and ⟨−feminine⟩. (The feature ⟨+animate⟩ is omitted for "he" and "she" since, in English, any noun that is masculine or feminine must be animate.) The features which define pronouns are generated in deep structures by the segment structure rules.

What evidence is there for the claim that pronouns are nouns in the deep structure? An earlier chapter contained a discussion of the process of *selection*, the process which prevents verbals from following incorrect deep structure subjects. Consider these two sentences:

> the boy laughed
> * the mortification laughed.

The second sentence is clearly anomalous because the verbal "laughed" is one which must have a subject noun carrying the feature ⟨+animate⟩ either explicitly or implicitly. What these cases reveal is that the features of nouns are the features relevant to the statement of the selectional restrictions. Furthermore, since no other constituent in the deep structure of noun phrases (the only other possible constituent being S) could be relevant, *only* the features of nouns are relevant in the statement of selectional restrictions.

Look now at the following strings:

> they gathered frequently in the park
> * I gathered frequently in the park.

What is wrong with the second string? The verbal "gather" requires a plural subject when used intransitively, and "I" is singular. But notice that pronouns, just like nouns, impose selectional restrictions upon verbals. The simplest analysis that agrees with the evidence is that pronouns are nouns in the deep structure. Pronouns are segments with the features ⟨+N⟩ and ⟨+PRO⟩ which are immediately dominated by N in deep structures.

Consider now some curiosities which suggest that pronouns, which originate as nouns in deep structures, become articles in surface structures. First, personal pronouns cannot be preceded by articles:

> * those they would like to see a movie
> * the he shouldn't do things like that
> * this you are often wrong.

In this respect, personal pronouns are different from nouns, most of which can be preceded by articles. Second, personal pronouns often seem to function as articles and not as nouns. The subject noun phrases italicized in the sentences below illustrate this phenomenon:

> *you strikers* don't know what you are doing
> *we doctors* have the responsibility to demand higher standards.

In the sentences above, the deep structure nouns in the subjects of these sentences are "strikers" and "doctors." So, what are "you" and "we"? They look a little like articles, do they not? If you inserted the adjective "young" between the pronoun and the noun:

> we young doctors

the whole group of words would look just like

> these young doctors.

(Constructions such as "we the young doctors" would seem to suggest that the "we" is not an article since the article "the" already exists. However, it is likely that both "we young doctors" and "we the young doctors" are derived from "we, who are young doctors" and "we, who are the young doctors" respectively. In this case, the pronoun as article analysis can be maintained. The "who are" is deleted and what remains either is "young doctors" if "doctors" is indefinite or "the young doctors" if "doctors" is definite.)

There is one way to explain what is going on here, even though the explanation may appear to be unlikely at first consideration. Personal pronouns, *in deep structures,* are nouns; but pronouns are not nouns in surface structures. *In surface structures, pronouns must be articles.* If, in surface structures, pronouns are articles, both of the problems mentioned above are explained. First, personal pronouns cannot be preceded by articles because they themselves are articles. Thus, *"those they" in the string *"those they would like to go to Japan" is ungrammatical. In English, articles cannot precede articles; they can only precede nouns. Second, certain personal pronouns can precede nouns because they are articles. This explains the grammaticality of "you strikers" in the sentence "You strikers don't know what you are doing." Thus, the assumption that personal pronouns (although nouns in the deep structure) are articles in the surface structure of noun phrases explains some curious facts about noun phrases in English.

This is all fine, but it does not explain *how* personal pronouns end up as articles. There must be a generative process which transforms deep structure personal pronouns, which are nouns, into surface structure articles. In fact, the process consists of two steps. The first step involves nothing more than the article transformation. This not only creates an article segment with the features already mentioned; it also copies the features of personal pronouns as well. For example, consider the deep structure of "I" in the sentence below:

I will sleep.

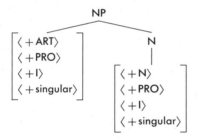

When the article transformation is applied, it generates the structure below:

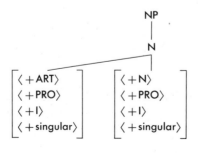

The second step is a new transformation: *noun segment deletion.* This transformation does two things. First, in the structure above, it adjoins the article segment to the noun segment under the domination of the noun:

NP
|
N

Second, it deletes the noun segment, leaving a noun dominating an article, as in the structure below:

$$
\begin{array}{c}
\text{NP} \\
| \\
\text{N} \\
| \\
\begin{bmatrix}
\langle +\text{ART} \rangle \\
\langle +\text{PRO} \rangle \\
\langle +\text{I} \rangle \\
\langle +\text{singular} \rangle
\end{bmatrix}
\end{array}
$$

In the second lexical pass, the article segment in the structure above is replaced by the word "I."

Personal pronouns have several forms. For example, "I" and "me" are different forms of the same pronoun. Traditionally, the "I" form is called *nominative;* the "me" form, *accusative.* These are distinguished by the features $\langle -\text{accusative} \rangle$ and $\langle +\text{accusative} \rangle$, respectively, in the lexicon. The lexical entries for the nominative pronouns under discussion here are as follows:

$$
\text{I} \qquad
\begin{bmatrix}
\text{I} \\
\langle +\text{N} \rangle \\
\langle +\text{PRO} \rangle \\
\langle +\text{I} \rangle \\
\langle -\text{accusative} \rangle \\
\langle +\text{singular} \rangle
\end{bmatrix}
$$

$$
\text{we} \qquad
\begin{bmatrix}
\text{we} \\
\langle +\text{N} \rangle \\
\langle +\text{PRO} \rangle \\
\langle +\text{I} \rangle \\
\langle -\text{accusative} \rangle \\
\langle -\text{singular} \rangle
\end{bmatrix}
$$

$$
\text{you} \qquad
\begin{bmatrix}
\text{you} \\
\langle +\text{N} \rangle \\
\langle +\text{PRO} \rangle \\
\langle +\text{II} \rangle
\end{bmatrix}
$$

he

$$\begin{bmatrix} \text{he} \\ \langle +\text{N} \rangle \\ \langle +\text{PRO} \rangle \\ \langle +\text{III} \rangle \\ \langle +\text{masculine} \rangle \\ \langle +\text{singular} \rangle \end{bmatrix}$$

she

$$\begin{bmatrix} \text{she} \\ \langle +\text{N} \rangle \\ \langle +\text{PRO} \rangle \\ \langle +\text{III} \rangle \\ \langle +\text{feminine} \rangle \\ \langle +\text{singular} \rangle \end{bmatrix}$$

it

$$\begin{bmatrix} \text{it} \\ \langle +\text{N} \rangle \\ \langle +\text{PRO} \rangle \\ \langle +\text{III} \rangle \\ \langle -\text{masculine} \rangle \\ \langle -\text{feminine} \rangle \\ \langle +\text{singular} \rangle \end{bmatrix}$$

they

$$\begin{bmatrix} \text{they} \\ \langle +\text{N} \rangle \\ \langle +\text{PRO} \rangle \\ \langle +\text{III} \rangle \\ \langle -\text{singular} \rangle \end{bmatrix}$$

Notice that there is only one entry for the pronoun "you" and that this entry is not marked for number. This will allow it to replace a segment marked either $\langle +\text{singular} \rangle$ or $\langle -\text{singular} \rangle$.

What is particularly interesting in the light of this analysis of personal pronouns is the evidence which suggests that the noun following the personal pronoun article is not always deleted, but takes on the form "ones," as in

you great ones who watch over us treat us like flies.

This suggests that the article analysis of personal pronouns is correct, since the appearance of this noun, usually "ones," can be explained by the assumption that personal pronouns are articles in the surface structure.

The form "ones" is used after personal pronouns in the plural. Such cases are not at all uncommon when an adjective intervenes, as in "you great ones." But in addition, the forms "we'uns" and "you'uns" are found in the dialects of certain Southern states, especially in the Ozarks. This indicates that "we ones" and "you ones," which is what "we'uns" and "you'uns" are, are nothing more than instances of personal pronouns as articles in the surface structure followed by noun segments which are not deleted by the noun segment deletion transformation.

One important characteristic of personal pronouns must be noted. As articles, they have the feature ⟨+definite⟩. For example, notice that only definite noun phrases can appear as subjects of sentences like the following:

> the analysis is Paul's
> those beads are Susan's
> this document is Ungaretti's.

If we introduce indefinite subjects into such constructions, the results are ungrammatical:

> * an analysis is Paul's
> * beads are Susan's
> * a document is Ungaretti's.

Notice, however, that the subjects of these sentences may be personal pronouns:

> *it* is Paul's
> *they* are Susan's
> *it* is Ungaretti's.

Thus, personal pronouns must be definite.

SUMMARY

Personal pronouns are not the same kind of constituent in deep structures as they are in surface structures. In deep structures, they are noun segments, represented by the feature ⟨+PRO⟩ and others. In surface structures, personal pronouns are article segments. Surface structures containing personal pronouns are generated through the application of the article transformation and the noun segment pronoun deletion transformation. As articles, personal pronouns are definite articles.

EXERCISE TWELVE

1. What is a "lexical pass"?
2. Explain the ambiguity of the sentence following:

   There are two books which you should read.

3. Draw deep structure trees for

   a. Those churches dominate the scene.
   b. The revolt Gibbon described was started by Servius.
   c. Albert refuses to reprimand Victoria.
   d. Adams believed that Roosevelt wanted to resign.
   e. Should Hayes be supported by patriotic citizens?
   f. He enjoys those motets.

4. How are the following items represented in the lexicon?

   a. socialist
   b. they
   c. existentialism
   d. swarthy
   e. ocelot
   f. desk
   g. Henry
   h. Prague

5. It has been claimed that pronouns are actually definite articles. Explain how the following data suggests that pronouns are definite:

   a. Strong though the boy was, he couldn't lift it.
   b. Strong though John was, he couldn't lift it.
   c. * strong though a boy was, he couldn't lift it
   d. * strong though some horse was, he couldn't lift it
   e. Strong though he was, he couldn't lift it.
   f. Strong though I am, I can't lift it.

6. What is

   a. a segment structure rule?
   b. a segment transformation?

7. How do pronouns differ from nouns in the surface structure?

8. Traditional school grammarians claimed that *pronouns* take the place of nouns. Is their claim supported by the following sentences? If so, what is the evidence?

   a. The Greeks, influenced by Aristotle, claimed that they were the first to distinguish between words and their referents.
   b. Anyone who pleads the Fifth Amendment must show that he is not protecting others.
   c. The monk told the indignant actress that she sang atrociously.

9. Show how the deep structure tree drawn for 3e becomes a surface structure.

CHAPTER 13

Verbals and Particles

Like noun phrases, verb phrases may vary considerably in their surface structures. They may contain one noun phrase, two noun phrases, or no noun phrase at all; they may contain embedded sentences, and so forth. Perhaps the most interesting characteristics of the surface structure of verb phrases have to do directly with verbal elements—that is, verbs and adjectives. These are represented as verbals (VB) in the deep structure, with the features ⟨ + V⟩ and ⟨ − V⟩ respectively. For example, an abbreviated deep structure for the sentence

silver shines

would look like this:

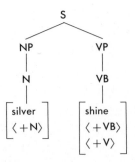

while an abbreviated deep structure of the sentence

silver is heavy

would be

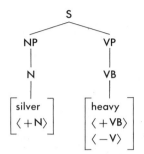

(The auxiliary constituent and many features of the noun segment have been ignored in this diagram.)

The latter sentence is generated from the deep structure by a segment transformation. As you can see from its diagram, the constituent structure lacks an appropriate form of "be," known as the *copula.* The copula "be" does not appear in the deep structure of verbals which are ⟨−V⟩, but its appearance in surface structures is predictable, since a form of the copula must appear in the surface structure whenever the verbal in a deep structure is an adjective, marked ⟨−V⟩.

The transformation which introduces the copula into deep structures, the *copula transformation,* does not actually introduce the word "be" or any of its forms, but rather introduces a segment containing the feature ⟨+COPULA⟩. Thus, from the deep structure above, the copula transformation will generate

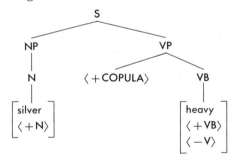

Notice that the interrogative transformation discussed earlier brings "is" to the front of the sentence in the formation of the "yes-no" question

is silver heavy?

Since, in the most general formulation of the interrogative transformation, that constituent which is permuted to the front of the sentence is the auxiliary, it is seen that a second transformation must apply after the copula transformation.   This transformation, which will be discussed in more detail later, brings the copula under the auxiliary to give the structure below:

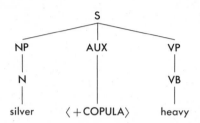

After all transformations have been applied, the correct form of the copula, i.e., "is," replaces the copula segment to give the following structure:

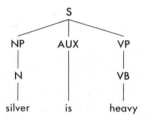

(The way in which the correct form of the copula is determined will be discussed in a later chapter.)

Some sentences contain words known as *verb particles* in their verb phrases.   The verb particles in the two sentences below are the words "up" and "out":

1. the chemist shook *up* the mixture
2. the telegraph operator bawled *out* the clerk.

In the presentations of English grammar with which you are probably familiar, words such as "up" and "out" are often considered to be *prepositions*.   But such an analysis is misleading.   Compare the two sentences above with the two below:

3. the chemist walked up the street
4. the telegraph operator walked out the door.

There is little advantage in considering the words "up" and "out" to be prepositions in sentences 1 and 2 and also in 3 and 4.   These words function very differently in the two pairs of sentences. In the first place, in sentences 1 and 2, the words "up" and "out" can be moved around to the other side of the object, giving the sentences below:

> the chemist shook the mixture up
> the telegraph operator bawled the clerk out.

On the other hand, in sentences 3 and 4, these words cannot be moved around to the other side of the noun phrases which follow them. If this permutation is carried out, two ungrammatical strings result:

> * the chemist walked the street up
> * the telegraph operator walked the door out.

Thus, despite their superficial similarity, sentences 1 and 2 are somehow different from sentences 3 and 4.

There are other differences between the way the words "up" and "out" behave when they function as particles and the way they behave when they function as prepositions. Prepositions may be shifted (or preposed) to the front of sentences when questions are asked. Thus, both of the sentences below are fully grammatical:

> up what did the chemist walk?
> out of what did the telegraph operator walk?

On the other hand, particles may not be preposed in a question. If they are, ungrammatical strings result:

> * up what did the chemist shake
> * out who did the telegraph operator bawl.

When question sentences containing verb particles are generated, the particle *must* remain in its original position. It cannot be preposed:

> what did the chemist shake up?
> who(m) did the telegraph operator bawl out?

One can imagine at least two ways in which particles could be represented in deep structures. First, they could be represented as actual constituents in the deep structure. Second, particles could be represented as verb features that cause the application of a transformation which introduces a particle segment into the structure. This question has not yet been resolved by grammarians. Since, in other situations, new evidence is being found for feature analysis rather than constituent analysis, the feature representation of particles is adopted here. But it should be kept in mind that such acceptance must be tentative at the present time.

In terms of this analysis, the deep structure of sentence 1, "the chemist shook up the mixture," is

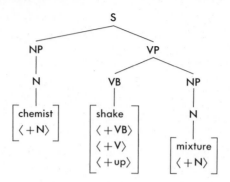

In other words, particles appear in the deep structure neither as constituents, such as NP or VP, nor as segments, but as features on the verbal segments.

The transformation responsible for introducing a particle segment into the structure is called the *particle segment transformation,* or more simply, the particle transformation. By now, you should be familiar with what such a transformation accomplishes. It introduces a segment into the verb phrase which contains the feature ⟨+particle⟩, together with whatever particle feature is specified in the verb segment. Thus, when the particle transformation is applied to the deep structure above, it generates the following structure:

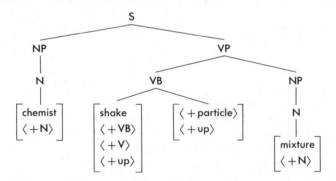

If no other transformations are applied to this structure, the segments in this surface structure are replaced by actual words from the lexicon. In this case, the particle segment is replaced by the word "up." (The surface structure below assumes that the article transformation and the

agreement transformations have already been applied. In all surface structures to follow, features of segments shall not be presented, inasmuch as they have no further syntactic consequences.)

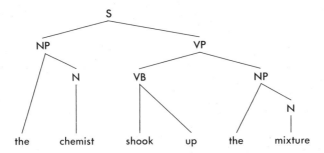

What can you discover about another transformation of English from the following two sentences:

> the chemist shook up the mixture
> the chemist shook the mixture up.

The word "up" is a particle in both sentences, and both sentences have exactly the same deep structure, the deep structure discussed earlier in this chapter. Both sentences are synonymous. The transformation which relates them is the *particle movement transformation.* This transformation moves the particle segment introduced by the particle transformation around to the other side of the object of the verb phrase, creating the structure below:

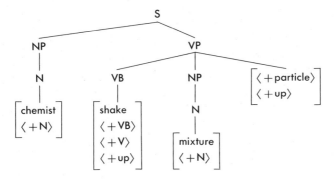

After the lexicon has been drawn on, the result is the structure of the sentence "the chemist shook the mixture up."

It is important to notice this new illustration of the ordering of transformations, an ordering which must hold if particles originate as features of verbals. It is obvious that the particle movement transformation could not apply if a particle segment had not previously been generated by the particle transformation.

The particle movement transformation is normally optional; that is, it may or may not be applied. This explains why English contains both of the sentences below:

> the chemist shook up the mixture
> the chemist shook the mixture up.

In the first sentence, the particle movement transformation has not been applied. In the second, it has. But there are certain cases in which the transformation is obligatory:

> the chemist shook it up
> * the chemist shook up it.

The second string is ungrammatical because the particle movement transformation has not been applied. Whenever the object noun is a pronoun, the particle movement transformation is obligatory. You can test this by constructing other pairs where the object noun is a pronoun:

> * the landlord put out him
> the landlord put him out
> * the visitor looked up them in the telephone directory
> the visitor looked them up in the telephone directory.

SUMMARY

This chapter has been concerned with some of the transformational processes affecting adjectives and verbs—in particular, the introduction of the copula before adjectives through the *copula transformation*. Another transformation, to be discussed in a later chapter, incorporates the copula into the auxiliary. For verbs which have particles, the *particle transformation* introduces a particle segment into the deep structure. Furthermore, the *particle movement transformation* moves the particle segment around to the right of the object—obligatorily if the object is a pronoun, optionally otherwise. Finally, particles have been shown as distinct from prepositions, even though the words may be the same, because of a difference in syntactic functions between the two. The particle is more closely associated with the verb. We have suggested here that particles be represented as verb features in the deep structure. Prepositions, which are more closely associated with nouns, are represented as features of nouns in the deep structure.

EXERCISE THIRTEEN

1. What is the evidence for the article nature of personal pronouns?

2. Why is it advantageous to assume that, in deep structures, singular and plural are features rather than constituents?

3. Draw deep structure trees for the following:

   a. This educational system is independent.
   b. The irate electorate voted the Board out.

4. Show how the deep structures for 3 become surface structures.

5. When is the particle movement transformation obligatory?

6. Why is the first representation of a sentence structure below better than the second? (Hint: Review the difference between constituents and constituent functions.)

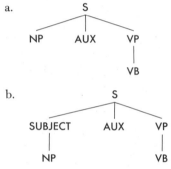

7. Are the transformations in the following pairs ordered with respect to one another? If so, why?

   a. article transformation, negation transformation
   b. particle transformation, particle movement transformation
   c. passive transformation, particle movement transformation

8. Explain the necessity of distinguishing between prepositions and particles even though each may be represented by the same word, e.g., "up."

CHAPTER 14

Aspect—Perfect and Progressive

Verbals, like nouns, have *inherent* syntactic properties represented as features. You have already seen that verbals may be either verbs or adjectives and that certain verbals have particle features. If a verbal is an adjective ⟨ − V⟩, a copula segment is introduced by the copula transformation to generate sentences such as

the moon is blue.

One of the most complex inherent properties of verbals is traditionally referred to as *aspect*. This chapter will investigate both the aspect properties and the transformations through which these properties are converted into words in the surface structure.

There are two aspect properties: *perfect* and *progressive*. The progressive is illustrated by *b* in the following sentence pairs:

1. a. Leonardo designed a submarine
   b. Leonardo *was* design*ing* a submarine
2. a. our cat sits on the mantle
   b. our cat *is* sitt*ing* on the mantle
3. a. civil servants work very hard
   b. civil servants *are* work*ing* very hard
4. a. the pirates fought for their lives
   b. the pirates *were* fight*ing* for their lives.

The progressive adds to the meaning of the sentence. Notice in the above sentences that the use of the progressive conveys the idea of an ongoing activity.

What is it in the *b* sentences which informs us that these sentences are in the progressive aspect? Each sentence contains some form of the copula preceding the verb. In each sentence the verb ending is "ing." In other words, a progressive sentence contains the sequence "be . . . ing," where the three dots are either a verb or, as you will see, another copula. The question to answer now is how a progressive sentence acquires this sequence.

Once again the problem arises as to whether a certain item exists as a constituent in the deep structure or as a feature on either a noun or, in this case, a verbal. Once again, grammarians have not yet obtained definitive answers. Thus, if some account is to be given of the various syntactic facts involving aspect and related phenomena, it is necessary to make an arbitrary choice between one alternative and the other. The analysis which follows assumes that aspect is represented in terms of features in the deep structure. Once again, it should be kept in mind that, although many important syntactic facts can be explained in these terms, the critical assumption, i.e., that aspect is representable in terms of features, is debatable.

The progressive aspect appears as the feature ⟨+progressive⟩ on a verbal in the deep structure. Thus, the sentence

Undergraduates are studying

would have roughly the following deep structure:

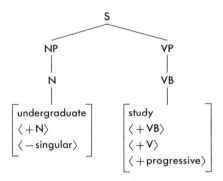

The transformation which introduces the copula segment whenever the verbal contains the feature ⟨+progressive⟩ is the *progressive segment transformation,* or simply, the progressive transformation. It introduces, to the left of the verbal, a segment containing the features ⟨+progressive⟩ and ⟨+copula⟩. The first feature identifies the segment as having been generated through the progressive transformation, and the second indicates that this segment is ultimately to be replaced by the correct form of the copula. The structure generated is as follows:

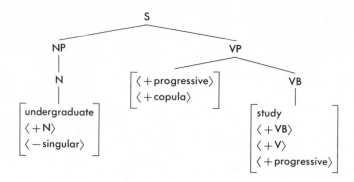

This transformation generates the progressive segment, but more is required. As things stand, only the ungrammatical string below has been generated:

* undergraduates are study.

The procedure required for introducing "ing" to the right of the verb, called the *affix transformation,* is one of the key transformations in English. This transformation introduces a segment with the features ⟨ +affix⟩ and ⟨ +progressive⟩ to the *right* of the segment following the progressive segment. In the above structure, this happens to be the verbal segment "study," but it need not have been, as you will see. When the affix transformation is applied to the structure above, the following is generated:

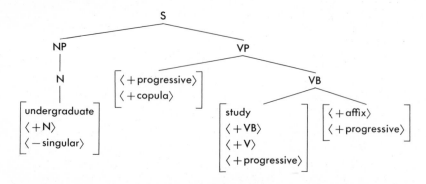

The progressive segment is ultimately replaced by the appropriate form of the copula, "are"; the verbal segment, by "study"; and the affix segment, by "ing." Thus, the progressive and the affix transformations have correctly generated the verb phrase "are studying."

An affix segment, as you have seen, is adjoined to the right of whatever segment follows the progressive segment.   The segment to the right of the progressive segment, however, may not always be the verbal segment.   When the verbal is an adjective instead of a verb, things are different.   The progressive sentence

Souza is being honest

has the deep structure:

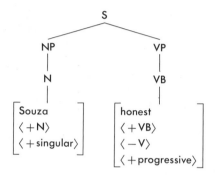

To generate a surface structure from this deep structure, the copula transformation must be applied as well as the progressive and the affix transformations.   The ordering of these three transformations is crucial. The only order in which they can apply is:

1. Progressive transformation
2. Copula transformation
3. Affix transformation.

First, the progressive transformation is applied to generate the following structure (the words which ultimately replace the segments are included inside quotation marks to help you follow the derivation):

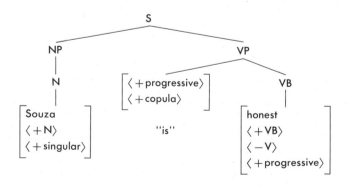

The derivation is still not complete.   The progressive segment must in this case precede another copula segment, and then the rule introducing the suffix "ing" must be applied.   So, after the progressive segment is introduced by the progressive transformation, the copula transformation is applied.   This introduces the copula segment, required by adjectives, between the progressive segment and the verbal segment:

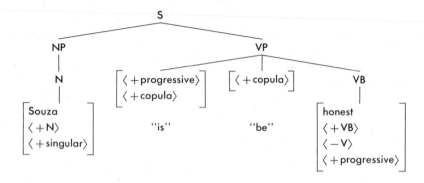

Notice that the segment to the right of the progressive segment is *not* the verbal segment, but a copula segment.   Remember how the affix transformation must be applied: Place an affix segment to the right of the constituent, *any constituent,* which is to the right of the progressive segment.   Thus, application of the affix transformation places the affix to the right of the copula segment, generating the structure below:

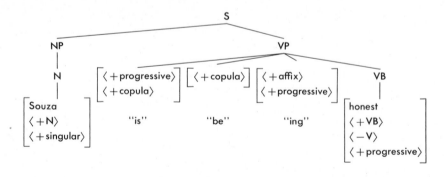

In a more complete derivation, the progressive segment would end up under the domination of the auxiliary through the application of the auxiliary incorporation transformation, to be discussed in the following chapter.   Thus, after the segments are replaced by items from the lexicon, the following final structure results:

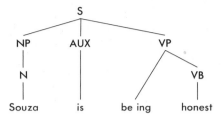

The case of the so-called *predicate nominative* is worth considering briefly. In a sentence like

John is a hero

the copula "is" is not introduced into the deep structure by a transformation. It is there all along as a peculiar type of transitive verb.

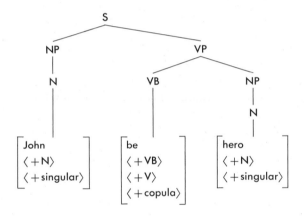

If the copula as a verb is neither progressive nor perfect, the copula itself is incorporated into the auxiliary. But if, for instance, it is progressive in the deep structure, the relevant transformations apply to produce the sentence

John is being a hero.

Here, the progressive affix "ing" is attached to the right side of the copula verb.

If you have mastered the transformational apparatus required to generate the progressive verb phrases, the subject matter of this chapter to this point, you will have no difficulty with anything else in this book, since no other component of English syntax discussed in this book is more complex.

Earlier in this chapter it was stated that there are two aspect properties. The *perfect* aspect is illustrated by *b* in the following sentence pairs:

1. a. no one eats mud
   b. no one *has* eat*en* mud
2. a. we struggled with the giraffe
   b. we *have* struggl*ed* with the giraffe
3. a. etymologists study words
   b. etymologists *have* studi*ed* words.

Like the progressive, which consists of the copula and the ending "ing," the perfect consists of two parts. The first is a form of "have" ("have," "has," and "had"), and the second is an ending which is usually either "ed" or "en," depending upon the word to which it is to be attached.

It is interesting that the traditional grammarian Jespersen, in his *Essentials of English Grammar,* traces the use of "have" in this construction back to a time when "have" had its full meaning, "possess," or "hold." He points out that a sentence like "I have caught the fish" was equivalent to "I hold (have) the fish as caught," rather like the modern sentence "I have you beaten."

Generating the perfect aspect involves transformations of a type familiar to you. First, the perfect is represented in deep structures by the feature ⟨ +perfect⟩ on the verbal segment. Thus, the rough deep structure of sentence 3*b* above would be the following (the auxiliary is again excluded):

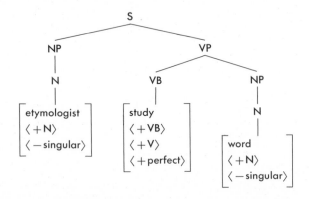

The basic transformation which applies to this structure is the *perfect segment transformation,* or more simply, the perfect transformation. This introduces a perfect segment, with the feature ⟨ +perfect⟩, to the left of the verbal, giving

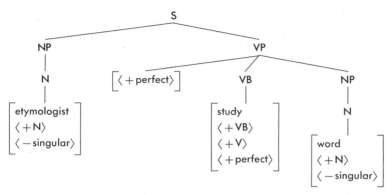

If no other transformations were applied, the string generated would be

* etymologists have study words.

However, as in the case of the progressive, the affix transformation is applied. But this time, instead of introducing an affix segment with the feature ⟨ +progressive⟩ to the right of the segment following the perfect segment, it introduces a segment with the feature ⟨ +perfect⟩, thereby giving the structure below:

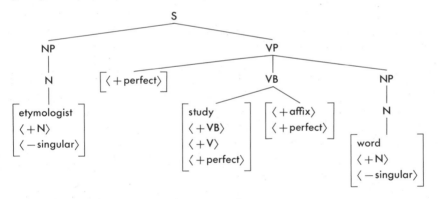

When these segments are replaced by words from the lexicon, the following structure results (assuming the application of the noun suffix and other transformations):

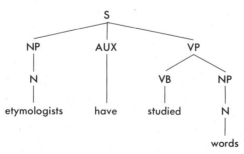

Perhaps the most interesting case involving aspect arises when a sentence contains *both* the progressive and the perfect, as do the sentences below:

1. Olaf has been learning Greek
2. Sven has been painting.

You should have no trouble at all generating these sentences if you keep in mind that three ordered transformations must apply: the perfect, the progressive, and the affix.   The deep structure of sentence 2 contains both the features ⟨+progressive⟩ and ⟨+perfect⟩:

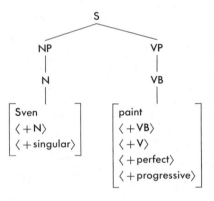

First, the perfect segment is introduced via the perfect transformation:

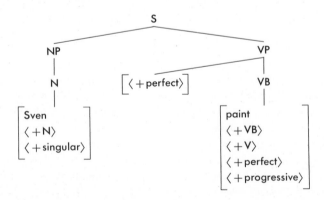

Second, the progressive segment is introduced to the left of the verbal by the progressive transformation:

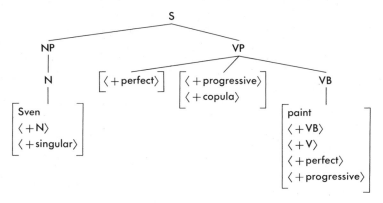

Finally, the affix transformation must be applied. This transformation will apply to both the perfect and the progressive segments existing in this structure. Thus, this transformation introduces an affix segment, with the feature ⟨+progressive⟩, to the right of the verbal segment *and* an affix segment, with the feature ⟨+perfect⟩, to the right of the progressive segment. This application generates

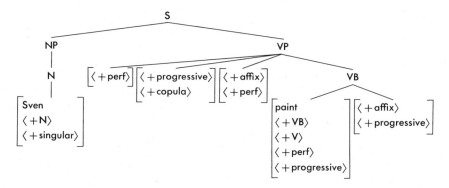

If no more transformations are applied, the perfect segment is replaced by the correct form of "have"—"has"; the progressive segment, by "be"; the affix segment with the feature ⟨+perfect⟩ is replaced by "en"; the verbal segment, by "paint"; and the affix segment with the feature ⟨+progressive⟩ is replaced by "ing." The perfect segment, which is the leftmost segment of the verb phrase, later becomes "has." The word "has," in such a position, becomes an auxiliary capable of being shifted around the subject noun phrase if the presence of the QUESTION constituent necessitates the application of the interrogative transformation. After the auxiliary incorporation process takes place, we have the structure at the top of the following page.

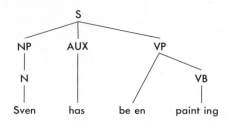

The above shows how sentences with both the progressive and the perfect aspects are generated, with the assumption that aspect is marked in deep structures in terms of features of verbals.

SUMMARY

The progressive aspect and the perfect aspect are represented in deep structures by the features ⟨+progressive⟩ and ⟨+perfect⟩. These features are specified on verbal segments by the segment structure rules. Basically, their surface structures are generated by the progressive transformation, the perfect transformation, and the affix transformation, all of which are segment transformations.

EXERCISE FOURTEEN

1. Draw a deep structure tree for

   a. We have administered recreational activities.
   b. Caradon was being evasive.
   c. Control yourself!

2. Explain in detail how the deep structures for 1*a* and 1*b* are converted into surface structures.

3. What arguments are there for the assumption that verbs and adjectives should be treated as the same kind of constituent in the deep structure?

4. You were told in this chapter that "in a more complete derivation, the progressive segment would end up under the domination of the auxiliary." What justifications are there for assuming that both progressive and perfect segments may end up as auxiliaries?

5. Describe the differences between noun phrase complements and verb phrase complements.

6. Draw a deep structure tree for

   It amuses Shaw that Englishmen ridicule their emotions.

7. Define, with examples:

   a. adjunction
   b. substitution
   c. deletion
   d. intransitive verbal
   e. intermediate structure

8. Describe briefly some tests which identify noun phrases, mentioning where these tests fail as well.

CHAPTER 15

The Auxiliary

Until now the auxiliary constituent has been more or less ignored in most sample phrase structures. Still, the role of the auxiliary is a major one in English.

In earlier chapters it was asserted that words such as "can," "may," "must," "will," and a few others function as auxiliaries in such sentences as those below:

> You *can* leave now
> He *will* find only trouble there
> What goes up *must* come down.

Auxiliaries of this type are called *modals*. The deep structure of the sentence

Artemis must leave

might be represented in the following way:

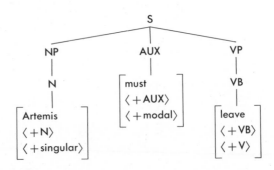

The auxiliary segment contains other features besides the defining feature $\langle +\text{AUX} \rangle$. To see this, look at the following sentences:

1. a. you can leave now
   b. you could leave now
2. a. he will find only trouble here
   b. he would find only trouble here
3. a. what goes up may come down
   b. what goes up might come down.

Notice how the modals have changed their form in the *b* sentences above. This change illustrates the phenomenon of *syntactic tense.* Traditionally, the "can," "will," and "may" forms of the modals are said to be in the present tense, while the "could," "would," and "might" forms are said to be in the past tense. It is very important to remember that syntactic tense, referring specifically to present or past time (as in a modal), does not necessarily yield the tense of the sentence as a whole. For example, the sentence

what goes up might come down

has a modal in the syntactic past tense, but the sentence does not convey the meaning of past time at all. You could add adverbials referring to present or even future time without creating a meaningless sentence. In fact, past time adverbials are the only ones that are excluded:

what goes up might come down today
what goes up might come down tomorrow
* what goes up might come down yesterday.

Thus, when we speak about syntactic tense, we are speaking about a purely syntactic phenomenon, the alteration of the actual form of a word. Of course, syntactic tense does have some semantic significance; it does have meaning, but this meaning is not directly correlated with time.

Syntactic tense is represented in deep structures by $\langle +\text{present} \rangle$ for the syntactic present, and $\langle -\text{present} \rangle$ for the syntactic past. The tense feature is generated by the segment structure rules on the auxiliary segment. Thus, the deep structure of the sentence

Artemis might leave

would be given as

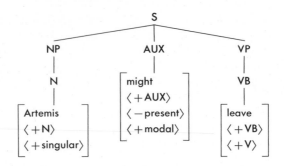

You have already seen what happens to this constituent in the generation of interrogative sentences like those below:

<blockquote>
can you leave now?
would he find only trouble here?
</blockquote>

In earlier chapters, in the discussion of the interrogative transformation,
which generates the surface structures for sentences like those above,
you learned that words like "can" and "would" were shifted to the left
of the subject noun phrase of the sentence.   What is permuted to the
left of the subject noun phrase is not just a word; it is the entire auxiliary
constituent.   The deep structure of a sentence like

<blockquote>
may Artemis leave?
</blockquote>

is roughly given by the following tree diagram:

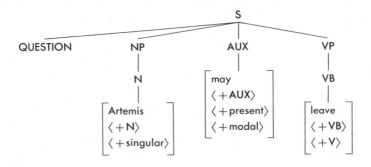

The constituent QUESTION indicates that the surface structure is
interpreted semantically as a question.   The interrogative transformation interchanges the auxiliary constituent with the subject noun phrase
to give the structure below:

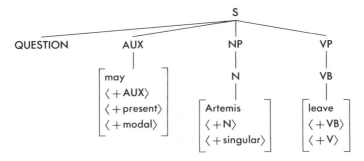

Finally, the QUESTION constituent is deleted, giving the surface structure below:

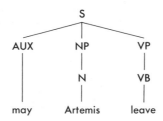

But what happens when there is no auxiliary modal like "can," "may," "shall," "will," or "must"? The interrogative transformation must have some constituent to shift around the surface subject. To answer this, we must look at some example sentences of a kind dealt with in earlier chapters. Since the interrogative transformation shifts only the auxiliary constituent, the following sentences are particularly interesting:

1. is Zeus honest?
2. is Zeus eating?
3. has Zeus eaten?

In each sentence, a segment has been introduced by a different transformation: (1) the copula transformation, (2) the progressive transformation, and (3) the perfect transformation. If only auxiliaries are permuted by the interrogative transformation, how did these segments become auxiliaries? They were not auxiliaries in the deep structure, since they originated as features of verbals.

The deep structure of the sentence

is Zeus honest?

is roughly the following:

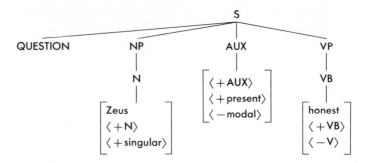

Notice first of all that the auxiliary is not a modal in this deep structure. It is simply an abstract entity containing the feature ⟨ +present⟩, which indicates that the sentence is in the syntactic present tense. The first transformation to be applied is the copula transformation, giving

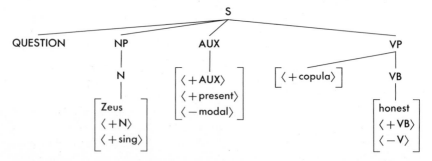

At this point, the *auxiliary incorporation transformation,* which was mentioned but not discussed earlier, is applied. This new transformation shows how the copula comes to be an auxiliary. The auxiliary incorporation transformation copies the features of the first segment of the verb phrase, *if this segment is not a verbal,* onto the auxiliary segment and then deletes the first segment of the verb phrase. The following structure results:

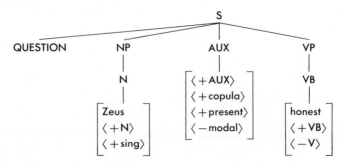

Now the interrogative and the QUESTION deletion transformations are applied. For the future, it is necessary to remember that when a segment which will ultimately end up as either a form of "be" or a form of "have" is the first segment of the verb phrase, the features of this segment are incorporated into the auxiliary, *unless* the auxiliary is a modal. In the latter case, the transformation may not be applied. As sentences like

<blockquote>Zeus could be honest</blockquote>

and

<blockquote>could Zeus be honest?</blockquote>

show us, the auxiliary incorporation transformation could not apply in such a situation.

Another interesting syntactic phenomenon involving the auxiliary constituent is negation. A negative sentence, like

<blockquote>O'Brien will not behave</blockquote>

contains a deep structure in which the constituent NEGATIVE appears:

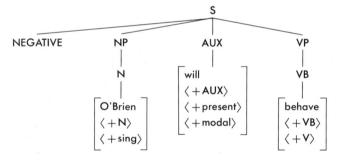

The negative element is placed immediately after the auxiliary by the *negative placement transformation,* creating the following structure:

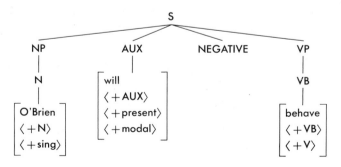

If no other transformations apply, NEGATIVE is replaced by "not." An optional transformation exists, however, which adjoins the NEGATIVE to the auxiliary segment under the domination of AUX. In this instance, when the *negative adjunction transformation* applies, the negative element is replaced by the contraction "n't." This is the source of sentences like those below:

O'Brien can't leave now

he mustn't do that.

Consider now a new situation. Suppose that the auxiliary is not a modal and that the first element of the verb phrase is the verbal itself, as in the sentence below:

Joad likes philosophy.

The deep structure of this sentence could be abbreviated as follows:

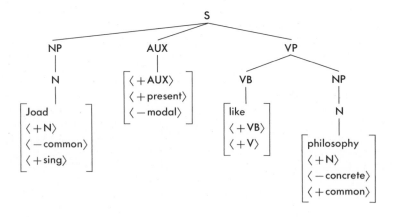

The verbal is not incorporated into the auxiliary, as can be seen from the fact that the string

* likes Joad philosophy

is ungrammatical. If this analysis is essentially correct, it must be assumed that in such sentences as "Joad likes philosophy," the auxiliary is deleted from the surface structure, since it leaves no trace. (As will be seen later, this deletion takes place amidst the transformations which determine the agreement of verbals with the tense of the auxiliary and the number of the surface subject.)

What reason is there to believe that the auxiliary exists in the deep structure of such sentences in the first place? As mentioned earlier, the reason is that this assumption helps us to explain certain interesting facts, facts which emerge upon consideration of the following sentences:

>does Joad like philosophy?
>Joad does not like philosophy.

The existence of "does" in these two sentences can be explained very nicely on two assumptions. First, the deep structure of "Joad likes philosophy" does contain an auxiliary. Second, this auxiliary must be deleted under certain special conditions:

1. the auxiliary contains neither the feature ⟨ + modal⟩ (since "can" in "John can go" cannot be deleted), nor the feature ⟨ + copula⟩ (since "is" in "John is eating" or "John is honest" cannot be deleted), nor the feature ⟨ + perfect⟩ (since "have" in "they have eaten" cannot be deleted)
2. the auxiliary immediately precedes a verbal segment, one marked ⟨ + VB⟩.

Consider the derivation of the sentences above in terms of these assumptions. For the first sentence, the interrogative transformation will move the auxiliary around the subject noun phrase. The auxiliary will *not* be deleted because it does not immediately precede a verbal. What then happens to the auxiliary? It is replaced by the appropriate form of "do," in this case "does," from the lexicon. For the second sentence, the negative element is placed between the auxiliary and the verbal. Thus, once again, the auxiliary is not deleted and is replaced by "does." However, in the deep structure of "Joad likes philosophy," the auxiliary ends up immediately preceding the verbal and, since the conditions stated under 1 above are met, the auxiliary is deleted. Thus, the existence of "does" in the sentences above can be taken as evidence of the existence of an auxiliary in all deep structures.

SUMMARY

The auxiliary segment, as generated in a deep structure, either is or is not a modal. In the latter event, a number of important transformational processes can affect it. In general, if a non-modal auxiliary immediately precedes a verbal, it must be deleted through a transformation to be discussed further in the following chapter. There are, however, a number of conditions which could prevent a non-modal auxiliary from immediately preceding a verbal. First, either the perfect segment or a copula segment (e.g., the progressive segment, the adjective copula) can intervene. Then the auxiliary incorporates into itself the features of the first non-verbal segment following it, deleting the segment in the process. Second, neither the perfect nor the copula segment may be present, but the sentence may be negative or interrogative. In both cases, the auxiliary will not end up immediately preceding a verbal and will not be deleted.

If the auxiliary is a modal, it will be a word such as "can," "may," and so forth. If the auxiliary is not a modal, it will be either a form of the perfect, "have," or a form of the copula, "be," in the event that the auxiliary incorporation transformation has applied, or a form of "do" otherwise.

One exceptional fact is not explained by this analysis. This is the fact that "have," when it is a verbal in the deep structure,

1. they have money

seems to act like an auxiliary, giving the interrogative,

2. have they money?

On the other hand, an equivalent sentence exists in which "have" acts like a normal verbal:

3. do they have money?

The proposed analysis accounts for sentences 1 and 3, but not for sentence 2.

EXERCISE FIFTEEN

1. Explain the difference between syntactic tense and temporal tense.
2. Draw deep structure trees for
   a. Wasn't Simpson appointed by Volpe?
   b. Bismarck was demanding an unconditional surrender.
   c. Has the new computer been operating?
3. Show in detail how the deep structure for 2c is converted into the surface structure.
4. Write out nine modals.
5. Why must the auxiliary incorporation transformation be applied after rather than before the progressive transformation?
6. Name a condition which would prevent the application of the auxiliary incorporation transformation.
7. Why is it necessary to say that sentences like

   Volpe appointed Simpson.

have auxiliaries in the deep structure which are deleted later?   Why not claim that some sentences start out without auxiliaries?

8. How does the appropriate form of "do" get into many sentences which don't have this form in their deep structures?

9. What is the relative ordering in the following sets of transformations and why?

    a. interrogative transformation, auxiliary incorporation transformation
    b. progressive transformation, affix transformation
    c. perfect transformation, progressive transformation, affix transformation

CHAPTER 16

Agreement

If you had ever written a sentence in school like

* one of the soldiers carry ammunition

your paper was probably returned with the stern, red-inked injunction, "AGREEMENT." Your teacher must have written this on hundreds of papers and wondered just how to teach "agreement." In fact, even then you knew quite a lot about agreement and probably got things right more often than wrong.

You normally ensure that the form of the verbal agrees with the number of the surface subject. For example, when the surface subject is third person singular, the present tense form of the verb ends in "s." In some cases, the verb is a kind of carbon copy showing a plural form when the surface subject is plural, and a singular form when it is singular. In other cases, when the verb is in the past tense for example, the form of the verb is the same regardless of whether its surface subject is singular or plural. Thus we have

the ballerina laughed

and

the ballerinas laughed

but not

* the ballerina laugheds.

Since the "s" is only added to present tense verbs whose surface subjects are not merely ⟨ +singular⟩, but also in the third person ⟨ +III⟩, the person feature must be considered in transformations affecting agreement.

How may this kind of information be presented in terms of the kind of feature analysis used here?   What processes are involved in agreement?

At least two steps are involved in agreement.   The first affects the auxiliary segment.   Remember that the copula transformation introduces a copula segment before adjectives such as "hungry" in the deep structure for

the crocodiles are hungry.

The auxiliary incorporation transformation then incorporates the copula segment into the auxiliary.   As yet, however, there is no indication about which form of the copula is to be used in the structure, since both person and number features are missing from the auxiliary.

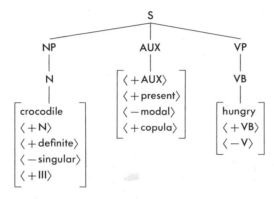

The third person plural form of the copula is needed if the auxiliary is to agree with its surface subject.   The auxiliary must have, then, the features ⟨ +III⟩ and ⟨ −singular⟩, the last two features marked on the subject.   So the first transformation required for agreement, the *auxiliary agreement transformation,* as it may be called, copies the number and person features of the subject onto the auxiliary segment:

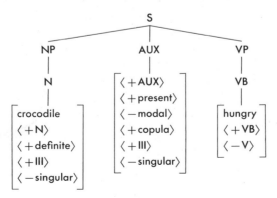

The word in the lexicon with features matching that of the auxiliary segment is "are."

The sentence "the ballerina laughs" has no surface structure auxiliary. But this sentence, like all others, does contain an auxiliary in its deep structure. The auxiliary agreement transformation copies the relevant features of the subject onto the auxiliary segment:

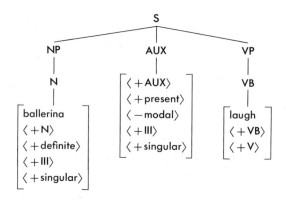

You will remember the last chapter specified that a non-modal auxiliary immediately preceding a verbal is deleted if it does not carry either the ⟨+copula⟩ or the ⟨+perfect⟩ feature. As the auxiliary in the above structure does not meet the conditions for retention, the *verbal agreement transformation* copies the relevant features of number, person, and *tense* onto the verbal from the auxiliary and deletes the latter segment. Application of this transformation to the above structure generates:

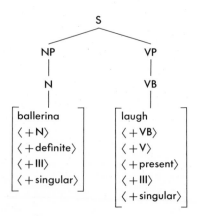

For most verbals all that is needed now is a *verb suffix transformation* which may add an affix segment that later becomes "s" or "ed." This is a process similar to the noun suffix transformation. When the verbal has the features ⟨+III⟩, ⟨+singular⟩, and ⟨+present⟩, the transformation creates a verb affix with these features:

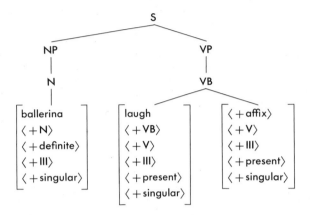

Note that the affix segment contains the feature ⟨+V⟩ to show that it is a verb affix, not a noun affix. When all other necessary transformations have been applied, the lexicon supplies the suffix "s" to replace the affix segment:

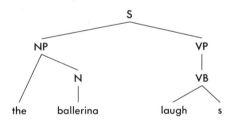

Another occasion when the verb suffix transformations may be applied is when the verbal has the feature ⟨−present⟩. In this case the affix segment is

$$\begin{bmatrix} ⟨+\text{affix}⟩ \\ ⟨+\text{V}⟩ \\ ⟨-\text{present}⟩ \end{bmatrix}$$

This affix is later replaced from the lexicon by "ed." The number and person features are irrelevant here:

> the ballerina laughed
> the ballerinas laughed.

These transformations, the auxiliary agreement transformation, the verbal agreement transformation, and the verb suffix transformation, can finally account for number and tense agreement, it seems. The transformations are simple and general. Unfortunately, there is one minor snag. These rules generate correct forms in

> The rain in Spain *falls* mainly in the mountains
> Seven purposeful seamen *dragged* in a porpoise.

But they also generate, as teachers often find out,

> * I swimmed the Atlantic in 1966
> * he knowed that he was wrong.

A number of common verbs—"tell," "buy," "sell," "take," "make," and "sink," for example—have irregular past tense forms. No firm solution to this problem has been found yet. Possibly these verbs show their idiosyncrasy as a feature in the lexicon. Such a feature would block the application of the verb suffix transformation, and the appropriate past tense form would be drawn from the lexicon to replace the verbal segment. It is not yet understood exactly how to incorporate exceptions into a grammar. For now it is sufficient to remember that the three simple transformations discussed here account for *most* kinds of agreement.

The ordering of these transformations is quite important. For example, the verbal agreement transformation cannot precede the copula transformation and the aspect transformation *if* they are applicable. The *deep* structure of

> the crocodiles are green

for example, does not contain a copula. If the copula transformation is not applied first, the verbal agreement transformation will copy the person, number, and tense features of the auxiliary segment onto the verbal and delete the auxiliary. The verb suffix transformation will then generate something that eventually becomes

> * the crocodile greens

or

> * the crocodile greened.

If the copula transformation is applied first, a copula precedes the verbal, and the auxiliary cannot be deleted.

SUMMARY

Agreement, in English, involves three transformations. The first is the auxiliary agreement transformation, which copies the features of number and person of the subject onto the auxiliary segment. The second is the verb agreement transformation, which 1) copies the same features plus the tense feature of the auxiliary onto a verb segment just in case the auxiliary immediately precedes the verb segment and is neither ⟨ +modal⟩ nor ⟨ +copula⟩ nor ⟨ +perfect⟩, and 2) deletes the auxiliary. Finally, the verb suffix transformation adds a suffix to the verb segment 1) when the segment is singular, third person, and in the present tense, or 2) when the segment is regular and in the past tense.

EXERCISE SIXTEEN

1. State the elementary transformation or transformations (i.e., substitution, deletion, adjunction) employed in the following transformations:

   a. article transformation
   b. affix transformation
   c. auxiliary incorporation transformation

2. Why do the transformational rules of English not generate sentences with plural adjectives?

3. Draw deep structure trees for

   a. The crocodiles are green.
   b. That grasshopper crackles.
   c. A tall Mexican had been painting that mural.

4. Show in detail how the deep structures for 3*a* and 3*b* become surface structures.

5. Look up the topic "Tense" in a traditional grammar and then write a comparison of the ways in which that grammar and the present book treat the same forms.

6. What evidence is there that agreement depends on the surface subject rather than the deep subject?

7. When is a non-modal auxiliary deleted?

8. How are particles represented in deep structures?

9. Describe the dialect which would result from a grammar which did not contain the *verbal agreement transformation*.

CHAPTER 17

Prepositions

To grammarians there seem to be almost as many unanswered questions about prepositions as there are about any other single topic in English syntax. Are prepositions represented as constituents or as features of constituents in deep structures? Are there special preposition phrase nodes in surface structures, as you have in effect been taught in school, or are so-called prepositional phrases actually noun phrases? Conclusive answers to questions of this sort cannot be given at present. The purpose of this chapter is to illustrate certain interesting facts about prepositions and, wherever possible, to suggest how these facts might be accounted for.

To begin with, one interesting fact about prepositions is that all noun phrases, in their deep structures, seem to have prepositions associated with them, even though these prepositions are frequently deleted from surface structures. The sentence

the army destroyed the fortress

contains no prepositions in its superficial form. However, prepositions can be seen to be associated with both the subject and the object noun phrases at some point during the generation of the sentence. Prepositions are revealed, for instance, when sentence structures are nominalized and turned into noun phrases. The above sentence, when nominalized, becomes the noun phrase given below:

the army's destruction *of* the fortress.

The cleft sentence test shows that this is a noun phrase:

the army's destruction of the fortress was ruthlessly carried out

> what was ruthlessly carried out was the army's destruction of
> the fortress.

In this nominalization, the preposition "of" has been introduced to the left of "the fortress." Where has this preposition come from? One simple explanation is to assume that it was really there all along and that this preposition was simply deleted in the sentence

> the army destroyed the fortress.

But there is an alternative which might occur to you. Suppose it was the case that the preposition was not there all along and that it was introduced by the transformation which did the nominalizing. What is less than satisfactory about this second proposal is that it would require one to believe that there are two nominalization transformations and not just one. Consider the following pair of strings:

1. the mathematician concentrated on the problem
2. the mathematician's concentration on the problem.

The second string in the pair is a nominalization of the first, which is a sentence. Observe that the preposition "of" has not been introduced. Had it been, the ungrammatical nominalization below would have been generated:

> * the mathematician's concentration of on the problem.

So, it would be necessary to suppose one nominalization transformation for the situation in which the underlying sentence has a preposition associated with the object noun phrase, as in the pair above, and one other nominalization transformation for the situation in which no preposition is associated with the object. The latter would introduce "of" into the nominalization. If it is assumed, however, that the "of" is really there all along in nominalizations like

> the army's destruction of the fortress

then one nominalization transformation suffices. Thus, the latter analysis is adopted here.

The subject noun phrase "the army" also does not contain a preposition in the surface structure. But if this sentence had undergone the passive transformation, the preposition "by" would appear before the original deep subject:

> The fortress was destroyed *by* the army.

Once again, this may be accounted for by the assumption that the preposition is there all along, in the deep structure, and that it is deleted whenever the subject noun phrase remains in its original position; that is, when the passive transformation has not been carried out.

As to the origin of prepositions, the tentative position taken here is that they originate as features in deep structures—in particular, as features of noun segments. This would certainly explain why there are prepositional constructions in which the choice of preposition seems to be dependent upon a noun:

> The tournament is on Monday
> The tournament is at noon
> The tournament is in May.

The three prepositions above are dependent upon the nouns following them. This is indicated by the ungrammaticality of the following strings:

> * the tournament is at Monday
> * the tournament is in Monday
> * the tournament is on noon
> * the tournament is in noon
> * the tournament is at May
> * the tournament is on May.

The ungrammaticality of these strings can be explained if it is assumed that the prepositions "on," "at," and "in" are uniquely associated with the nouns "Monday," "noon," and "May" as features. Thus the ungrammaticality of the strings above is much the same as that of the noun phrase "a pants." Here, "pants" is a plural noun carrying the feature ⟨ − singular⟩, and therefore it may not be preceded by a singular article.

However, the choice of particular prepositions seems to depend on verbals as well as on nouns. This is why only the *a* sentence of the following pairs is grammatical:

1. a. Rusk flew to Bombay
   b. * Rusk approved to Bombay
2. a. Rusk approved of Bombay
   b. * Rusk flew of Bombay.

Here it seems that the noun has little to do with the choice of preposition, since the only difference between the two strings is the verbal itself. It is important to account for these varied restrictions on prepositions. The hypothesis that prepositions originate as features on noun segments does help to account for these restrictions.

Verbals are quite commonly chosen on the basis of the nouns surrounding them as subjects, objects, and indirect objects:

1. Napoleon smiled
   * the salt smiled
2. Cleopatra lifted the silver
   * Cleopatra lifted the metabolism.

It is easy to see what is wrong with the ungrammatical sequences above. The verbal "smile" must be preceded by a noun marked $\langle +\text{human}\rangle$, while the verbal "lift" must be followed by an object marked $\langle +\text{con-}$ crete$\rangle$. The selection of a verbal depends upon the features of the noun segments surrounding the verbal—in particular, the subject noun segment, the object noun segment, and the noun segment which may follow the object noun segment (the indirect object).

This method of stating selectional restrictions can be used to explain ungrammatical strings like

> * Rusk approved to Bombay
> * Rusk flew of Bombay

if prepositions originate as features on noun segments. The verbal "approve" requires an object noun with the feature $\langle +\text{of}\rangle$ and no other preposition features. Thus, the string

> * Rusk approved to Bombay

is predictably ungrammatical, since the object noun contains the feature $\langle +\text{to}\rangle$ and not the feature $\langle +\text{of}\rangle$. Similarly, "flew" requires a noun with features like $\langle +\text{to}\rangle$, $\langle +\text{around}\rangle$, $\langle +\text{over}\rangle$, $\langle +\text{through}\rangle$, and so forth, but not the feature $\langle +\text{of}\rangle$. Thus, a sentence like

> Rusk flew around Bombay

is grammatical, and the string

> * Rusk flew of Bombay

is ungrammatical. Part of the semantic interpretation of sentences containing prepositions is given by the features on nouns.

The analysis of prepositions in the deep structure may be profitably compared with the analysis of particles presented in an earlier chapter. Particles, you will recall, were said to be represented as features of verbs. When a particle feature exists, a particle in the form of a particle segment is introduced into the structure by the particle transformation. When prepositions of the sort under discussion are represented as features of nouns in the deep structure, the process by which prepositions actually get into sentence structures is presumably somewhat similar. However, this can only be speculation at the present time since there are a great many questions about the kind of structure created when a preposition segment is actually introduced. What is "of the city" in the following sentence?

Jones approves *of the city.*

It is difficult to suppose that "of the city" is a noun phrase. For example, cleft sentences like

* what Jones approves is of the city

are ungrammatical. In other words, "of the city" simply does not function like an NP. Thus, it seems best to assume that this is a different kind of constituent, in particular a *prepositional phrase,* abbreviated PP. In terms of this suggestion, the sentence above could be represented as in the tree diagram below.

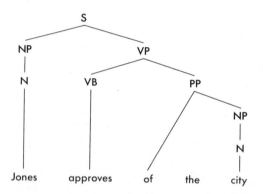

At the present time, it simply is not known how constituents which are not terminal constituents can be introduced by transformation. So, the transformational derivation of prepositional phrases is something of a mystery. Hopefully, grammatical research will resolve this difficulty within the near future.

In this connection, there is one respect in which prepositional phrases might be supposed to be noun phrases. This is in questions such as the two below.

What are you talking about?
About what are you talking?

If the question transformation involved in the generation of such sentences as those above moves questioned *noun phrases* to the front of the sentence, then "about what" is a noun phrase and it would follow that "of the city" in

> Jones approves of the city

is a noun phrase.   However, it is not obvious that this transformation moves only noun phrases.   Perhaps it moves noun phrases and prepositional phrases.   What is particularly suspicious is that this transformation seems to operate on verb phrases, or at least verbals, as well as noun phrases.

> What is John, sad or happy?

So, the issue is in doubt.   There is no very good reason to argue that constituents such as "of the city" are anything but special constituents which we call prepositional phrases.   On the other hand, grammarians do not, at the present time, have an understanding of the way in which prepositional phrases are generated from deep structures.

SUMMARY

It has been suggested here that prepositions are present in deep structures as features of nouns and that prepositions are introduced into sentence structures by transformation.   However, this transformational process is not understood at present.   The particular difficulty is that a preposition and its following noun phrase do not function like noun phrases but rather like special constituents identified as prepositional phrases.   How non-terminal constituents are transformationally introduced into the deep structure of sentences is currently not known.

Prepositions often do not appear in the surface structure of sentences because they have been deleted by either the subject or the object preposition deletion transformations.

EXERCISE SEVENTEEN

1. How do particles differ from prepositions?
2. Examine these sentences.   They are identical except for one word.   What observations can you make about the string "when the party arrived" in the two sentences?   Are they different in terms of their syntactic properties?

   a. Dr. Wynder discovered when the party arrived.
   b. Dr. Wynder left when the party arrived.

3. Draw deep structure trees for

   a. Joyce wrote about that Irish city.
   b. Will the folk singer tell Orpheus about the demonstration?
   c. Landor promised to write an ode.

4. Draw the deep structure for

    Eliot enjoyed publicizing himself.

   and then explain the presence of the reflexive pronoun in terms of this deep structure.
5. How does the hypothesis that prepositions originate as features on noun segments help account for the varied restrictions on prepositions?
6. Explain simply the ambiguity of the following voter registration test question:

   Will you give aid and comfort to the enemies of the United States government or the government of this state?
7. How are the following items represented in the lexicon?

   a. aggressive
   b. rhinoceros
   c. fantasy
   d. linguist
   e. I

Prepositions, Indirect Objects, and the Cross-over Principle

Verb phrases, as you saw in Chapter 8, may contain not only an object noun phrase but also a second noun phrase. You were told then that the second noun phrase sometimes contained a preposition:

> the economist convinced me *of the truth*
> a spectator threw the pamphlets *into the area*
> the folk singer told Orpheus *about the demonstration.*

In fact, the second noun phrase in a verb phrase, like the first noun phrase, invariably has a preposition in the deep structure. The prepositions are often deleted by transformations referred to in Chapter 17. A large part of this chapter deals with the type of double object construction traditionally referred to as the *indirect object* construction. These constructions differ somewhat from other double object constructions.

Contrast the following sentences:

1. Ian gave a lecture to the class
2. Ian followed the detective to the city.

The difference in meaning is clear enough. But these two sentences also differ as to the transformations which may be applied to them. In sentence 1, the noun phrase containing the preposition, "to the class," can be moved around the object noun phrase, and its preposition can be deleted, giving the sentence below:

3. Ian gave the class a lecture.

But, if the same is done to sentence 2, an ungrammatical string results:

4. * Ian followed the city the detective.

The deep structure for sentence 3 is (in abbreviated form):

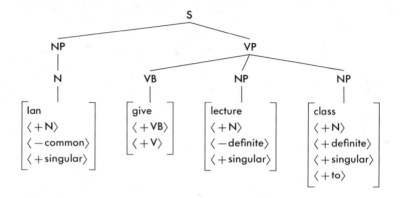

One could now apply the preposition transformation to create a preposition segment to the left of the second noun phrase in the VP:

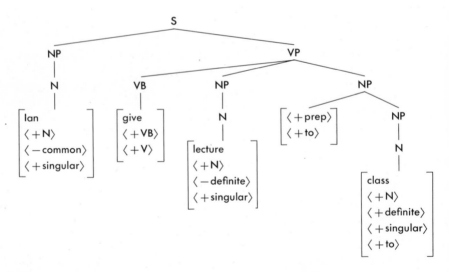

Once such other transformations as the article and the agreement transformations are carried out, the surface structure for the sentence following is generated:

Ian gave a lecture to the class.

How, then, does one generate sentence 3?   After the preposition transformation, a second transformation, the *indirect object inversion transformation,* is applied.   This transformation reverses the order of the object and indirect object noun phrases and deletes the preposition segment of the indirect object.   The result is

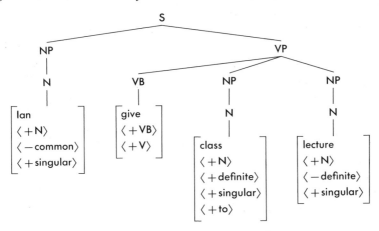

which becomes

Ian gave the class a lecture.

The indirect object inversion transformation is usually optional, which is why both sentences 1 and 3 are grammatical.

There is one case in which indirect object inversion cannot be applied (except in some dialects of British English):

5. a. you should send it to Ross
   b. * you should send Ross it
6. a. Robin took it to him
   b. * Robin took him it
7. a. you should send the book to Ross
   b. you should send Ross the book
8. a. Robin took the book to him
   b. Robin took him the book.

These data show that the transformation cannot be applied when the object is a pronoun.

The following sentences have the same deep structure, and consequently the same meaning:

9. a. Swift sent a note to Stella
   b. Swift sent Stella a note

    c. a note was sent to Stella by Swift
    d. Stella was sent a note by Swift.[6]

Two optional transformations may be used:

      the passive transformation
      the indirect object inversion transformation.

Neither of these was used to generate the first of the four sentences. In sentence 9*b*, the indirect object inversion transformation has been applied. The passive transformation was used for sentence 9*c*, while both transformations were applied to generate sentence 9*d*.

    Is the passive transformation applied before or after the indirect object transformation? One way to find out is to try both orderings. First, suppose that the passive transformation, which operates on the noun phrase immediately after the verbal, precedes the indirect object inversion transformation. The following string may, for this purpose, represent the deep structure:

    9. a. Swift sent a note to Stella.

If the passive transformation is applied, it generates

    9. c. a note was sent to Stella by Swift.

But how, then, can the sentence below be generated?

    9. d. Stella was sent a note by Swift.

For the sentence above to be generated, the passive transformation would have to move the indirect object to the front of the sentence. But it cannot, since the indirect object does not immediately follow the verbal in 9*a*. Thus, this ordering could not be correct.

    Now try the second possible order, in which the indirect object inversion transformation precedes the passive transformation. From the deep structure represented by 9*a*, the indirect object inversion transformation could, if it is applied, generate

    9. b. Swift sent Stella a note.

If the passive transformation is now applied, the sentence

    9. d. Stella was sent a note by Swift,

which could not be generated by the first order given, is correctly gen-

---

[6] Note that this sentence could have come from a different deep structure and is therefore ambiguous. Someone else could have sent Stella a note written by Swift.

erated. Suppose now that the indirect object inversion transformation had not been applied, leaving the structure of the sentence

9. a. Swift sent a note to Stella.

The passive transformation applied here will generate

9. c. A note was sent to Stella by Swift.

Thus, all possibilities have been generated, and it is seen that when both transformations are to be used, indirect object inversion transformation must precede the passive transformation.

Passive and double object constructions reveal a very interesting phenomenon, one that may well be the case for all languages. This has to do with the reflexive transformation. What conclusion can you draw from the following strings?

10. a. Captain Carpenter admired Eustacia
    b. Eustacia was admired by Captain Carpenter
11. a. Captain Carpenter admired himself
    b. * himself was admired by Captain Carpenter
    c. * Captain Carpenter was admired by himself.

The passive transformation may only be performed if the subject noun phrase is *not* identical to the noun phrase following the verbal. Now look at the operation of a new transformation which involves the inversion of noun phrases in verb phrases:

12. a. I argued with Captain Carpenter about Eustacia
    b. I argued about Eustacia with Captain Carpenter
13. a. I argued with Captain Carpenter about himself
    b. * I argued about himself with Captain Carpenter
    c. * I argued about Captain Carpenter with himself.

The strings 13*b* and *c* are ungrammatical in the same way as the ungrammatical passive strings 11*b* and *c*.

What is going on here? Are the phenomena observed in 10 and 11 related to the phenomena in 12 and 13? The transformation involved in 10 and 11 is different from the one for 12 and 13. But are the observed facts a reflection of a deeper principle? From the two cases, there does appear to be a similarity between the passive transformation and the transformation inverting two noun phrases inside of a verb phrase. Both transformations invert noun phrases. It seems to be the fact that *transformations cannot invert identical noun phrases.* This fact, called the *cross-over principle,* explains the ungrammaticality of 11*b* and *c* and 13*b* and *c*. Observe that 11*a* contains identical subject and object noun phrases in the deep structure.   The cross-over principle predicts that these two noun phrases cannot be inverted.   This prediction is confirmed by the fact that, when the passive transformation is applied to this deep structure, ungrammatical strings result.   Exactly the same is true of sentences 13*b* and *c*.   In 13*a*, the verb phrase contains two identical noun phrases in the deep structure.   Since these two noun phrases cannot be inverted, it follows that 13*b* and *c* must be ungrammatical.   In 12*a*, on the other hand, where the two noun phrases are not identical, inversion is possible, and, when it happens, the result is a grammatical sentence.[7]

SUMMARY

The second of the two noun phrases in a verb phrase has, like other noun phrases, a preposition feature in the deep structure.   In the case of indirect object construction, the second noun phrase in the verbal has the feature ⟨ +to⟩ in the deep structure.   Thus, the preposition transformation creates a preposition segment to the left of this noun phrase, and the two together are dominated by another noun phrase. However, it is also possible to apply the indirect object inversion transformation when the object noun is not a pronoun.   This transformation inverts the object and indirect object noun phrases and deletes the preposition of the indirect object segment.   Finally, there appears to exist a cross-over principle which prohibits the inversion of identical noun phrases.   This prohibition holds for all transformations which invert noun phrases, e.g., the passive transformation and the transformation which reverses the order of noun phrases inside of verb phrases.

EXERCISE EIGHTEEN

1. Account for the ambiguity of

    Stella was sent a note by Swift.

2. Draw the deep structure tree for

    Melanie awarded Christopher the cup.

---

[7] It is impossible at the present time to give a precise formulation of the cross-over principle, since a number of difficulties have not yet been explained.   For example, if in 13*a* "with Captain Carpenter" and "about Captain Carpenter" are noun phrases, there is no obvious reason why they should not be capable of being inverted, since they are not identical.   Still, they contain identical noun phrases, and apparently it is this fact which makes inversion impossible.

3. Explain in detail how the deep structure for 2 becomes a surface structure.

4. State three other sentences which could have been generated from this deep structure and show how these sentences are generated.

5. When can indirect object inversion not take place?

6. What justifications are there for assuming that

> Swift sent Stella a note.

and

> Swift sent a note to Stella.

come from the same deep structure?

7. Explain why the passive and the indirect object inversion transformations can only be applied in a certain order. Use examples.

8. Describe the cross-over principle, and illustrate the facts which this principle seeks to explain.

CHAPTER 19

Questions

Of the two main types of question sentences, only the yes-no questions have been discussed. These are the question sentences which might normally elicit a "yes" or "no" answer:

> did Columbus discover America in 800 A.D.?
> is Benedict unusually tall?
> can the compound be isolated?

The other kind of question sentence is the WH question. These are never answered by "yes" or "no":

> who is Godot?
> when is the next solar eclipse?
> what is the name of that artist?

The answers to most yes-no questions may be given by paraphrasing the questions themselves, in sentences beginning with "It is true that..." and "It is the case that..." or "It is not true that..." and "It is not the case that...." The answer to a WH question is normally a noun phrase, as you see from the possible answers to the WH questions above:

> the Creator
> at 5 o'clock
> Matisse.

Remember that there is a corresponding yes-no question for almost every declarative sentence.

> May they leave?
> They may leave.

However, it is sometimes the case that transformations must be applied to question sentences which need not necessarily be applied to declarative sentences. For example, one may apply the *extraposition transformation* to the sentence

> that she ran away worried her mother

and generate

> it worried her mother that she ran away.

As will be seen in a later chapter, this transformation moves the string "that she ran away" from the beginning to the end of the sentence. Apparently this transformation must be applied if a grammatical yes-no question is to be generated:

> * did that she ran away worry her mother
> did it worry her mother that she ran away?

The deep structure of any question sentence differs in one important respect from that of a declarative, or statement, sentence: It possesses the additional constituent QUESTION. If there were no differences in the deep structures of the two, the grammar would not be able to account for the ability of all normal native speakers to distinguish between questions and statements. Thus, the deep structure of

> they may leave

is

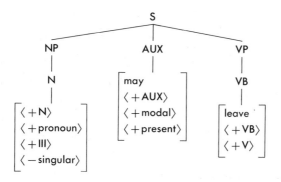

whereas that of

> may they leave?

is

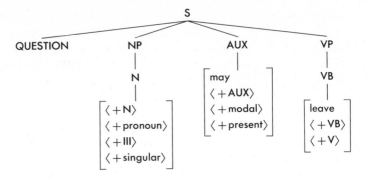

Then the structure below is generated by the interrogative and the QUESTION deletion transformations:

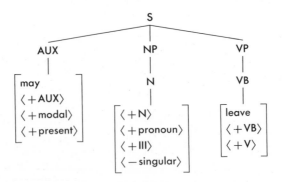

The final structure is

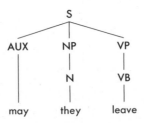

In the example above, the auxiliary was the modal "may." But the auxiliary might not have been a modal. In that case, if the verbal contains the feature ⟨+progressive⟩, the progressive transformation creates a copula segment to the left of the verbal, while an affix transformation puts an affix segment after the verbal. Then the auxiliary incorporation transformation applies to transfer the features of the progressive segment to the auxiliary segment (cf. Chapters 14 and 15). The interrogative transformation shifts the auxiliary (which is eventually spelled out as "is") in front of the subject noun phrase. The constituent QUESTION is deleted later and a structure like the following is generated:

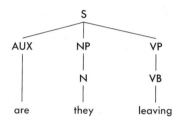

A form of "have" will fill the auxiliary position if the verbal has the feature $\langle +\text{perfect} \rangle$ instead of $\langle +\text{progressive} \rangle$ and if the auxiliary contains no modal. If there were no aspect features nor any modal, the auxiliary would eventually have been replaced by a form of "do." Sentences like the following are generated in this way:

Does astronomy supersede astrology?

WH questions are questions about noun phrases. The WH question words "who," "what," "when," "where," and "which" are *interrogative pronouns*. These pronouns, like all other pronouns, originate in terms of features on noun segments in the deep structure.

But it is not enough simply to show a pronoun like "what" with the features $\langle +\text{N} \rangle$, $\langle +\text{pronoun} \rangle$, and $\langle -\text{human} \rangle$. It is necessary to distinguish between the pronouns "it" and "what" in the deep structure. The pronoun "it" has exactly the same features as those listed above for "what." One important difference between the two is that "it" is definite and "what" is indefinite. However, it would seem that the marking $\langle -\text{definite} \rangle$ on "what" is still not wholly adequate, since it is necessary to distinguish "what" from the pronoun "one," as in "One doesn't make silly gestures in a classroom." "One" here is indefinite and therefore not distinct from "what." A tentative solution would be to propose a new feature, the feature $\langle +\text{WH} \rangle$. In deep structures, then, interrogative pronouns possess the feature $\langle +\text{WH} \rangle$; all others possess the feature $\langle -\text{WH} \rangle$.

When a noun segment contains $\langle +\text{WH} \rangle$ in deep structures, it is being questioned. The features $\langle +\text{WH} \rangle$ and $\langle -\text{WH} \rangle$ must also accompany pronouns in the lexicon in order that the correct pronoun, i.e., interrogative versus personal, may be chosen.

it
$$\begin{bmatrix} \text{it} \\ \langle +\text{N} \rangle \\ \langle +\text{pronoun} \rangle \\ \langle -\text{WH} \rangle \\ \langle -\text{human} \rangle \\ \langle +\text{singular} \rangle \\ \langle +\text{definite} \rangle \end{bmatrix}$$
what
$$\begin{bmatrix} \text{what} \\ \langle +\text{N} \rangle \\ \langle +\text{pronoun} \rangle \\ \langle +\text{WH} \rangle \\ \langle -\text{human} \rangle \\ \langle -\text{place} \rangle \\ \langle -\text{definite} \rangle \end{bmatrix}$$
one
$$\begin{bmatrix} \text{one} \\ \langle +\text{N} \rangle \\ \langle +\text{pronoun} \rangle \\ \langle -\text{WH} \rangle \\ \langle -\text{definite} \rangle \end{bmatrix}$$

With this interpretation, the interrogative pronouns "who," "when," and "where" all contain the feature $\langle +\text{WH} \rangle$. However, "who" is marked in the lexicon with the feature $\langle +\text{human} \rangle$; "when" is marked with the feature $\langle +\text{time} \rangle$; "where" is marked with the feature $\langle +\text{place} \rangle$.

who(m)
$$\begin{bmatrix} \text{who(m)} \\ \langle +\text{N} \rangle \\ \langle +\text{pronoun} \rangle \\ \langle +\text{human} \rangle \\ \langle +\text{WH} \rangle \end{bmatrix}$$
when
$$\begin{bmatrix} \text{when} \\ \langle +\text{N} \rangle \\ \langle +\text{pronoun} \rangle \\ \langle -\text{human} \rangle \\ \langle +\text{time} \rangle \\ \langle +\text{WH} \rangle \end{bmatrix}$$
where
$$\begin{bmatrix} \text{where} \\ \langle +\text{N} \rangle \\ \langle +\text{pronoun} \rangle \\ \langle -\text{human} \rangle \\ \langle +\text{place} \rangle \\ \langle +\text{WH} \rangle \end{bmatrix}$$

It is easy to see why these pronouns must contain these features. A possible answer to the question

Whom did you see?

is

I saw the janitor

(which contains a $\langle +\text{human} \rangle$ noun "janitor"), but not

I saw the rock

(which contains a $\langle -\text{human} \rangle$ noun "rock"). Similarly, an appropriate answer to the question

When did you see the movie?

could be

I saw the movie on Friday

(which contains a $\langle +\text{time} \rangle$ noun "Friday"), but not the sentence

I saw the movie on my father's recommendation

(because "recommendation" has the feature $\langle -\text{time} \rangle$). Finally, a possible answer to the question where is your report?

is

my report is *in my desk*

(which contains a ⟨ +place⟩ noun "desk"), but not

my report is *in an unusual form*

(because the noun "form" has the feature ⟨ −location⟩).
   WH question sentences are generated by two question transformations. The sentence

what will Darcy buy?

has the deep structure

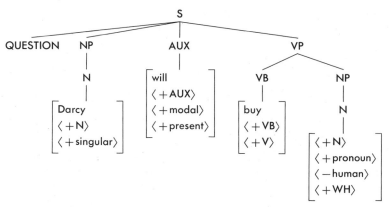

As in all question sentences, the interrogative transformation moves the
auxiliary in front of the subject noun phrase. The application of this
transformation to the structure above produces

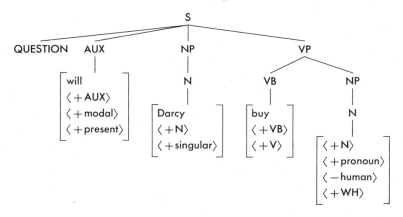

The *WH question transformation* replaces the QUESTION constituent with the noun phrase containing a noun with the feature ⟨+WH⟩.

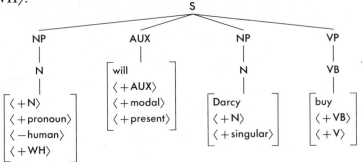

When the segments in this structure are replaced by words from the lexicon, the following surface structure is generated:

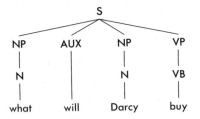

Sentences like the one below

who will leave?

do not seem to have been affected by the interrogative transformation. In fact, both transformations are employed, but the effect of the interrogative transformation is nullified because the WH question transformation is being applied to the subject noun phrase. Here is the deep structure of the sentence above:

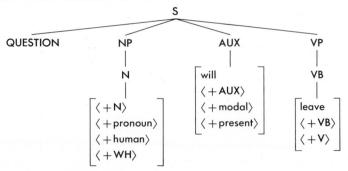

The interrogative transformation generates the structure

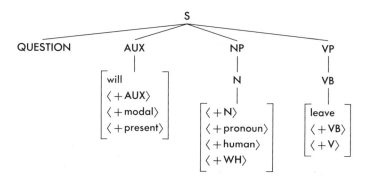

At this point, the WH question transformation replaces the QUESTION constituent with the subject noun phrase of the sentence. Thus, the subject noun phrase is once again in front of the auxiliary, and the effect of the interrogative transformation is nullified:

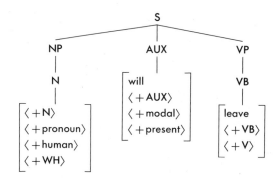

When words replace segments in the second lexical pass, the sentence following is generated:

who will leave?

A final type of WH question which should be considered is a sentence like

which book did you read?

Phrases like "which book" occur because not only pronouns but also ordinary nouns may be marked with the feature ⟨ +WH⟩ in deep structures. When this happens, the article transformation introduces an article segment with the feature ⟨ + WH⟩. This segment will be spelled in the lexicon as either "which" or "what." Presumably, the same sort of mechanism is involved in the generation of noun phrases like "what boy" in sentences like

what boy are you talking about?

You will detect a semantic difference between the two sentences below:

which boy are you talking about?
what boy are you talking about?

Such differences as exist in the semantic interpretation of the two sentences have not yet been explained by grammarians.

SUMMARY

The generation of yes-no questions depends upon the application of the interrogative transformation, which moves the auxiliary in front of the subject noun phrase. WH questions involve not only the interrogative transformation but also the WH question transformation, which replaces the QUESTION constituent with a noun phrase in which the noun carries the feature ⟨+WH⟩. If the WH question transformation does not apply, as is the case in yes-no questions, the QUESTION constituent is subsequently deleted by the QUESTION deletion transformation, which is one of the very last transformational rules to apply. When questions appear in embedded sentences (as so-called *indirect questions*), their transformational properties are slightly different from those described in this chapter. These properties will be discussed in some detail in Chapter 22.

EXERCISE NINETEEN

1. Define the following:

   a. reflexivization
   b. aspect
   c. immediate domination
   d. the WH question transformation

2. Why are the deep structures of negative and interrogative sentences shown with the constituents NEGATIVE and QUESTION, respectively? Why couldn't we just use negative and interrogative transformation without having these constituents in the deep structure?

3. Draw deep structure trees for

   a. What must I say?
   b. Whom will Oscar choose?
   c. I will look this word up.

4. Explain in detail how the deep structures for 3*a* and 3*b* become surface structures.

5. What is a noun phrase complement?

6. What semantic difference can you detect between

   a. Which book are you talking about?
   b. What book are you talking about?

7. What is the semantic and syntactic importance of the time and place features? These features may also be important in sentences which are not interrogative. Try to list some examples.

8. What is the derivation of the following sentence:

   Who is Harry?

SECTION FOUR

Sentence Embedding

CHAPTER 20

Noun Phrase Complements and Complementizers

In Chapter 7, we discussed the embedding of sentences in noun phrases, and in Chapter 8, we focussed on the embedding of sentences in verb phrases. We used the giant sentence beginning

> Epstein had mentioned the fact that Kant believed the rumor that Descartes rejected the hypothesis that matter had originated . . .

to show that there is no limit on the number of embedded sentences possible in a grammatical sentence of English. The number is, in fact, determined only by the limitations of human memory, concentration, and similar factors. This possibility of sentences recurring inside various constituents of other sentences, described as *sentence recursion*, is one of the two explanations for the infinite number of possible sentences in a human language. The second source of recursion is the conjunction of sentences.

The constituent structure of the sentence

> Mulligan is reckless

is embedded in a noun phrase in

> that Mulligan is reckless worries Stephen.

This sentence might be shown as the following constituent structure (the auxiliary and other details are excluded):

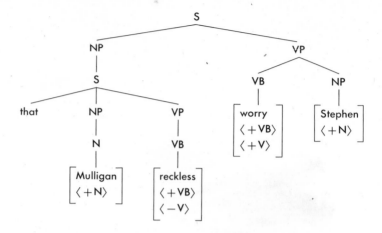

(In actuality, the structure above is not a deep structure, for the subject noun phrase lacks a *head* noun preceding the complement sentence. The syntactic evidence for this head noun will be discussed shortly. For the purposes of the present chapter, however, discussion based upon intermediate structures such as the one above will suffice.)

The embedded sentence here is said to function as a *noun phrase complement*. This was one of the six syntactic functions described in Chapter 10. As you learned then, every noun phrase, no matter where it appears in a deep structure, may contain a sentence functioning as a noun phrase complement. Noun phrase complements may appear in subject noun phrases, as in the sentence above, or in object noun phrases, as in the sentence below:

> Stephen denied that Mulligan was reckless.

The word "that," one of the characteristic signals of the noun phrase complement, is called a *complementizer*. Complementizers are introduced into deep structures by the *complementizer transformation*. The most common complementizers in English are:

a. the *clause complementizer*, "that":

> that Mulligan had behaved recklessly worried Stephen

b. the *infinitive complementizer*, "for . . . to":

> *for* Mulligan *to* have behaved recklessly worried Stephen
> *for* Metternich *to* leave Austria was astonishing

c. the *gerundive complementizer*, the genitive or possessive form of the noun (or pronoun) and "ing," spelled as either " 's . . . ing," generally for singular nouns:

Mulligan*'s* hav*ing* behaved recklessly worried Stephen
Metternich*'s* leav*ing* Austria was astonishing

or "'. . . ing," generally for plural nouns:

the boys' eat*ing* was a matter for concern.

The cleft sentence test shows that

for Mulligan to have behaved recklessly
for Metternich to leave Austria
Mulligan's having behaved recklessly
Metternich's leaving Austria

are all *noun phrase* complements:

what worried Stephen was for Mulligan to have behaved
recklessly
what was astonishing was for Metternich to leave Austria
what worried Stephen was Mulligan's having behaved recklessly
what was astonishing was Metternich's leaving Austria.

Look now at an abbreviated intermediate structure for

for Metternich to leave Austria was astonishing.

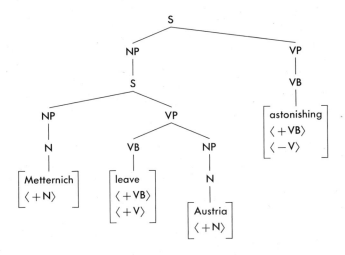

The complementizer transformation introduces "for" in front of the
subject noun phrase of the embedded sentence and "to" before the
verb phrase. The result is the constituent structure below:

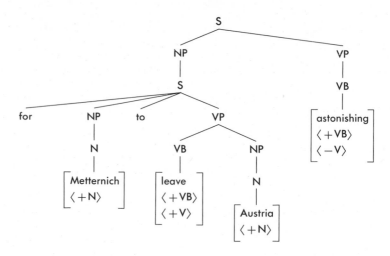

The sentence

> Metternich's leaving Austria was astonishing

is generated in much the same way. To avoid confusion, the embedded noun phrase complements will be tagged as "clause ... ," "infinitive ... ," and "gerundive . . . ."

The infinitive and gerundive noun phrase complements share several properties. You might be able to identify one of them from the following strings:

1. a. Metternich prefers for Garibaldi to leave
   b. * Metternich prefers for Metternich to leave
   c. Metternich prefers to leave
2. a. Metternich prefers Garibaldi's leaving
   b. * Metternich prefers Metternich's leaving
   c. Metternich prefers leaving.

In both 1c and 2c the subject noun phrase of the embedded sentence, "Metternich," has been deleted, together with the "for" or " 's" part of the complementizer. Such deletion is not possible for 1a and 2a, and thus it is evident that the transformation deleting the noun phrase is the *identical noun phrase deletion transformation* referred to in Chapter 4. (This transformation, you will recall, never applies when the clause complementizer "that" appears. In this case, pronominalization rather than deletion of the second identical noun phrase takes place.) The identical noun phrase deletion transformation is applied to a constituent structure like the simplified one below:

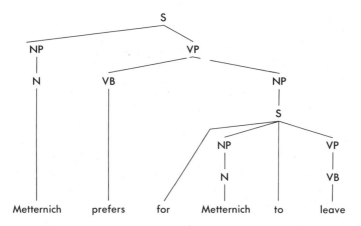

and converts it into:

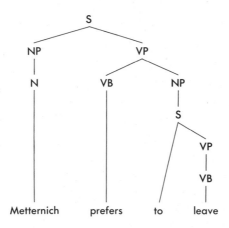

Notice that the surface structure is understood exactly as if "Metternich" had not been deleted from the deep structure.

It has been assumed that the identical noun phrase deletion transformation deletes the "for" part of the infinitive complementizer. Strictly speaking, this assumption is probably false. In all likelihood, the "for" is deleted by a separate transformation when it occurs immediately in front of "to." Thus, the structure represented by the string

> * Metternich prefers for Metternich to leave

first becomes, by the identical noun phrase deletion transformation,

> * Metternich prefers for to leave

and then

> Metternich prefers to leave.

It is interesting in this respect that dialects of English survive to this day where this transformation which deletes "for" before "to" does not exist. In such dialects, sentences such as

> I want for to go

are completely grammatical. In the present illustrations, however, no further mention of the transformation deleting "for" before "to" will be made. We shall assume that this transformation applies whenever the identical noun phrase deletion transformation applies.

In our last example, the embedded sentence was an infinitive noun phrase complement in the object noun phrase. A gerundive noun phrase complement in, say, the subject noun phrase would reveal the same properties. Thus the identical noun phrase deletion transformation has obviously been applied in the generation of

> discovering gold made the boys famous

in which the deleted subject of the noun phrase complement must have been identical to the noun phrase "the boys" in the main sentence.

One other property gerundive and infinitive noun phrase complements share is illustrated here:

3. a. I like the carnation's *being* fresh
   b. I like the carnations' *being* fresh
4. a. I like the carnation *to be* fresh
   b. I like the carnations *to be* fresh
5. a. I was glad that the carnation *was* fresh
   b. I was glad that the carnations *were* fresh.

Only in 5a and 5b, in a clause noun phrase complement, does the form of "be" show *agreement* with the subject of the embedded sentence. The infinitive and gerundive complementizers appear to block the application of the verbal agreement transformation.

The final complementizer property to be dealt with in this chapter involves deletion:

6. a. Joseph thinks *that* rhetoric is superior to honest reasoning
   b. Joseph thinks rhetoric is superior to honest reasoning
7. a. Metternich preferred *for* Garibaldi to leave
   b. Metternich preferred Garibaldi to leave

8. a. I dislike Joseph's staying out so late
   b. I dislike Joseph staying out so late.

In each case the first part of the complementizer (the whole of the clause complementizer) has been removed by optional *complementizer deletion transformations*. The syntactic conditions under which such deletions take place are somewhat different for each complementizer and are often very idiosyncratic. Perhaps you can work out for your own dialect under what circumstances this sort of complementizer deletion can optionally (or even obligatorily) take place.

SUMMARY

Noun phrase complements are marked by three different complementizers—clause, infinitive, and gerundive—introduced into deep structures by the complementizer transformation. When the subject noun phrase in an infinitive or gerundive complementizer is identical to a relevant noun phrase in the main sentence, the subject noun phrase and the first element of the complementizer are deleted. The infinitive or gerundive complementizers will also prevent the application of the agreement transformation to the embedded sentence. Finally, the clause complementizer and the first element of the infinitive and the gerundive complementizers may—and sometimes must—be deleted by an optional transformation called complementizer deletion.

EXERCISE TWENTY

1. What properties, shared by the gerundive and infinitive complementizers, are not possessed by the clause complementizer?

2. Explain briefly each of the following:

   a. sentence recursion
   b. noun phrase complements
   c. complementizer
   d. perfect aspect

3. Draw deep structure trees for the following sentences:

   a. The opportunity for Wolfe to defeat Montcalm presented itself.
   b. Stephen is worried by the fact that Mulligan is reckless.

4. Show, in detail, how the deep structures drawn for 4a and 4b become surface structures.

5. Under what circumstances can the complementizer deletion transformation be applied? When can it never be applied?

6. Describe one other kind of embedded sentence than the noun phrase complement and the verb phrase complement.

7. How would the following be represented in the lexicon:

   a. ambition
   b. handsome
   c. mud
   d. Harold
   e. shoe

CHAPTER 21

Extraposition and "It" Deletion

One important syntactic process in noun phrase complement constructions is that of *extraposition*. Because of its key role in the complement
system, it will be considered in some detail in this chapter.

Begin by looking at the sentence below:

Columbus made the claim that the world was round.

The string "the claim that the world is round" is a noun phrase complement construction containing the sentence

the world was round.

The structure of the initial sentence could be abbreviated as follows:

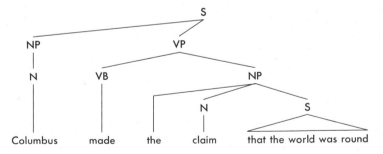

If we apply the passive transformation to this structure, we get

The claim that the world was round was made by Columbus.

This sentence would have the following (highly abbreviated) structure:

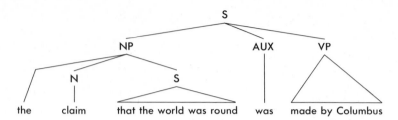

The process of extraposition is illustrated when we compare the passive sentence

the claim *that the world was round* was made by Columbus

with the sentence

the claim was made by Columbus *that the world was round.*

What does the *extraposition transformation* do?

When a noun phrase complement follows its "head" noun (e.g., "claim"), this transformation detaches the embedded sentence from under the domination of the noun phrase of which it is a complement and moves it to the end of the main sentence. When the extraposition transformation is applied to the structure above, it generates

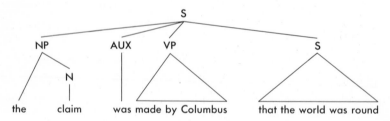

In the light of the extraposition transformation, we must revise certain parts of the analyses of the noun phrase complement suggested in the preceding chapter. The analysis provided for sentences like the one below:

that Mulligan is reckless worries Stephen

must be revised. In the last chapter, the string "that Mulligan is reckless" was described as a sentence embedded inside the subject noun phrase with roughly the structure given at the top of page 173.

Notice that the subject noun phrase is missing something that you should have come to expect as a necessary constituent of every noun phrase in the deep structure: the constituent N. All noun phrases contain nouns in the deep structure. But noun phrase complement construc-

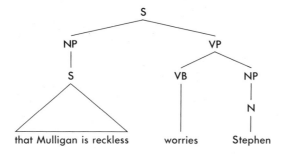

tions like the one above do not seem to contain a noun, only a sentence. In fact, in the deep structure of sentences like

> that Mulligan is reckless worries Stephen

there *is* a noun in the deep structure of the subject noun phrase; in the surface structure this noun is deleted. If there is assumed to be a noun in the deep structure of sentences such as the one above, then the synonymy of the sentences

1. *that Mulligan is reckless* worries Stephen
2. it worries Stephen *that Mulligan is reckless*

can easily be explained. Both of these sentences would have exactly the same deep structure, just as the sentences below have the same deep structure.

3. the claim *that the world was round* was made by Columbus
4. the claim was made by Columbus *that the world was round.*

Knowing what extraposition does, we need only assume that sentence 2 results from the application of the extraposition transformation in order to explain the relatedness of sentences 1 and 2. In other words, we assume that the subject noun phrase in the deep structure of sentences 1 and 2 actually contains a noun and that this noun is the pronoun "it," as shown in the tree diagram below:

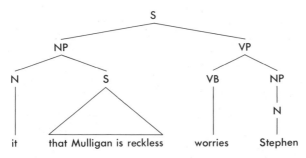

Recall that extraposition applies when a complement sentence follows the *head* noun of a noun phrase complement construction, that noun dominated immediately by NP. Thus, the extraposition transformation may be applied to the structure above, the head noun being the pronoun "it," to generate the structure below:

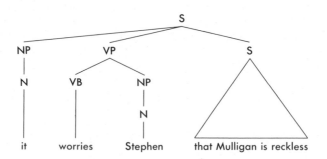

Thus sentence 2 is generated.

The extraposition transformation is usually optional. This explains why both sentences 3 and 4 may be generated.

3. The claim that the world was round was made by Columbus.
4. The claim was made by Columbus that the world was round.

In sentence 3 the extraposition transformation has not been applied; in 4, it has. Suppose, now, that "it" is the head noun of a noun phrase containing a noun phrase complement sentence. What happens if the extraposition transformation is not applied in such constructions? Look again at the deep structure for sentence 2. If the extraposition transformation had not been applied, the ungrammatical string below would have been generated:

* it that Mulligan is reckless worries Stephen.

However, this string can be made grammatical by application of the third important noun phrase complement transformation, the "it" *deletion transformation*. This normally obligatory transformation deletes the pronoun "it" *whenever this pronoun appears immediately before its noun phrase complement*, that is, before the constituent S dominated by the same noun phrase which dominates the pronoun, as is the case in the deep structure diagram for sentences 1 and 2 above. Thus, if the extraposition transformation has not been used, "it" deletion is obligatory. The foregoing deep structure is converted into the following surface structure by the "it" deletion transformation:

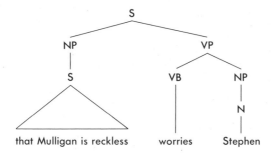

Likewise, all of the sentences below, which contain only an S in their surface structures, have a noun in their deep subjects as well as the S. The noun is the pronoun "it" in each case:

> finding you in this library astonishes me
> to find you in this library astonishes me
> that you are in this library astonishes me.

The first of these, for example, can be derived from an intermediate structure abbreviated as "it my finding you in this library astonishes me." The extraposition and the "it" deletion transformations are ordered so that extraposition precedes pronoun deletion. Extraposition is usually optional, but pronoun deletion is normally obligatory. Sentences like

> I dislike *it* for you to stay up late
> I wouldn't guarantee *it* that he will be late,

which are common in many dialects of English, are examples of cases where pronoun deletion is optional; but such cases are exceptions.

The extraposition and the "it" deletion transformations are so important in English syntax that it is worthwhile to consider, in some detail, the derivation of three sentences involving these transformations:

5. Carlo argues that Columbus discovered America
6. that Columbus discovered America is argued by Carlo
7. it is argued by Carlo that Columbus discovered America.

The order of the three transformations involved in the generation of these three sentences is:

a. passive transformation (optional)
b. extraposition (optional)
c. "it" deletion (obligatory).

The deep structure for sentences 5, 6, and 7 is

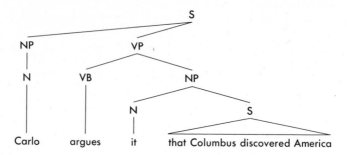

Begin with sentence 5. Neither the first nor the second optional transformations has been applied. Thus, the pronoun "it" still immediately precedes the complement sentence "that Columbus discovered America." Therefore, the "it" deletion transformation applies to generate the surface structure for sentence 5:

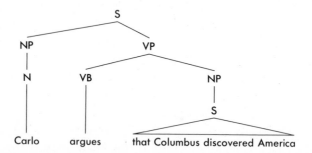

In the generation of sentence 6, the passive transformation has been applied, moving the noun phrase "it that Columbus discovered America" to the front of the sentence:

* it that Columbus discovered America is argued by Carlo.

Since extraposition has not been applied, "it" deletion generates:

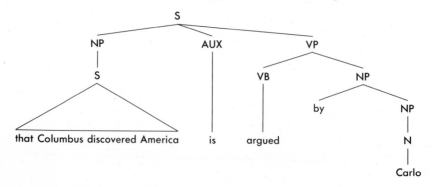

Finally, in the generation of sentence 7, the passive transformation has been applied. This time, however, the extraposition transformation is applied to move the complement to the end of the sentence:

it is argued by Carlo that Columbus discovered America.

Since extraposition separates the complement from the pronoun "it," "it" deletion will not apply. Thus, we generate the surface structure below:

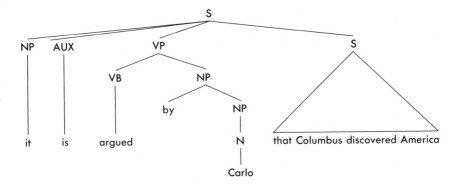

SUMMARY

All noun phrases containing noun phrase complements also contain a head noun. Deletion often occurs if this head noun is the pronoun "it." Extraposition is an optional transformation which moves the complement to the end of the sentence and which may be applied when a complement sentence follows a pronoun head. When extraposition is not applied, and the head of the noun phrase complement is a pronoun, the pronoun must be deleted by the "it" deletion transformation.

EXERCISE TWENTY-ONE

1. Draw deep structure trees for

   a. It was claimed by Culligan that the patent was fraudulent.
   b. The child he adopted became a podiatrist.
   c. The poet hates to write sonnets.

2. Explain in detail how the deep structure trees for 1a and 1c become surface structures.

3. What are the conditions for extraposition to apply as this transformation was discussed in this chapter?

4. Distinguish between the uses of "that" in the following sentences:

   a. The news *that* the Cambodians had protested aroused only a cynical smile.
   b. The problem *that* Trilling discussed concerned the nature of the literary experience.
   c. *That* problem is insoluble so long as psychology remains behavioristic.

5. What evidence is there for positing an "it" as the head noun of a noun phrase containing a complement when the noun phrase has no "it" in the surface structure? Use examples.

6. When must the "it" deletion transformation be applied?

7. Draw the deep structure tree for

   Viola tends to drink milk.

   Remember to check first whether "to drink milk" is a noun phrase complement or a verb phrase complement.

8. There is a common dialect of English for which the following sentences are accepted as perfectly normal by speakers of that dialect:

   a. I would dislike it for you to do that.
   b. I can't guarantee it that you are right.

   Compare this dialect with the following dialect in terms of the rules discussed in this chapter:

   c. I would dislike for you to do that.
   d. I can't guarantee that you are right.

9. For both of the dialects mentioned above, the following sentences are ungrammatical:

   a. * it for you to do that is difficult
   b. * it that you are right is obvious.

   Does this fact alter your conclusion about the way in which the transformations are operating in the first dialect described in 8?

CHAPTER 22

Indirect (or Embedded) Questions

In Chapter 19, two different types of interrogative sentences, yes-no and WH questions, were described. So far, only *main sentence* interrogatives have been discussed—that is, interrogative sentences which were not embedded sentences. In this chapter, you will see that both yes-no and WH questions may be noun phrase complement sentences. Their behavior as embedded sentences is only slightly different.

To begin with, we will review briefly the transformations essential to the generation of non-embedded interrogative sentences. The interrogative transformation shifts the auxiliary to the position before the subject noun phrase. The WH question transformation replaces the QUESTION constituent with a noun phrase in which the noun carries the feature ⟨+WH⟩. The QUESTION constituent is subsequently deleted by the QUESTION deletion transformation if the WH question transformation is not applied.

How do these yes-no question sentences

1. can you stay?
2. is it true?

differ from the sentences below:

3. I don't know whether you can stay
4. I wonder if it is true.

In the first place, although compelling syntactic evidence is as yet scanty, it seems that the strings "whether you can stay" and "if it is true" are actually yes-no questions equivalent to sentences 1 and 2. In this respect, it is especially interesting that sentences 3 and 4 may be paraphrased by sentences 5 and 6, in which the yes-no questions actually appear:

5. I don't know the answer to the question, "Can you stay?"
6. I wonder what is the answer to the question, "Is it true?"

Secondly, these same strings, "whether you can stay," and "if it is true," are noun phrase complements—sentences embedded in noun phrases. The cleft sentence test for noun phrases yields positive results for both sentences 3 and 4.

Thus, such phrases can be viewed as interrogative sentences embedded as noun phrase complements. This means that sentence 3 has roughly the structure given below:

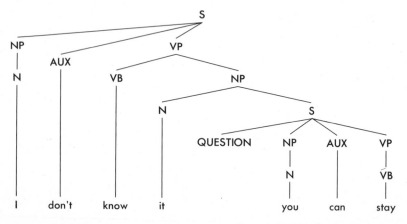

A look at this structure should show you the major differences between interrogative sentences which are not embedded and interrogative sentences which are embedded. For example, how does the derivation of the sentence

I don't know whether you can stay

differ from the derivation of the sentence below:

can you stay?

In interrogative sentences embedded as noun phrase complements, the interrogative transformation is not applied; in such sentences, the auxiliary and the subject noun phrase are not inverted. Moreover, the QUESTION constituent is not deleted in such sentences, but is replaced by either "whether" or "if" from the lexicon. QUESTION is thus not an imaginary constituent after all; it has actual substance in embedded sentences: "whether" or "if."

In view of these considerations, we must reconsider the formulation of the interrogative transformation and the QUESTION deletion transformation. The former inverts the subject noun phrase and the auxiliary. The latter deletes the QUESTION constituent. But *both of these transformations apply just to main sentences,* never *to embedded question sentences.*

What happens when WH questions are embedded as noun phrase complements? The WH questions

7. what can you see?
8. who can see?

can be embedded as noun phrase complements:

9. I don't know what you can see
10. I wonder who can see.

Generating WH questions embedded as noun phrase complements is no more complicated than generating such sentences when they are not embedded. The (abbreviated) deep structure of sentence 10 is

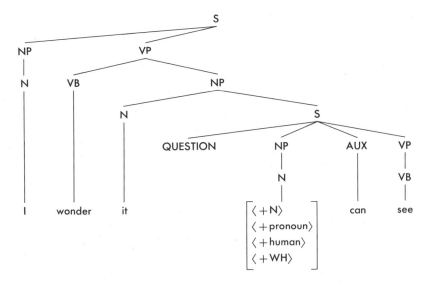

As the question sentence is an embedded sentence, the interrogative transformation cannot be applied. The WH question transformation applies and replaces the QUESTION constituent with the NP containing a noun with the feature ⟨+WH⟩. This gives us the structure below (in which the ⟨+WH⟩ segment has been replaced by the pronoun "who"):

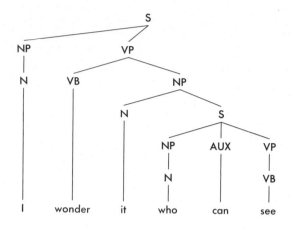

Application of the pronoun deletion transformation deletes the pronoun "it" appearing before the noun phrase complement sentence. Thus, the correct surface structure of the sentence

I wonder who can see

has been generated.

SUMMARY

Question sentences may be embedded as noun phrase complements. The interrogative transformation, obligatory for non-embedded questions, cannot be applied to embedded questions. In embedded WH questions, however, the WH question transformation must still be applied. The constituent QUESTION, which you may have thought of as an imaginary or "understood" constituent, turns out to have the physical shape "if" or "whether" in embedded yes-no questions. The QUESTION deletion transformation may not be applied to embedded questions.

EXERCISE TWENTY-TWO

1. Which transformation is not applied to embedded questions and is applied in non-embedded questions?
2. Under what conditions may noun phrases be deleted?
3. Why would any semantic theory based upon transformational grammar be concerned with deep structures and the lexicon rather than surface structures?

4. Draw deep structure trees for

   a. Heathcliff asked whether Darcy admired Herzog.
   b. That Jane could prefer Bingley shocked Tarzan.
   c. Colby wanted to shoot himself.

5. Show how the deep structure for 4a becomes a surface structure.

6. What are the elementary transformations employed in extraposition and pronoun deletion?

7. What evidence is there for assuming that embedded interrogative sentences are noun phrase complements?

8. Give one semantic reason and one syntactic reason for believing that the constituent QUESTION appears in the deep structure of interrogative sentences.

"It" Replacement, Reflexives, and Synonymy

Three major transformations of the complement system have been discussed: identical NP deletion, extraposition, and "it" deletion. There is one other, whose existence is not nearly so apparent from a casual examination of surface structures as are the other three: *"it" replacement.* This transformation helps to explain the synonymy of the sentences below:

> it happens that Scopes is honest
> Scopes happens to be honest.

Let us begin our explanation of the above with a discussion of the sentences

1. for Scopes to have done that surprises me
2. that Scopes did that surprises me.

Do these two sentences have the same deep structure? The answer is "yes." Notice that the strings

> for Scopes to have done that

and

> that Scopes did that

are actually noun phrase complements in the subject noun phrases of these sentences; this can be demonstrated by applying the cleft sentence test. Thus, the only difference between the two sentences has to do with the complementizer. Sentence 1 has a noun phrase complement in its subject with the infinitive complementizer; sentence 2 has the clause complementizer. Thus, the sentences have virtually the same deep structure, abbreviated below:

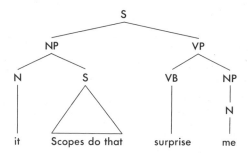

Sentences 1 and 2 are generated from this deep structure through the application of the complementizer transformation (introducing the infinitive complementizer in the first sentence and the clause complementizer in the second) and the "it" deletion transformation.

Now, consider the following two sentences in the light of this analysis:

3. I believe that I am honest
4. I believe myself to be honest.

Notice, once again, that these two sentences mean exactly the same thing, and we would expect them to have identical deep structures— thus, sentence 3 should differ from sentence 4 only in the choice of complementizer. It is not easy, however, to establish this. What must first be shown is that both sentences contain noun phrase complements in their object noun phrases. But here the cleft sentence test fails us. It works for the first sentence

what I believe is that I am honest

but turns in a negative result for the second:

* what I believe is (for) myself to be honest.

The ungrammaticality of the latter sentence shows that the string "my-self to be honest" is not a noun phrase in sentence 4. This fact reduces the chances of showing that both sentences 3 and 4 have the same deep structure.

If we are to show that these sentences have the same deep structure, we must show that something happens to the noun phrase complement in sentence 4, something which destroys its structure as a noun phrase and which creates a new structure which cannot pass the cleft sentence test. The critical clue is in sentence 4—the existence of the reflexive

pronoun "myself." A brief study of reflexives reveals two basic properties. First, two identical noun phrases are necessary for reflexivization
of the second by the first. Second, and for the present more important,
it is necessary for the two identical noun phrases to be *in the same simple
sentence*, as demonstrated by the sentences below:

5. a. * I hurt I
   b. I hurt myself
6. a. * I think that myself will go now
   b. I think that I will go now
7. a. * I think that they like myself
   b. I think that they like me.

Compare the deep structures of sentences 5*b* and 7*b*.

5*b*

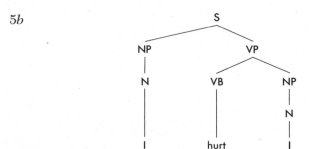

Notice that here both noun phrases containing "I" are in the same
simple sentence. To put it another way, no S node dominates one NP
which does not dominate the other as well.

7*b*

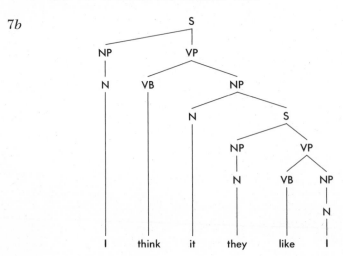

Notice that the two identical NP's in this structure are not in the same simple sentence. In particular, the object NP for "I" is dominated by an S node which does not dominate the subject NP to which it is identical. Thus, the fact that the two noun phrases are identical means nothing from the point of view of reflexivization. Under such circumstances, the reflexive transformation cannot be applied.

Now, to show that sentences 3 and 4 have the same deep structure, the existence of the reflexive form in sentence 4 must be explained. If the second "I" originates in the complement sentence, how could it be reflexivized? Look at the rough (much abbreviated) deep structure for sentence 3:

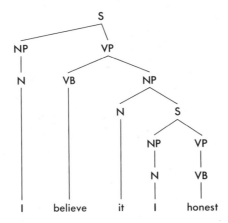

Notice that the subject of the embedded sentence and the subject of the main sentence are identical, but cannot be reflexivized, since they are not in the same simple sentence. At this point, let us consider the *"it" replacement transformation,* for it is this transformation which will resolve the difficulties here. The "it" replacement transformation does two things. First, it detaches noun phrase complements with infinitive and gerundive complementizers from underneath the NP's which dominate them and reattaches them under the domination of VP's. Applied to the structure above, this stage of the "it" replacement transformation generates the structure at the top of page 188.

(Notice that the infinitive has been excluded in the above structure, but this is only for convenience. This complementizer is assumed to be present, since the "it" replacement transformation can apply only when an infinitival or gerundive complementizer is present.) The second stage of "it" replacement replaces the pronoun head of the noun phrase

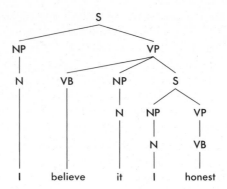

which contained the noun phrase complement, namely "it," with the subject noun phrase of the complement sentence. This gives the structure below:

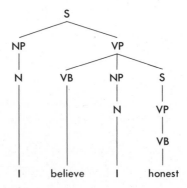

With the infinitive complementizer present, and assuming the application of the copula transformation, the structure generated would be the one below:

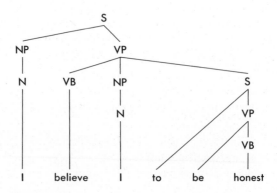

Now, what about reflexivization? What you observe is that the "it" replacement transformation has created a structure to which the reflexive transformation can, in fact, be applied. This is because the "it" replacement transformation has moved the subject of the complement sentence into the main sentence. Thus, the two identical noun phrases are now in the same simple sentence, and reflexivization can, therefore, apply. (This assumes an ordering of rules, of course. Reflexivization must follow "it" replacement.) When reflexivization applies, we end up with the desired structure:

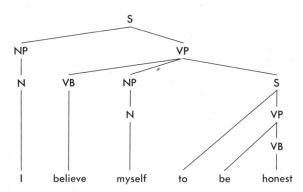

What does this analysis using the "it" replacement transformation accomplish with respect to the two sentences under discussion? First, our analysis explains that the two sentences have the same meaning because they have the same deep structure. Second, it explains the reflexivization in the second sentence of the pair by demonstrating how the second identical noun phrase is brought into the same simple sentence as the first identical noun phrase. Third, it explains why the cleft sentence test succeeds for sentence 3:

> what I believe is that I am honest

but fails for sentence 4:

> * what I believe is myself to be honest.

If you look at the surface structure for the second string above, you will see that "myself to be honest" is not a noun phrase at all, but two constituents, a noun phrase followed by the remains of a complement sentence. Thus, the cleft sentence test, which works only on noun phrases, will predictably fail.

Consider finally, the first two sentences given in this chapter:

8. it happens that Scopes is honest
9. Scopes happens to be honest.

We can now easily explain the synonymy of these two sentences. Both originate with a noun phrase complement construction in subject position. But, in the case of sentence 9, the complementizer is infinitival. For verbs like "happen," the "it" replacement transformation is obligatory under such circumstances. Thus the lexical string below, representing the deep structure of sentence 9,

> * it for Scopes to be honest happens

is transformed into the following string when the first stage of "it" replacement moves the complement sentence, "for Scopes to be honest," to the end of the verb phrase:

> * it happens for Scopes to be honest.

Then the "it" is replaced by the subject noun phrase of the complement sentence, with the concomitant deletion of "for," giving the sentence below:

> Scopes happens to be honest.

SUMMARY

This chapter has introduced the last transformation of the complement system, the "it" replacement transformation. This transformation explains how complement constructions with very similar or the same deep structures can end up with very distinct surface structures. You have seen, furthermore, that the "it" replacement transformation must precede the reflexivization transformation.

EXERCISE TWENTY-THREE

1. Draw deep structure trees for
    a. Brigid happens to enjoy sausages.
    b. Jonathan thought himself to be perceptive.
    c. Sonia took Raskolnikov soup.
    d. The constable asked what Jonathan wanted.
    e. Wadsworth enjoys looking at the scenery.
    f. It is unusual for these plants to flower.

2. Explain carefully how the deep structures for 1a and 1b become surface structures.

3. Under what circumstances can reflexivization take place if a tree structure contains two identical noun phrases?

4. What do you notice about the following set of sentences?

    1. a. I know the place where he lives.
       b. I know where he lives.

    2. a. He knows the time when he should be here.
       b. He knows when he should be here.

    3. a. I met him on the street where he lives.
       b. I met him where he lives.

    4. a. He saw me arrive at the hour when I should have been in Chichester.
       b. He saw me arrive when I should have been at Chichester.

5. How would the following be represented in the lexicon?

    a. mountain   d. amaze
    b. Moses   e. amazing
    c. fertility   f. lizard

6. Explain concisely how the *agreement transformations* work.

7. Explain what is wrong with the following strings. Try to describe what is wrong in terms of features.

    a. * Rosemary brought his own cousin
    b. * she had always thought highly of himself
    c. * Forbes washed despair
    d. * the road heaved a sigh of relief
    e. * the dinner enjoyed Newmark
    f. * Schlesinger amazed the door

8. What is the relative ordering of the "it" replacement transformation and the passive transformation, and why?

CHAPTER 24

Verb Phrase Complements

One of the basic reasons for assuming the existence of such entities as noun phrase complements is the fact that embedded sentences seem, very often, to act like noun phrases under such tests as the passive test, the cleft sentence test, and others. Reviewing briefly, the phrase

> that Henry Adams visited the Paris Exposition of 1900

in the sentence

> few people know that Henry Adams visited the Paris Exposition of 1900

must be a sentence embedded inside of a noun phrase because of the fact that this phrase passes both the passive test:

> that Henry Adams visited the Paris Exposition of 1900 is known by few people

and the cleft sentence test:

> what few people know is that Henry Adams visited the Paris Exposition of 1900.

There are embedded sentences in English, however, which cannot be said to be embedded in noun phrases if these tests are reliable. The following sentence contains an embedded sentence:

1. Joan prefers to work at the museum.

By now, you should be able to recognize that "to work at the museum" is what remains of an embedded sentence—

> * Joan prefers for Joan to work at the museum

with the subject of the embedded sentence, "Joan," deleted because it is identical to the subject of the main sentence. Had the subject of the complement sentence been different from the subject of the main sentence, it would not have been deleted, a fact illustrated by the sentences below:

> Joan prefers for Peter to work at home
> Joan prefers Peter to work at home.

What else can be determined about the embedded sentence in 1? In what constituent was this sentence embedded in the deep structure? If you apply the cleft sentence test, you will find that the sentence was embedded in a noun phrase:

> what Joan prefers is to work at the museum.

However, what do you make of the sentence below:

2. Joan condescended to work at the museum.

Superficially, just looking at the surface structure of this sentence, it appears to be identical (except for the verb) to our original sentence. But the cleft sentence test fails:

> * what Joan condescended was to work at the museum.

Assuming the reliability of the cleft sentence test, we must conclude that the string "to work at the museum" in sentence 2 is not a noun phrase complement at all—an embedded sentence, yes, but not a sentence embedded inside a noun phrase.

In this case the sentence is a *verb phrase complement*. It has been embedded directly under the immediate domination of a verb phrase, as in the following tree diagram:

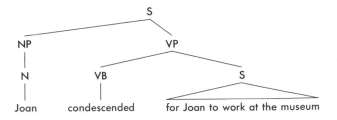

When identical phrase deletion is applied, as study of verb phrase complements has shown always to be necessary, the subject of the embedded sentence is deleted, giving the structure that follows:

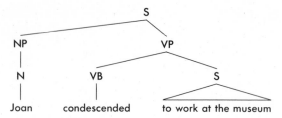

The cleft sentence test fails because the embedded sentence is not dominated by a noun phrase.

If this analysis is correct, it is predictable that verb phrase complements will not undergo the passive transformation. This transformation, you will recall, inverts only noun phrases. Since what follows the verbal is not a noun phrase, the passive transformation cannot take place. Thus, the ungrammaticality of the string

* to work at the museum was condescended by Joan

is to be expected.

Verb phrase complement constructions of the sort under discussion are called *intransitive verb phrase complement constructions* because they contain no object noun phrase. In such constructions, the complement sentence simply follows the verbal. However, the *transitive* verb phrase complement construction has a verbal followed by a noun phrase which in its turn is followed by a complement sentence, all under the immediate domination of VP. An example of such constructions is given below:

Guido tempted Daisy to adopt the rat.

What evidence is there that this sentence has the structure given below?

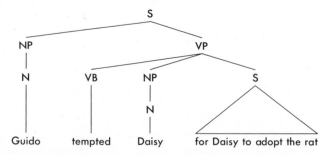

You can check that the string "Daisy to adopt the rat" is not a noun phrase complement in the sentence above because the cleft sentence transformation fails:

* what Guido tempted was for Daisy to adopt the rat.

However, might not this sentence be similar to those sentences involving the "it" replacement transformation:

I believe Daisy to be greedy.

Compare the sentences:

3. a. I believed the vet to have examined Daisy
   b. I believed Daisy to have been examined by the vet
4. a. I persuaded the vet to examine Daisy
   b. I persuaded Daisy to be examined by the vet.

The sentences in 3 are synonymous; they have exactly the same meaning. The deep structure of the sentences in 3 is roughly the following:

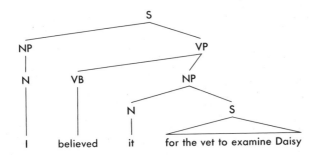

"It" replacement must be applied to this structure to replace the "it" by the subject of the complement sentence. However, the "it" replacement transformation does not necessarily take the deep subject; it may also take the surface subject. If the passive transformation has been applied to the complement sentence:

* I believe it for Daisy to have been examined by the vet,

the "it" replacement transformation will replace "it" by the surface subject of the sentence, "Daisy":

I believe Daisy to have been examined by the vet.

Thus, the only difference between sentences 3a and 3b is whether or not the passive transformation has been applied. The deep structures of the two are identical; they thus have exactly the same meaning.

But what about sentences 4a and 4b, which are not synonymous? It is quite possible to persuade the vet to examine Daisy without persuading Daisy to be examined by the vet, and conversely. If they are not synonymous, we may assume that the two sentences have different deep structures.   Sentences 4a and 4b are instances of transitive verb phrase complements in which the verb is followed by a noun phrase which is in turn followed by an S, all under the domination of the verb phrase, VP.   This formulation would give us the following structure for 4a:

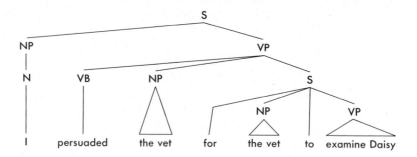

Identical noun phrase deletion is applied to generate:

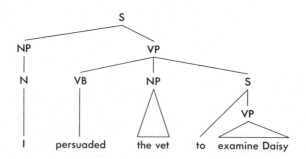

Now compare the deep structure of sentence 4a with that of sentence 4b:

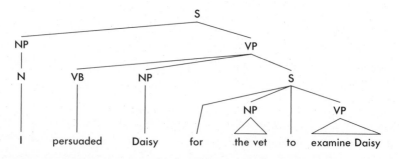

Notice the very important difference between the deep structures.   In that of 4a, the object of the verbal is "the vet."   In the deep structure of sentence 4b, the object of the verbal is "Daisy."   Thus, the two deep structures are different, and their difference in meaning can be explained in these terms. The only question remaining concerns the generation of sentence 4b from the deep structure above. First, the passive transformation is applied to the verb phrase complement, giving roughly the following structure:

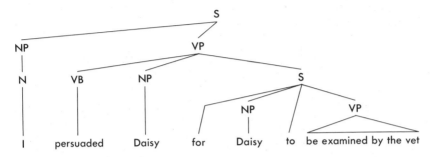

Following the application of the passive transformation, the identical noun phrase deletion transformation deletes the subject noun phrase of the complement sentence. This gives the final structure below:

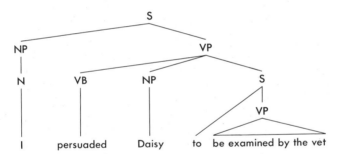

There are two facts to keep in mind regarding verb phrase complements, both transitive and intransitive. First, these complements require the infinitive complementizer "for . . . to." No convincing cases of verb phrase complements seem to exist which take the clausal complementizers. The italicized string below

I had him going around in circles

seems to be a case of transitive verb phrase complementation where the gerundive complementizer is used, but we can find very few such cases. Second, the identical noun phrase deletion transformation is obligatory. There are no exceptions to this rule. Thus, the subject of the verb phrase complement sentence must always be identical to the appropriate noun phrase in the main sentence. For intransitive verb phrase complements, the noun phrase in question is the subject noun phrase of the main sentence. For transitive verb phrases, the noun phrase is always the object noun phrase of the main sentence. When these conditions are not satisfactorily met, the generative process fails, and no grammatical sentence is generated.

SUMMARY

There exist complement sentences which are not noun phrase but verb phrase complements. Such sentences are immediately dominated by verb phrases. Such constructions always have the infinitive complementizer, and identical noun phrase deletion is obligatory.

EXERCISE TWENTY-FOUR

1. What conclusions can you draw from the strings below?

   1. a. * take a pill and are you sick?
      b. Take a pill and go to bed.

   2. a. * I painted the garage and don't threaten me
      b. I painted the garage, and Lucille washed the Olds.

   3. a. * are you ready and he went yesterday
      b. Are you ready and is the plane waiting?

2. Explain how the "it" replacement transformation works.

3. How do verb phrase complements differ from noun phrase complements?

4. Explain how articles get into sentences.

5. Summarize the arguments for regarding pronouns as articles.

6. Distinguish between semantic and syntactic tense.

7. Draw deep structure trees for

   a. Napoleon refused to sign this compact.
   b. The green book stated that the hippopotamus symbolized the Church.
   c. The porter wondered who was at the gate.
   d. Are you threatening a strike?

8. Are the following sentences synonymous?

   a. I convinced the man to photograph Daisy.
   b. I convinced Daisy to be photographed by the man.

Are the following sentences synonymous?

   c. I suspected the man to have photographed Daisy.
   d. I suspected Daisy to have been photographed by the man.

In your own words, offer an explanation for your observations.

CHAPTER **25**

Relative Clauses

Thus far, two types of embedded sentences have been discussed in detail: noun phrase complements—sentences embedded in a noun phrase following a noun:

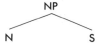

and verb phrase complements—sentences embedded in a verb phrase either following the verbal directly or following an object noun phrase which follows the verbal:

One other kind of embedded sentence needs discussion: *relative clauses.* These sentences are embedded in noun phrases, and they follow a noun phrase, *not* a noun:

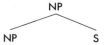

The sentence below contains this kind of construction as the subject noun phrase:

the argument which Palmerston presented disconcerted the protesters.

The string "the argument which Palmerston presented" is a noun phrase, as you will see if you apply the cleft sentence and passive tests. The actual relative clause, "which Palmerston presented," contains a transitive verbal, "presented," which requires an object noun phrase in the deep structure. Although one does not appear in the surface structure, you can tell from the sense of the clause that what Palmerston presented was "the argument" and that this noun phrase must have been the object noun phrase in the deep structure. In other words, the relative clause

which Palmerston presented

has, as its deep structure, what is abbreviated below as a string:

Palmerston presented the argument.

Underlying all relative clauses, then, are sentence structures.

The subject noun phrase of the sentence

the argument which Palmerston presented disconcerted the protesters

is structured as follows (again the auxiliary and much feature material have been omitted, since they are not relevant to the discussion):

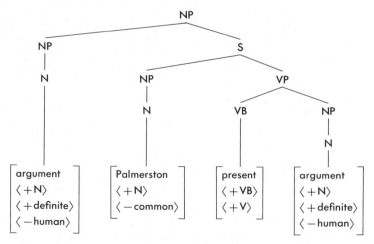

Thus, this subject noun phrase itself contains a noun phrase and a sentence.

Several transformations are involved in generating the surface structure of relative clauses. Perhaps the most important is the *relative clause transformation* itself. This transformation operates on a relative clause structure in which the head noun phrase, the one to the left of the embedded sentence, is identical to an appropriate noun phrase inside the embedded sentence. In the structure above, these identical noun phrases are the deep structure noun phrases for "the argument." The transformation does two things under such conditions. It adds the features ⟨ + WH⟩ and ⟨ + pronoun⟩ to the noun segment in the identical noun phrase of the relative sentence and it moves this noun segment to the front of the sentence, giving the structure below:

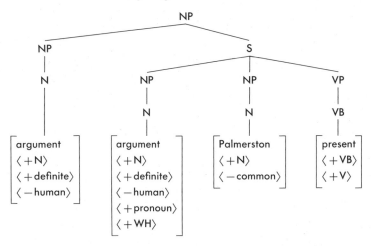

The addition of the features ⟨ + WH⟩ and ⟨ + pronoun⟩ results eventually in the replacement of this noun segment by the relative pronoun "which."

The relative clause transformation thus establishes the order of the parts of the relative clause. The next structure is a consequence of the double application of the article transformation:

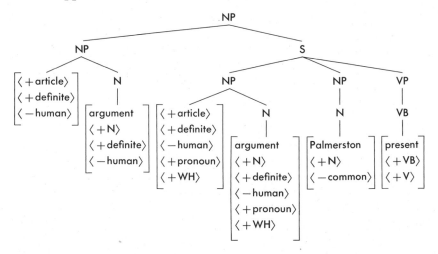

The first article segment will be replaced by "the" from the lexicon; the second, which contains a ⟨+WH⟩, must be replaced by the WH word "which." The resulting string

> * the argument which argument Palmerston presented

is now ungrammatical in most dialects of English, although such noun phrases were quite common in the sixteenth, seventeenth, and eighteenth centuries. The second "argument" is deleted by the *relativized noun deletion transformation*. This transformation deletes noun segments with the features ⟨+pronoun⟩ and ⟨+WH⟩ when they occur at the front of relative clauses *and* are preceded by an article segment with the features ⟨+pronoun⟩, ⟨+definite⟩, and ⟨+WH⟩. Thus the final structure of the noun phrase containing the relative clause is

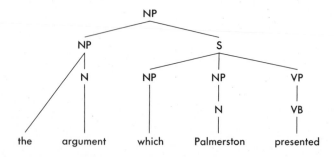

This is basically how relative clauses are generated from deep structures. The form of the relative pronoun depends upon the features of the ⟨+WH⟩ noun in the noun phrase. For example, the relative pronoun "which" occurs only when the deleted noun is ⟨−human⟩. The relative pronoun "who" is restricted, in all dialects, to noun phrases in which the head noun has the feature ⟨+human⟩. Note that this restriction does not apply when a proper name is given to an animal, when it is treated as if it were human. The relative pronoun "that" is not affected by any such restrictions. Thus both of the following are grammatical:

> the boy that Tarkington searched for was in the loft
> the plough that Tarkington searched for was in the loft.

No grammarian has yet been able to explain one other property of the relative pronouns "who" and "which" (but not of the relative pronoun "that"). If the relative pronoun is "who" (or "whom") or "which," and is preceded by a preposition, the relative transformation may move the preposition as well:

1. a. the boy who(m) I spoke to
   b. the boy to whom I spoke
2. a. the book which I spoke about
   b. the book about which I spoke
3. a. the boy that I spoke to
   b. * the boy to that I spoke
4. a. the book that I spoke about
   b. * the book about that I spoke.

The surface structures of relative clauses vary considerably because different optional transformations have been applied. Yet the relationship between alternative forms is not hard to account for. Take, for example, these pairs of sentences:

1. a. the situation which you describe depresses me
   b. the situation you describe depresses me
2. a. I am using the vibrator that you bought for me
   b. I am using the vibrator you bought for me
3. a. men who(m) you respect should be listened to
   b. men you respect should be listened to.

It is easy to pick out the relative clauses in the *a* sentences above. The question to be answered is how these relative clauses are related to the *b* strings below:

> you describe
> you bought for me
> you respect.

The difference between the *a* sentences and the *b* sentences is that the *relative pronoun deletion transformation* has deleted the relative pronouns "which," "that," and "who(m)." The only question remaining is to determine the circumstances under which this optional transformation may be applied. In the three *a* sentences above, the relative pronouns come between the head noun phrase and the subject noun phrase of the relative clause; e. g., the structure of the first *a* is given below:

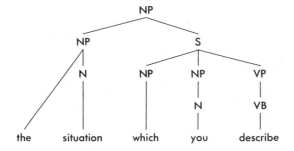

This configuration of constituents, *when the pronoun follows directly after the head noun phrase and precedes the subject noun phrase of the relative clause,* is the only one in which the relative pronoun deletion transformation can apply.

If a preposition has been brought to the front of the sentence along with the relative pronoun, the relative pronoun cannot be deleted:

1. a. the radio telescope which Holmes boasts about is superb
   b. the radio telescope Holmes boasts about is superb
2. a. the radio telescope about which Holmes boasts is good
   b. * the radio telescope about Holmes boasts is good.

If the relative pronoun is the subject of the relative clause itself, as in the sentence

> the situation which bothers John depresses me

the relative pronoun cannot be deleted:

> * the situation bothers John depresses me.

The relative pronoun subject of a relative clause may, however, be deleted by a *relative clause reduction transformation* if it precedes a segment with the features ⟨ +copula⟩ and ⟨ +present⟩, which indicate some form of the copula "be":

1. a. the girl who is sitting on the rock is selling lemonade
   b. the girl sitting on the rock is selling lemonade
2. a. unicorns which are captured at midnight turn into princesses
   b. unicorns captured at midnight turn into princesses
3. a. artists who rely on the sales of their works are unfortunately rare
   b. * artists rely on the sales of their works are unfortunately rare.

The third *b* string above is ungrammatical because the relative pronoun subject did not precede a copula segment. Usually, relative clause reduction also generates ungrammatical strings when the relative pronoun subject precedes a copula segment followed by an adjective—that is, a verbal with the feature ⟨ −V⟩:

1. a. plays which are controversial rarely appear on Broadway
   b. * plays controversial rarely appear on Broadway
2. a. actors who are gifted sometimes despise playwrights
   b. * actors gifted sometimes despise playwrights.

Another transformation, the *adjectival VP shift,* or, more simply, the adjective transformation is needed here to shift the adjective to the left of the noun in the main sentence noun phrase:

> controversial plays rarely appear on Broadway
> gifted actors sometimes despise playwrights.

Thus the structure

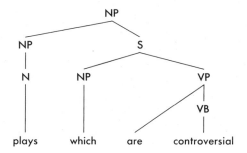

becomes, through relative clause reduction,

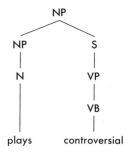

This, in turn, is transformed by the adjective transformation into:

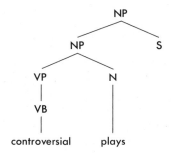

Structures of this sort are governed by a convention known as *tree-pruning*, which deletes one node of any type when it immediately dominates either nothing or another node of exactly the same type. Thus, the S and then one NP are deleted to generate diagram *a*:

a

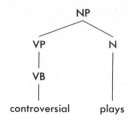

If there were an article before the noun in the main sentence noun phrase, however, only the S could have been deleted—diagram *b*:

b

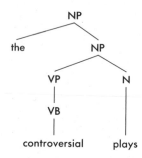

What justification is there for representing the structure as in *b* rather than *c*? What does *b* tree explain that *c* does not?

c

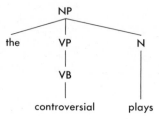

In *b*, "controversial plays" is a constituent. In *c*, it is not. Now when you read the sentence

this controversial play outdoes that one

you understand the pronoun "one" to mean "controversial play." The pronoun transformation converts *noun phrases* into pronouns, not *nouns* into pronouns. Since it has converted the structure of "controversial play" into the pronoun "one," you either have to accept that "controversial play" is a noun phrase constituent, or invent a separate pronoun transformation just to deal with this case. The simpler and more intuitive solution is to treat "controversial play" as a noun phrase within a noun phrase.   Tree diagrams are not arbitrary gimmicks; they should represent relationships intuitively perceived by the native speaker.

Now, what about sentences like this:

this controversial play outdoes that uncontroversial one.

if the pronoun transformation converts noun phrases (not nouns) into pronouns, it seems that "play" itself must be a noun phrase and the structure of "this controversial play" something like the following:

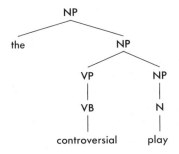

But if this analysis is correct, the derivation of "the controversial play" must be somewhat different from the derivation presented earlier. Starting with the intermediate structure identical to that in the middle of page 205,

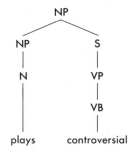

the adjectival shift transformation must cause the introduction of a new NP to dominate the VP containing "controversial" and the NP "plays."

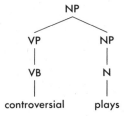

Finally, the article transformation itself must create a new NP node dominating the article segment and the NP above.

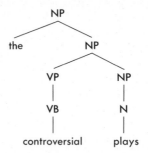

This analysis would explain the facts about pronominalization. (Keep in mind, now, that the article transformation has a new formulation. Earlier in this text, it was said simply that the article transformation introduces an article segment. Now, it is being asserted that this transformation introduces a new NP node as well. The introduction of this new node seems necessary if one is to understand how pronominalization works in sentences like

this boy knows more than that one.)

The adjective transformation must move verb phrases. If only the verbal were moved, the relative clauses in the following noun phrases

the child *who is quietly sleeping*
the city *which is totally destroyed*

would become

* the sleeping child quietly
* the destroyed city totally.

The adverbials "quietly" and "totally," however, are adjoined to verbals underneath the domination of verb phrases. Since they are moved as units, the following strings result:

the *quietly sleeping* child
the *totally destroyed* city.

In English, relative pronouns and interrogative pronouns almost always have the same form. When interrogative pronouns occur in embedded question sentences, it is sometimes hard to tell them from relative pronouns. In the sentences

1. Ludwig knows when her plane arrived
2. Ludwig laughed when her plane arrived

the word "when" has a function in 1 different from that in 2. For example, the cleft sentence test shows that the string "when her plane arrived" is a noun phrase complement in sentence 1; in fact, it is an embedded WH question:

> what Ludwig knows is when her plane arrived.

But the same test applied to sentence 2 shows that here the string is not a noun phrase complement:

> * what Ludwig laughed was when her plane arrived.

In sentence 2, the string is a relative clause contained in a noun phrase whose head noun phrase has been deleted. The full prepositional phrase was, in its original form, "at the time when her plane arrived":

> Ludwig laughed at the time when her plane arrived.

"When" and "where," like "who," "which," and "that," can function as relative pronouns. One of the facts which supports this claim is that "when" and "where" delete in the same way as the other relative pronouns:

1. a. the man whom you saw
   b. the man you saw
2. a. the time when you came
   b. the time you came
3. a. the place where you were
   b. the place you were.

The word "when," in its function as a relative pronoun, is always at the front of a clause modifying a noun which has the feature ⟨ +time⟩:

> the time when John arrived
> the day when John arrived
> the minute when John arrived.

The relative pronoun "where" is always at the front of a clause modifying a noun which has the feature ⟨ +place⟩:

> the place where you are sitting
> the town where I was born
> a location where I can find you.

Noun phrases of this sort often seem to be transformed by what might be called the *time-place deletion transformation*. This transformation takes noun phrases like

> at the time when . . .

and

at the place where . . .

and transforms them, by deleting the head noun phrase along with the preposition, into the strings below:

when . . .
where . . . .

This transformation only deletes the head noun of noun phrases when that noun is either the word "time"or the word "place." Thus, noun phrases where the head noun is, for example, either "hour" or "street" are unaffected by this transformation.

The time-place deletion thus allows the reduction of

Ludwig laughed at the time when her plane arrived

to the sentence below:

Ludwig laughed when her plane arrived.

This explains, then, why there may be difficulty in distinguishing between embedded sentences and reduced relative clauses of this type; both have the same surface structure. The cleft sentence test will show, as it did for sentences 1 and 2 above, whether a particular clause is a noun phrase complement or not.

There is one other test, one which shows that a clause is an adverbial clause: the *time-place test*. This test is based upon the existence of an *adverb preposing transformation* which moves adverbials to the front of the sentence, as demonstrated below:

1. a. I was sleeping at the time when she arrived
   b. at the time when she arrived, I was sleeping
2. a. I was sleeping when she arrived
   b. when she arrived, I was sleeping
3. a. I walked to town because my car broke down
   b. because my car broke down, I walked to town
4. a. he bought the jacket even though it was too small
   b. even though it was too small, he bought the jacket.

If a string is an adverbial clause of the sort we have been discussing, it can be shifted by the adverb preposing transformation to the front of the sentence. Thus, if you are asked to distinguish between the sentences

Ludwig knows when her plane arrived

and

Ludwig laughed when her plane arrived

you can make use of the time-place test as well as the cleft sentence test. The former yields a grammatical sentence only for the second sentence:

> * when her plane arrived, Ludwig knows
> when her plane arrived, Ludwig laughed.

So far, the relative pronoun "that" has been given scanty attention. Primarily this is because this particular relative pronoun raises a number of as yet unanswered questions. As mentioned earlier, "that" can appear with either ⟨+human⟩ or ⟨−human⟩ nouns. The unresolved problem arises in the event that the relativized noun phrase contains an initial preposition. In such cases, "that" cannot be used. As yet, grammarians have found no way to state this restriction in terms of the transformational rules for relative clause formation.

SUMMARY

To generate a relative clause, a sentence is embedded in a noun phrase which contains another noun phrase. Both this other noun phrase and the embedded sentence are dominated by the same higher noun phrase:

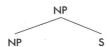

Such constructions are called relative clauses, a term referring to the function played by the embedded sentence. As you have seen, relative clauses require that a noun phrase in the embedded sentence be identical to the noun phrase to the left of the relative clause. The key transformation in the generation of the surface structure of relative clauses is the relative clause transformation, which adds the features ⟨+WH⟩ and ⟨+pronoun⟩ to the second noun phrase *and* which moves the identical noun phrase to the front of the embedded sentence. This noun phrase ultimately becomes a particular relative pronoun.

Several of the important transformations which apply to relative clauses are:

relative pronoun deletion—relates noun phrases like those below:

> the problems which you raise

and

> the problems you raise

relative clause reduction—relates noun phrases like

> those people who are leaving now

and

> those people leaving now

adjectival VP shift or adjective transformation—relates noun phrases like

> plays which are controversial

and

> controversial plays

time-place deletion—reduces relative clauses like

> at the time when you came home

to

> when you came home.

Such reduced adverbial clauses can be distinguished from embedded questions by the cleft sentence test and a new test, the time-place test, which makes use of the adverb preposing transformation. This transformation converts sentences like

> the hero was dead when the play ended

into

> when the play ended, the hero was dead.

EXERCISE TWENTY-FIVE

1. Using your imagination and your knowledge of the relative clause system, explain as fully as you can the ambiguity of the following noun phrase:

> the invisible man's deodorant.

(Hint: Genitive constructions such as "John's book" are related to relative clauses such as "the book which John has." Furthermore, you will need to make use of multiple embeddings, i.e., relative clauses within relative clauses.)

2. What property distinguishes "who" and "which" from "that"?
3. When may the relative pronoun deletion transformation not be applied?
4. Draw deep structure trees for
   a. A late rose ravages the casual eye.
   b. The generals who infested those cafés were arguing about the corrupt administration.

    c. The situation you described depressed Stanley.

    d. Johnson believed that a *coup* was being prepared by someone.

5. Show in detail how the deep structures for *4a, 4b,* and *4c* become surface structures.

6. Explain:

    a. auxiliary incorporation
    b. indirect object inversion
    c. reflexive transformation
    d. tests for verb phrases
    e. tree-pruning (in linguistics)

7. Write a brief essay justifying in your own words why it is the case that pre-posed adjective constructions, e.g., "the red rose," must be transformationally related to relative clause constructions, e.g., "the rose which is red."

8. How can embedded questions be distinguished from adverbial clauses of time and place?

SECTION FIVE

Simplicity and Linguistic Explanation

C H A P T E R 26

Pronouns and Case

In Chapter 12, the fact that pronouns should be analyzed as articles in surface structures was discussed in some detail. It was assumed in that chapter that all pronouns were marked in the deep structure with the feature ⟨ +pronoun⟩ on noun segments. However, while it is certainly true that pronouns may be introduced into a deep structure through the segment structure rules which specify segment features, it is also true that pronouns, or at least the feature ⟨ +pronoun⟩, may be introduced transformationally before the application of the article segment transformation.

In the sentence

Superman said that she would leave

it is clear that "Superman" and "she" refer to different objects. The sentence is quite unambiguous. However, the sentence

Superman said that he would leave

is ambiguous. The pronoun "he" could refer either to "Superman" or to some entirely different masculine referent.

Ambiguous sentences must have as many deep structures as they have interpretations. The sentence "Superman said that he would leave" has two interpretations and may, therefore, be expected to have two deep structures. One of these deep structures presents us with no difficulty at all. When "he" refers not to Superman but to some other masculine referent, the pronoun "he," or at least the features which define this pronoun, actually appears in the deep structure. Thus, the deep structure for this interpretation is approximately (with only the features of the pronoun represented):

217

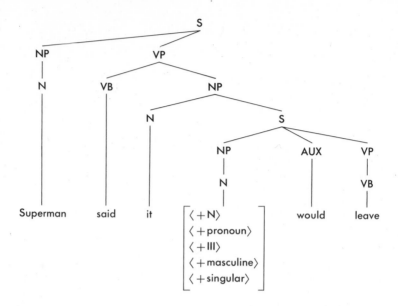

This gives one deep structure for the sentence, but what about the other? The two strings following provide a clue:

<blockquote>
Superman said that Robin would leave
* Superman said that Superman would leave.
</blockquote>

Although the meaning of the second string is perfectly clear, there is something syntactically peculiar about it. Something *must* happen to the subject noun phrase of the complement sentence, since it is identical to the subject of the main sentence. If there had been an infinitive or a gerundive complementizer instead of a clausal one, the subject noun phrase would have been deleted by the identical noun phrase deletion transformation. Here the *pronoun transformation* applies to convert the subject noun phrase of the embedded sentence into a pronoun, giving, ultimately, the same surface structure as that for a sentence with the pronoun already in the deep structure. In other words, the pronoun transformation changes the feature ⟨ −pronoun⟩ on nouns into the feature ⟨ +pronoun⟩ to give a structure like the one on page 219.

When a pronoun refers to some other noun phrase specified in the sentence, as is the case in the above example, it is called an *anaphoric pronoun.*

The pronoun transformation takes place before the article transformation and the other transformations which create the surface structure. Now that the subject noun of the complement sentence has been converted into a noun marked ⟨ +pronoun⟩, all of the transformations

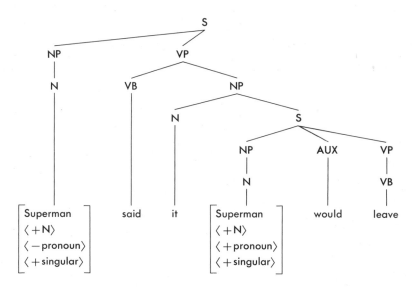

applying to such segments apply as if the segment had already been marked ⟨ +pronoun⟩ in the deep structure. When words are introduced from the lexicon, the subject noun segment of this complement sentence is replaced not by "Superman," but by "he." Thus, pronouns get into surface structures in two different ways: Either the pronoun is actually present in the deep structure or it is introduced by the pronoun transformation when two identical noun phrases appear in deep or intermediate sentence structures.

The pronoun transformation requires for its application that the two identical noun phrases *not* be in the same simple sentence. [Keep in mind that if the two identical noun phrases are in the same simple sentence, then one of two things will happen. If the second identical noun phrase is not contained inside another noun phrase, this noun phrase is reflexivized, as in

this tall boy hurt himself.

If the second identical noun phrase is contained inside another noun phrase, so-called *weak pronominalization* must take place, as in

this tall boy hurt that one   ("tall boy" pronominalized)
this tall boy hurt that short one   ("boy" pronominalized)]

Grammarians are currently searching for the generalization which would specify the positions of the two identical noun phrases relative to one another when pronominalization applies. To date, this problem is unsolved. Still, some general remarks on this problem can be made. A common case of pronominalization involves one identical noun phrase in the main sentence and the other in an embedded sentence. In this case, one normally pronominalizes the noun phrase in the embedded sentence:

> the boy said that *he* would go
> the boy said that they like *him*.

There are instances where either of the identical noun phrases may be pronominalized, as shown below:

> the fact that I hate *him* doesn't worry John
> the fact that I hate *John* doesn't worry him
> those who know *him* like John
> those who know *John* like him.

Furthermore, pronominalization may also apply to either of the identical noun phrases when two independent embedded sentences are involved:

> * people that know John think that John is smart
> people that know *him* think that John is smart
> people that know John think that *he* is smart.

So far there has been no attempt to account for the various forms of the personal pronouns:

I	me
he	him
she	her
we	us
they	them

Traditionally, pronouns in the first column are described as being in the *nominative* case; the pronouns in the second column are said to be in the *accusative* case. One way to represent the distinction between them in the lexicon is to suppose the existence of a feature ⟨ −accusative⟩ for the nominative forms and ⟨ +accusative⟩ for the accusative forms. (The use of ⟨accusative⟩ is completely arbitrary.)

In the deep structure, all pronouns (and nouns also, as you will see) are nominative, ⟨ −accusative⟩. Whether or not a noun segment acquires the feature ⟨ +accusative⟩ during the *case transformation* depends entirely on where in the constituent structure the segment happens to appear. For example, compare the following pairs of sentences:

1. a. * the white-necked ravens avoided I
   b. the white-necked ravens avoided me

2. a. I avoided the white-necked ravens
   b. * me avoided the white-necked ravens.

These examples reveal that the transformation converting a segment from ⟨−accusative⟩ to ⟨+accusative⟩ may not normally be applied to a segment in subject position. There are, however, certain exceptional cases when the case transformation must be applied to what seems to be the surface subject of an embedded sentence. Characteristically, such cases are noun phrase complement sentences in which the complementizer is infinitive or, on occasion, gerundive. For example,

> I prefer for him to stay

is grammatical, but the string

> * I prefer for he to stay

is not.

Whether or not a particular noun segment will become an accusative segment can be determined only after the application of the transformations which move noun segments around to create new structures. For example, the passive sentence

> some money was found by him

has the same deep structure as

> he found some money.

The case transformation does not apply until the passive transformation has moved the deep subject from its initial position. The case transformation will not apply to the sentence

> I believe that he is honest

until after the "it" replacement transformation has generated

> * I believe he to be honest

which has the following structure:

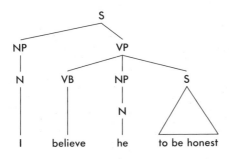

The transformations which create the surface structure for pronouns apply after the case transformation, with the features ⟨ +accusative⟩ and ⟨ −accusative⟩ determining the form introduced from the lexicon for any noun segment. Thus the string just above becomes

I believe him to be honest.

Is the case transformation applied just to pronouns or to all nouns in the proper environment? It is at least a possibility that it must apply to all nouns. In the following sentence,

Dr. Rank likes to have people talk about him

the "him" is ambiguous; it could refer either to "Dr. Rank" or to someone else. Unless this pronoun refers to "Jones" or some other male person than "Dr. Rank," the pronoun does not appear in the deep structure—"Dr. Rank" does:

* Dr. Rank likes to have people talk about Dr. Rank.

If the case transformation has to be applied before the pronoun transformation, the former must be applied to *all* nouns, not just those marked ⟨ +pronoun⟩. For if the second "Dr. Rank" were not marked with ⟨ +accusative⟩, it would be impossible to generate the correct form of the pronoun in the surface structure:

* Dr. Rank likes to have people talk about he.

Thus, it is possible that the case transformation is applicable to all nouns. To *prove* this, it must be proven that the case transformation precedes pronominalization. In fact, this particular issue has not as yet been resolved. So it is best, for the present, to accept the possibility without committing oneself to an acceptance of the general application of the case transformation to all nouns.

SUMMARY

This chapter has been concerned with two syntactic phenomena, pronominalization and case marking. The pronoun transformation converts one of two identical noun phrases into a pronoun, ⟨ +pronoun⟩, providing that the two noun phrases are not in the same simple sentence (in which case, as you saw earlier, reflexivization applies). The case transformation converts the basic nominative form of a noun, ⟨ −accusative⟩, into the accusative form, ⟨ +accusative⟩, most commonly when the noun is not a subject noun in the surface structure.

EXERCISE TWENTY-SIX

1. Why are some sentences containing pronouns ambiguous? Use examples to illustrate your answer.

2. Explain:

   a. anaphoric pronoun
   b. segment structure rules
   c. case transformation
   d. complementizer
   e. extraposition
   f. constituent functions
   g. feature
   h. constituent

3. Draw deep structure trees for the following:

   a. The pompous colonel declared that those *campesinos* preferred him (the colonel).
   b. For the peasants to avoid them is natural.
   c. I discovered what Helga was planning to do to herself.
   d. Open those doors!

4. When is the reflexive transformation applied to identical noun phrases?

5. Show in detail how the deep structures for 3*a* and 3*b* become surface structures.

6. Explain the arguments for applying the case transformation before the pronoun transformation.

7. How might a language which doesn't use the elementary transformation of deletion differ from English? What transformations would this language not have?

CHAPTER 27

Simplicity and the Search for Deep Structures

Arguments for the existence of particular transformations and particular deep structures are based upon the assumption that the simplification of the grammar (in the sense of a set of generative rules and an associated lexicon) leads to correct descriptions of syntactic phenomena which express significant generalizations. For example, a grammar in which, to describe a particular phenomenon, a certain amount of information is duplicated is less general than a grammar for the same phenomenon in which this information is stated only once.

In our earlier discussion of the passive transformation, no real justification for the passive transformation was given other than an appeal to one's intuition that active and passive versions of the same sentence have the same meaning. Now, it could quite easily be demonstrated that the passive transformation must exist; for, if it did not, the grammar would have to be made considerably more complex and less general. Let us see how this argument works.

To begin with, consider the following active sentences, the first of which is, aside from being fully grammatical, semantically well formed; the second of which is semantically very peculiar:

1. the critic praised the performance
2. * the performance praised the critic.

We have already discussed the peculiarity of the second sentence in terms of selectional restrictions on the verbal. The verbal "praise" is simply one which requires a subject noun specified as $\langle +$human$\rangle$. Since the noun "performance" is $\langle -$human$\rangle$, it follows that the introduction of such a noun as the subject of "praise" will result in an anomalous meaningless string.

Now consider the passive versions of sentences 1 and 2:

3. the performance was praised by the critic
4. * the critic was praised by the performance.

Sentence 4 is peculiar in exactly the same way as sentence 2. Now, let us imagine that passive and active sentences did not have common deep structures. This would mean that the grammar, somewhere in its rules, would have to contain two sets of selectional restrictions. First, for the active version, it would be necessary to state that the noun preceding "praise" must be ⟨ +human⟩. Second, when the verbal was passive and the noun "performance" followed it, as in sentence 4, it would be necessary to state exactly the same restriction, only in reverse.

It is possible to avoid stating this restriction twice if one simple assumption is accepted, namely, that the passive transformation exists and generates passive sentences from deep structures which are essentially active. Here, the restriction is stated solely for the deep structure, in particular, that "praise" must have a deep structure subject which is ⟨ +human⟩. Thus, we can predict that if the deep structure violates this restriction, the passive sentence will also violate this restriction because it is based upon the deep structure. Thus, assuming the existence of the passive transformation, the grammar can be considerably simplified.

English contains a number of extremely complex constructions for which neither the deep structures nor their generation is known with any degree of certainty. The purpose of this chapter is to acquaint you with some of these constructions and some of the observations which grammarians are currently making use of in attempting to determine correct deep structures and correct transformations operating on these deep structures. In general, these observations have to do with the simplicity of the grammar. That is, they concern properties which a correct grammar must have, even though the ways in which these properties are ultimately to be reflected in the grammar are not yet known.

NOMINALIZATIONS

One of the commonest features of human languages, and one which is still little understood, is *nominalization,* the syntactic process which relates sentences and noun phrases. In the first example below, nominalization has not taken place; in the second, it has:

5. Eliot refused the offer
6. Eliot's refusal of the offer.

In both cases, an English-speaking person knows that Eliot does the refusing, that what he does is refuse, and that what is refused is the offer. The relationships between the constituents are felt intuitively to be the same despite the surface differences in the two strings. You might say that "Eliot" is the deep subject of both sentences, that "offer" is the deep object of the verb phrase, and so forth. But there is other empirical evidence suggesting the relatedness between 5 and 6:

SENTENCES	NOUN PHRASES
Eliot refused the offer	Eliot's refusal of the offer
* Eliot refused consternation	* Eliot's refusal of consternation
* hopelessness refused the offer	* hopelessness's refusal of the offer
The offer was refused by Eliot	the refusal of the offer by Eliot
* the offer was refused by hopelessness	* the refusal of the offer by hopelessness

In each case, what is grammatical for the sentence is grammatical for the noun phrase. What is ungrammatical for one is also ungrammatical for the other. You can see from the "sentences" column that "refuse" has to have a ⟨+animate⟩ subject. But a ⟨+animate⟩ noun is also required for the noun phrase and bears the same logical relationship to the word "refusal." Similarly, noun phrases like "consternation" cannot be the object of "refuse," as you see from the second string on the left. But neither may they fill a semantically identical function in the noun phrase version, as you should be able to tell from the second string on the right. In other words, the restrictions associated with "refuse" bear a remarkable resemblance to those associated with "refusal." Either this is just a coincidence and both words appear independently in the lexicon (again coincidentally with the same syntactic properties), or the similarity between 5 and 6 is not coincidental and arises from the fact that the two structures share certain elements of deep structure. Acceptance of the latter point of view seems correct in that it would avoid unnecessary and counter-intuitive duplication of the restrictions on "refuse" and "refusal" somewhere in the grammar.

Two proposals for the solution of the problem raised by nominalizations have been made. The first assumes that nominalizations are actually derived from sentences through the application of a rule or set of rules which, for present purposes, could be called the *nominalization transformation*. Informally, this view holds that both 5 and 6 have roughly the following deep structure:

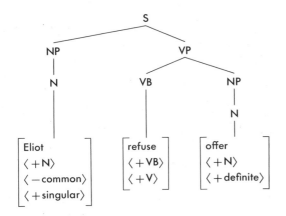

and that the nominalization transformation would presumably convert this structure into the structure of 6. On this analysis, it would not be necessary to list the identical restrictions on both "refuse" and "refusal," since only the verb form, "refuse," would appear in the lexicon. "Refuse" becomes the noun "refusal" transformationally, through the conversion of ⟨+VB⟩ and ⟨−N⟩ on "refuse" in the deep structure into ⟨−VB⟩ and ⟨+N⟩ in the surface structure of the nominalization, with the suffix "al" being added. Thus, whatever restrictions "refuse" has must be exactly identical to those for "refusal," since the latter has been generated from the former.

On this analysis of nominalization, several nominalization transformations would have to be posited. For example, a nominalized construction like

calculating machines

differs from the nominalized construction

eating apples (meaning "apples good for eating").

The semantic relationship of "machine" to "calculate" is subject to verbal, whereas the semantic relationship of "apples" to "eat" is object to verbal.[8]

When verbals are intransitive, a nominalization may result in which the positions of the subject and the verbal are reversed. Thus

the hunters shoot

---

[8] For a very interesting early transformational discussion of these problems, see R. B. Lees, *The Grammar of English Nominalizations,* Bloomington, Indiana (1960), Supplement to IJAL, 26.

has a nominalized counterpart:

the shooting of the hunters.

But this nominalized string is ambiguous, as it is not certain whether the hunters are shooting or someone is shooting the hunters. One interpretation, that in which "hunters" is the subject of "shoot," arises from the special nominalization transformation suggested above. The subject and verbal were interchanged and the preposition "of" introduced. The deep structure was basically that of

the hunters shoot something.

The other interpretation arises from the deep structure of an embedded sentence roughly equivalent to

someone shoots the hunters.

A nominalization transformation would convert this into something like

someone's shooting of the hunters.

Other transformations modify the structure so that it ends up as

the shooting of the hunters.

A second proposal, the details of which shall not be discussed here, has been made in which it is not assumed that nominalizations are derived from underlying sentences. In this proposal, it is assumed rather that the lexical entry for "refuse" and "refusal," which specifies the semantic and syntactic properties of these words, is simply not specified as to whether the entry is a noun or a verbal. What this entry becomes depends upon whether the entry is introduced under the domination of a noun or under the domination of a verbal. Without pursuing this analysis, which has not as yet been fully developed or sufficiently tested, you can still see that it would eliminate inelegant duplication, since the various syntactic properties of "refuse" and "refusal" would be stated only once, for the lexical entry common to both of these words. An important fact about this proposal, however, is that it avoids the difficult-to-justify claim that one of two or more derivationally related words is somehow basic.

MANNER ADVERBIALS

Look at the following sentences, some of which use adverbials of manner, while others use adjectives:

MANNER ADVERBIAL	ADJECTIVE	ADJECTIVE IN NOMINALIZED CONSTRUCTION
Plato analyzed his arguments ingeniously	Plato analyzed his arguments in an ingenious manner	Plato's analysis of his arguments was ingenious
Shawcross presented the case forthrightly	Shawcross presented the case in a forthright manner	Shawcross's presentation of the case was forthright
° Sam knew French ingeniously	° Sam knew French in an ingenious manner	° Sam's knowledge of French was ingenious
° Joseph resembled his brother forthrightly	° Joseph resembled his brother in a forthright manner	° Joseph's resemblance to his brother was forthright

Notice that selectional restrictions are shared by adjectives and corresponding adverbs of manner. For instance, one can analyze arguments "ingeniously" or in an "ingenious" manner. Furthermore, one's analysis can be "ingenious." On the other hand, not only is it impossible to resemble someone "ingeniously," it is impossible to resemble someone in an "ingenious" manner, and one's resemblance to something or someone cannot be "ingenious." These facts suggest that the constructions in the table above have elements of deep structure in common, which, if our assumption proves true, would make it unnecessary to state the selectional restrictions more than once.

We do not yet know exactly what these common elements of deep structure are. At first glance, it might be the adjectival form which appears in the deep structure with a noun phrase complement as subject. The deep structure of

Shawcross presented the case forthrightly

would be as shown on page 230.

If the nominalization transformation (yielding "Shawcross's presentation of the case was forthright") is not applied, a *manner adverbial transformation* may be applied instead to generate

Shawcross presented the case forthrightly.

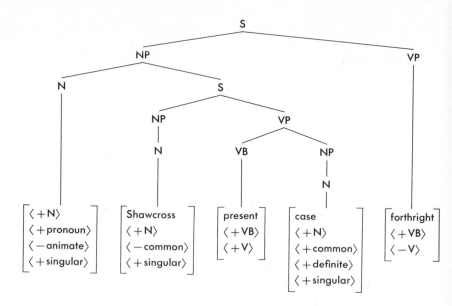

But this analysis immediately runs into difficulties. Compare the following two strings:

7. John rolled off the table ingeniously
8. * the rock rolled off the table ingeniously.

These strings show that there is a selectional restriction between "John" and "ingeniously"—one violated for "rock" and "ingeniously,"—and that if the manner adverbial is "ingeniously," the subject of such sentences as those above must be animate, never inanimate. Look back at the suggested deep structure for "Shawcross presented the case forthrightly," and you will see that we cannot state the selectional restrictions between "forthright" and "Shawcross," the subject of the complement sentence, since such selectional restrictions may only be stated for verbals and the nouns which surround them if they are in the same simple sentence. "Shawcross" is not in the same simple sentence as "forthright." Thus, if we assume that sentences 7 and 8 above have the same structure as the "Shawcross" sentence, we cannot state the selectional restrictions which would eliminate 8.

What this suggests is that the structure of sentences like 7 is more closely related to the deep structure for sentences like

John was ingenious in rolling off the table

in which, as you can see, "John" and "ingenious" are in the same simple sentence (thus allowing the statement of selectional restrictions). This general conclusion, although it has not yet been worked out in any detail, reflects the current thinking of many grammarians searching for deep structure analyses for the sentences in the table above.

THE GENITIVE

Consider the following data:

Eric has a dictionary	The dictionary which Eric has	Eric's dictionary
° the truth has consternation	° the consternation which the truth has	° the truth's consternation

Notice again that the selectional restrictions are constant for the constructions in the top row and the bottom row. Here, one would hope to explain the grammaticality of the former (and the ungrammaticality of the latter) in terms of a single selectional restriction stated on a shared deep structure.

This commonality of restrictions would be explained on the assumption that genitive constructions originate as relative clauses—that is, if the deep structure for "Eric's dictionary" was that given below:

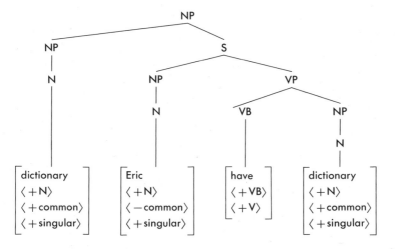

Clearly, as you have seen, this structure gives rise to the generation of the relative clause construction "the dictionary which Eric has." At this point, we could reasonably propose a genitive transformation (which, in reality, might consist of several transformational processes) that would generate "Eric's dictionary" from the relative clause structure. From this view, the grammaticality of the strings in the top row of the table and the ungrammaticality of those in the bottom row would stem from the fact that the relative clause sentence "Eric had a dictionary" is grammatical, whereas * "the truth has consternation" is not.

THE COMPARATIVE

Comparative constructions originate from deep structures containing at least two sentences.   The sentence

<blockquote>This book is heavier than the New York Times</blockquote>

is thus based upon a deep structure containing

<blockquote>this book is heavy
the New York Times is heavy.</blockquote>

What reason is there to believe that the comparative sentence is based upon the two adjective sentences, apart from the obvious relationship between "heavy" and "heavier"?   The following strings provide one answer:

This book is heavy The *New York Times* is heavy	This book is heavier than the *New York Times*
My cat is hungry Your mongrel is hungry	My cat is hungrier than your mongrel
° my pneumonia is hungry ° the *New York Times* is hungry	° my pneumonia is hungrier than the *New York Times*
My cat is hungry ° the *New York Times* is hungry	° my cat is hungrier than the *New York Times*
° the article transformation is angry My mother-in-law is angry	° the article transformation is angrier than my mother-in-law

The selectional restrictions are the same for "heavy," "hungry," and "angry" as they are for "heavier," "hungrier," and "angrier."   Both "heavy" and "heavier" (in this usage) require ⟨ +concrete⟩ noun subjects; both "angry" and "angrier" and "hungry" and "hungrier" require

⟨ +animate⟩ noun subjects. In comparative sentences the selectional restrictions apply to *both* the noun phrase to the left of the comparative adjective and to the noun phrase to the right. You know that in the sentence

> The article transformation is easier than the auxiliary transformation

the comparative adjective "easier" can take either "the article transformation" or "the auxiliary transformation" as its subject. You may thus infer that the deep structure contains both

> the article transformation is easy

and

> the auxiliary transformation is easy.

The *identical verb phrase deletion transformation* will delete the second verb phrase in sentences like

> * my father *is* more *big* than your father *is big*

to generate the sentence

> my father is bigger than your father

which also reflects the transformation of adjectives like "more big" into their correct comparative form.

SUMMARY

Transformations often provide the most general as well as the most intuitive way of accounting for many sentence constructions. Through transformations, a grammar achieves greater generality—one rule may account for many constructions. In some cases, such as the passive, something is known about deep structures and how transformations work on them. In other instances, some of which have been discussed in this chapter, considerably less is known. But even where precise formulations do not yet exist, as in manner adverbial, genitive, and comparative constructions, an approach like that described in this chapter provides a useful beginning for a detailed analysis within a grammatical framework intended to account for the linguistic intuitions of the native speaker. The purpose of this chapter has been to illuminate some of the considerations which a grammarian will take into account when he is attempting to formulate correct syntactic analyses.

EXERCISE TWENTY-SEVEN

1. What are the grounds for using transformations in the grammar of a human language?

2. What is the alternative to having nominalization transformations?

3. Draw deep structure trees for

   a. The sick surgeon ate a lobster which had been caught by Molineux.
   b. It is incredible that the man can evade prosecution.

4. Show in detail how the deep structures for 3a and 3b become surface structures.

5. How does an examination of selectional restrictions help in formulating a grammar?

6. What objections were presented to using a manner adverbial transformation to generate

   > Shawcross presented the case forthrightly.

   from the same deep structure as

   > Shawcross's presentation of the case was forthright.

7. Can you suggest any alternative to the manner adverbial transformation or the deep structure shown in this chapter? Look at these sentences for ideas:

   a. Shawcross was forthright in his presentation of the case.
   b. Shawcross was forthright in the manner of his presentation of the case.
   c. It was forthright of Shawcross to present the case in that manner.
   d. Shawcross was forthright in the manner in which he presented his case.

8. Explain how the simplicity criterion justifies the conclusion that pairs of sentences like the following are transformationally related to a common deep structure:

   > That he came late is strange.
   > It is strange that he came late.

CHAPTER 28

The Cyclic Principle

In many of the transformational analyses of various syntactic constructions, it has turned out to be the case that transformational rules are
ordered, i.e., certain transformations occur before other transformations.
If this order of rule application is not followed in such cases, the sentence generated by the rules will be ungrammatical. One of the topics
currently of interest to grammarians is whether rules apply cyclically, as
well as in a particular order. Consider the following sketch of a deep
structure with multiple embeddings:

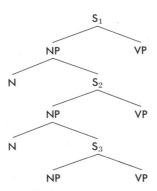

If the application of transformations is *not* cyclic, a particular transformation, when its turn comes, will be applied as many times as necessary to
the whole structure above, all at once. If the application of transformations *is* cyclic, then the set of cyclic transformations will be tested for
application as many times as there are S's in the deep structure. The
first cycle will attempt to apply the transformational rules to S_3 and
only to S_3. The second cycle will apply the rules to S_2 (which now in-

cludes S_3) and only to S_2. The third cycle will apply the rules to S_1 (which now includes S_2 and S_3). In other words, the set of transformations may be applied cyclically as many times as there are S's, starting with the lowest embedded S and working up to the highest, the main S. The question of the cyclic principle's existence is extremely important, and it will be worthwhile to consider two of the cycle's empirical foundations.

One argument for the existence of the transformational cycle can be presented fairly simply in terms of two transformations which should, by now, be familiar to you: the reflexive and the "it" replacement transformations. The former is responsible for the generation of a sentence like

John likes himself

which has a deep structure in which the subject and object noun phrases are identical. The important fact to keep in mind about reflexivization is that the two identical noun phrases must appear in the same simple sentence. One cannot, for example, be in the main sentence while the other is in a complement sentence or a relative clause.

The second transformation is involved (as a review of Chapter 23 will show you) in the generation of sentences like

John believes Mary to be honest.

Underlying this sentence is a deep structure in which the object noun phrase contains a complement, roughly according to the following tree diagram:

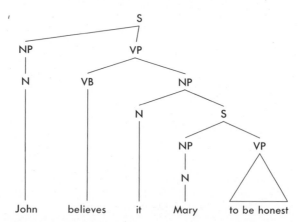

The "it" replacement transformation moves the S from under the domination of the NP and replaces the NP (which still dominates "it") by

the subject noun phrase of the complement sentence, giving the following structure:

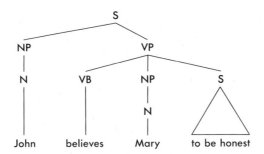

In effect, then, "it" replacement removes the subject of the complement sentence from the complement sentence and places it in the main sentence.

Now, consider the derivation of the sentence

1. I believe myself to be honest,

which, as you can see, requires the application of both the reflexive and the "it" replacement transformations. The rough deep structure for this sentence is given below:

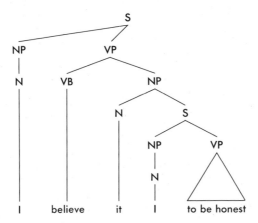

The important question in discussing the generation of sentence 1 from this structure concerns the ordering of the two transformations, a topic discussed in Chapter 23. If the ordering were

a. reflexive transformation
b. "it" replacement transformation,

the grammar would fail to produce sentence 1. In fact, it would generate the ungrammatical string

*I believe I to be honest.

Why is this the case? To begin with, given the ordering above, the reflexive transformation cannot apply because the two identical noun phrases are not in the same simple sentence at the time when this transformation must apply, if it is going to at all. Thus, reflexivization cannot take place. (Sentences like

*I believe that myself am honest

are predictably ungrammatical.) Now the "it" replacement transformation applies, bringing the subject noun phrase of the complement sentence into the main sentence. Since reflexivization has had its turn, nothing happens now to the "I" which has become the object of the main sentence. (It is not important here that later transformations will convert "I" to "me.") It simply remains, and the grammar has irrevocably generated the ungrammatical string given above. Thus, the ordering above fails.

Suppose now that the order is reversed. First, the "it" replacement transformation applies to take the subject noun phrase of the complement sentence and place it in the main sentence. Now, the two identical noun phrases are in the same simple sentence, the reflexive transformation can apply, and sentence 1 is generated. It would thus appear that *the "it" replacement transformation must precede the reflexive transformation.*

Here is a sentence containing a complement sentence, in which reflexivization takes place not in the main sentence but in the complement sentence:

2. I believe John to have hurt himself.

This sentence has the rough deep structure given at the top of page 239 (again omitting many details).

(The subject and object of the complement sentence are assumed to refer to the same person.) As you can see, the derivation of sentence 2 from the deep structure above requires, as did the derivation of sentence 1, the application of the "it" replacement and the reflexive transformations. For the derivation of sentence 1, you learned that these two transformation must be applied in the right order and that "it" replacement precedes reflexivization. Thus, you would naturally assume that this order of transformations will suffice for the generation of sentence 2.

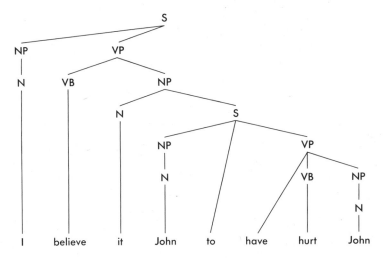

But it does not. When "it" replacement applies to the structure above, it moves the subject of the complement sentence into the main sentence, creating the structure below:

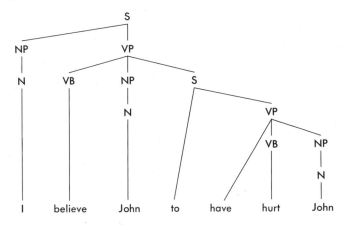

Now, the reflexive transformation should apply, but it cannot because the two identical noun phrases are no longer in the same simple sentence.[9]

---

[9] How is it possible to tell that the complement S label (node) has not been pruned, leaving only the VP node? Consider the consequences if the S node is pruned. Under such circumstances, it would be possible to generate the ungrammatical string

     * Sarah believes John to have hurt herself

from the deep structure represented by

     * Sarah believes it John to have hurt Sarah.

The reflexivization of the object of the complement sentence in the deep structure, "Sarah,"

Thus, you see that the order of transformations which was correct for sentence 1 is incorrect here. The correct order for the generation of sentence 2 is exactly the reverse: reflexive followed by "it" replacement. With this order of transformations, the reflexive correctly applies in the complement sentence, then "it" replacement applies, giving sentence 2.

A contradiction has arisen. Neither order can be said to be correct. Thus, the transformational formulation seems to fail, even though it is necessary to assume the existence of both the reflexive and "it" replacement transformations for a number of reasons discussed in earlier chapters.

This contradiction is resolved if we assume that transformations do not apply to complex deep structures (those containing embedded sentences) all at once, but rather that they apply to such structures cyclically. This assumption, referred to as the cyclic principle, was discussed at the beginning of this chapter. The principle asserts that transformations apply to the lowest embedded sentence first and proceed upward to the main sentence. Given the cyclic principle, a successful ordering for sentences 1 and 2 is that ordering in which "it" replacement precedes the reflexive transformation.

Consider the derivation of sentence 1 in terms of the cyclic principle by re-examining its deep structure. On the first cycle, the only sentence relevant to the application of transformations is the complement sentence, since this is the lowest sentence. Neither the "it" replacement nor the reflexive transformation can apply on the first cycle. The second cycle applies to the main sentence (including the complement sentence), and now "it" replacement can and does apply, bringing the subject noun phrase into the main sentence. Next, the reflexive transformation applies in its turn, since the two identical noun phrases have come to be in the same simple sentence, and thereby generates sentence 1.

Now consider the deep structure for sentence 2. On the first cycle, the "it" replacement transformation cannot apply, since the complement sentence contains no structure to which it could apply. However, the reflexive transformation can apply on this cycle, since both identical noun phrases are in the complement sentence. On the second cycle, applied to the structure as a whole, the "it" replacement transformation does apply and moves the subject noun phrase of the complement sentence into the main sentence, thus generating sentence 2. Reflexivization does not take place, as there are no identical noun phrases, and the

would come about, since it would be in the same simple sentence as the subject of the main sentence of the deep structure if the complement S node were pruned following the "it" replacement transformation. Since reflexivization does not take place, however, in sentences like the one above, it must be the case that the complement S node is still present to maintain the identical noun phrases in separate simple sentences.

derivation is complete. Thus, both sentences can be generated from "it" replacement preceding reflexivization if the transformations are applied cyclically.

It is particularly interesting to think about cases where reflexivization occurs both in the main sentence and in the complement sentence:

I believe myself to have defended myself well.

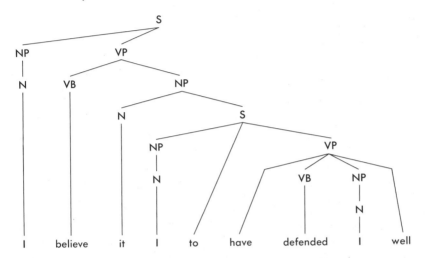

On the first cycle, the reflexive will apply to the complement sentence, since it contains identical noun phrases:

*I believe it I to have defended myself well.

"It" replacement, which could not apply on the first cycle, will operate on the main sentence (including the complement sentence) during the second cycle:

*I believe I to have defended myself well.

The reflexive will apply during the second cycle also, as the main sentence now contains two identical noun phrases, and the example sentence is correctly generated. One way for the rule of reflexivization to apply more than once, is for rules to be cyclically ordered. In fact, reflexivization must be applicable an indefinite number of times, as the following sentence illustrates:

John kept himself from expecting himself to prevent himself from believing himself to be proud of himself.

A second argument for the cycle's existence can be made in terms of two other transformations which should by now be very familiar to you:

extraposition and "it" deletion. These are involved in the generation of such sentences as

3. it is obvious that John is late

and

4. that John is late is obvious

from the same deep structure, very roughly that given below:

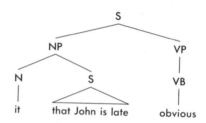

The extraposition transformation must precede "it" deletion and must be optional. The latter, on the other hand, is obligatory. Thus, the extraposition transformation may or may not be applied to the structure above. If it is applied, sentence 3 is generated and "it" deletion will not apply, since "it" no longer precedes the complement sentence. If the extraposition transformation is not applied, "it" deletion is applicable and generates sentence 4.

Now, consider the generation of a more complex sentence involving just these two transformations. This time the deep structure has a noun phrase complement embedded in another noun phrase complement to create two levels of embedding:

5. it is obvious that it is unnatural for Icarus to fly.

The complement sentence

6. it is unnatural for Icarus to fly

has the following deep structure:

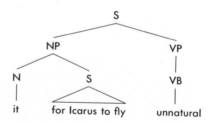

To this structure, extraposition is applied to give sentence 6. Sentence 5 has a deep structure which contains the deep structure for sentence 6:

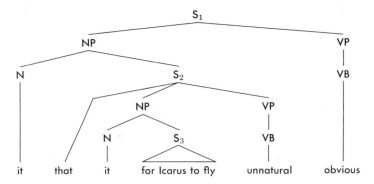

First, suppose that extraposition is applied to move S₂ to the end of the sentence:

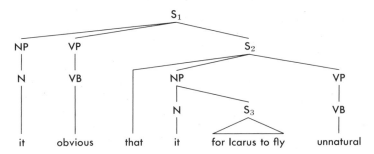

Extraposition now applies a second time to move S₃ to the end of the sentence, to give the surface structure for sentence 5:

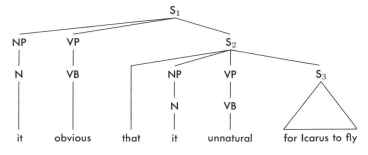

In this case, then, no difficulties arise. The extraposition transformation produces exactly the desired surface structure, even from such a complex deep structure.

But if transformations were not cyclical, then the optional extraposition transformation could apply either to S_2, S_3, both, or neither in the deep structure for sentence 5. If extraposition were applied only to S_3 and not to S_2, the following structure would be generated:

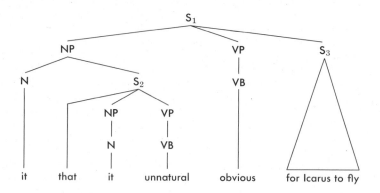

Now "it" deletion applies to the "it" preceding S_2, with the following result:

> * that it is unnatural is obvious for Icarus to fly.

The simple transformational rules which have correctly generated grammatical sentences in other instances apparently have failed here.

One of the sentences which should come from the deep structure for sentence 5 may present some problems. In this sentence,

> that it is unnatural for Icarus to fly is obvious

the extraposition transformation has not been applied to S_1, and the "it" deletion transformation has consequently deleted the highest "it," giving the following intermediate structure:

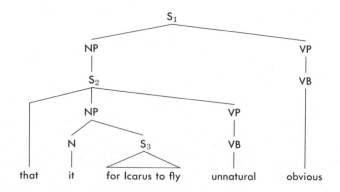

Now, to generate the desired sentence, there must be a way to move the complement sentence "for Icarus to fly" to the other side of "unnatural." But there is no transformation which does this. Extraposition will only move the complement sentence to the end of the sentence, generating the ungrammatical string

> * that it is unnatural is obvious for Icarus to fly.

If the rules are correct—and they have worked before—the difficulties in the last two attempts to generate sentences must lie elsewhere.

It turns out that the assumption of no cycle is misleading. First, it has led to the generation of non-sentences. Second, it has not allowed the generation of all the grammatical sentences which could be generated from a single deep structure.

Let's start again, with the assumptions this time that 1) the basic transformations, extraposition and "it" deletion, are correct and to be left unchanged, and 2) the transformations are ordered cyclically. On these terms, how may the generation of the ungrammatical string above be prevented? How may the grammatical string(s) be generated?

The deep structure for sentence 5, given earlier, is also the deep structure for the following synonymous sentences:

> that it is unnatural for Icarus to fly is obvious
> that for Icarus to fly is unnatural is obvious
> it is obvious that for Icarus to fly is unnatural.

Cyclic application of the transformations to this deep structure will allow generation of the first synonymous sentence, the one that was not producible when no cycle was assumed.

On the first cycle, extraposition and "it" deletion will be applied only to S_3. However, neither is relevant to this complement sentence, "for Icarus to fly." On the second cycle, where the relevant environment now includes S_2 and all that this S dominates, as given in the tree diagram below:

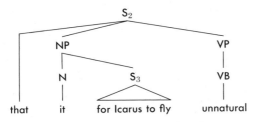

extraposition may apply. If it is applied, the following structure is generated:

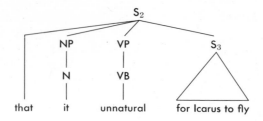

Once again, "it" deletion is not applicable. At this point, the inter-mediate structure for the sentence is as follows:

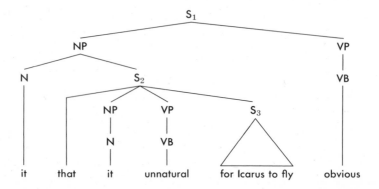

On the third cycle, the transformations are applied to S_1 and all that it dominates. Once again, the sentence contains as subject a noun phrase with a complement construction. Thus, the extraposition trans-formation may be applied, with S_2 being moved to the end of the sentence. However, this transformation need not apply, and, if it is assumed not to have applied here, the "it" deletion transformation will apply, to generate the surface structure of the desired sentence:

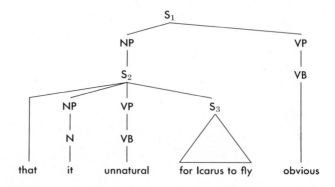

You will recall that the string generated on the assumption of no cycle was ungrammatical:

> * that it is unnatural is obvious for Icarus to fly.

Requiring the extraposition and the "it" deletion transformations to apply cyclically solves this problem. Look at the deep structure for sentence 5 once again.

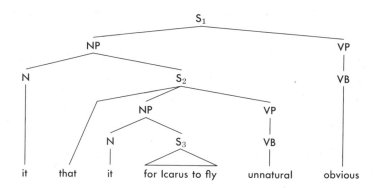

Note that the embedded sentence S_3, "for Icarus to fly," could be extraposed to the end of the sentence beyond the verb phrase "obvious" if there is no cycle and transformations may apply freely to the entire structure. This is where the problem lies, for there is no way to prevent the possibility that S_3 may be moved to the end of S_1. On the other hand, cyclic application of the transformations will only permit extraposition of S_3 to the end of S_2, and of S_2 to the end of S_1.

At this point you should make a copy of the deep structure given for sentence 5 and work through the four possibilities for surface structures:

1. it is obvious that it is unnatural for Icarus to fly
    first cycle   extraposition is not applied
                       "it" deletion does not apply
    second cycle   extraposition is applied
                       "it" deletion does not apply
    third cycle   extraposition is applied
                       "it" deletion does not apply
2. that for Icarus to fly is unnatural is obvious
    first cycle   extraposition is not applied
                       "it" deletion does not apply
    second cycle   extraposition is not applied
                       "it" deletion does apply

third cycle   extraposition is not applied
                 "it" deletion does apply
3. that it is unnatural for Icarus to fly is obvious
   first cycle   extraposition is not applied
                    "it" deletion does not apply
   second cycle   extraposition is applied
                    "it" deletion does not apply
   third cycle   extraposition is not applied
                    "it" deletion does apply
4. it is obvious that for Icarus to fly is unnatural
   first cycle   extraposition is not applied
                    "it" deletion does not apply
   second cycle   extraposition is not applied
                    "it" deletion does apply
   third cycle   extraposition is applied
                    "it" deletion does not apply

Try as you will, if the transformations are applied cyclically, you will not be able to generate ungrammatical sentences like the two below:

* for Icarus to fly is obvious that it is unnatural
* that it is unnatural is obvious for Icarus to fly.

SUMMARY

The transformational cycle is a principle which governs the application of transformational rules to phrase structures. It asserts, roughly, that transformations are applied cyclically, from bottom to top, beginning with the lowest S in a deep structure and proceeding to the highest. The cyclic principle explains a number of important facts, some of which have been investigated in this chapter. As grammatical research advances, it may, of course, turn out that the facts explained by the transformational cycle can be explained in other ways. However, since it explains a great many major syntactic facts with great precision, the hypothesis of the transformational cycle is a particularly fruitful one.

EXERCISE TWENTY-EIGHT

1. Summarize the arguments for the existence of the transformational cycle.
2. Draw deep structure trees for
   a. Give me that gun!
   b. Hank's leaving was intolerable.

    c. Albert refused to smile.

    d. Will Superman escape the monster?

3. Show in detail how the deep structures for 2*a* and 2*b* become surface structures.

4. What is the relevance of semantic arguments to grammar? Use examples.

5. What is the grammatical importance of the features of number and gender?

6. Give grammatical explanations for the ambiguity of

    a. Flying planes can be dangerous.

    b. The lamb is too hot to eat.

7. Explain why the following sentences are synonymous:

> A hard time was given John by his wife.
> His wife gave John a hard time.
> His wife gave a hard time to John.
> John was given a hard time by his wife.

SECTION SIX

Conjunction

CHAPTER 29

Conjunction and Non-restrictive Clauses

Few syntactic phenomena in English are as complex and as little understood as the formation of *conjunctive* ("and") or *disjunctive* ("or") sentences. Sentences are described as *compound* if their deep structures contain two or more conjoined sentences.

> Conjunctive compound: The cow jumped over the moon *and* the dish ran away with the spoon.
>
> Disjunctive compound: On Sunday evenings I play chess *or* I drive up to Corfe Castle with Lena.

This chapter deals with some of the basic properties of compound sentences and with analyses of the deep structure of such sentences. In some cases, transformations to account for the surface structures will be discussed.

All compound sentences have deep structure sentences which consist of a number of sentences equal to the number of constituents connected in the surface structure. The conjunctive compound sentence above might be represented approximately as follows:

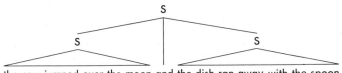

Even greater reduction is possible for some deep structures containing two conjunctive sentences. They may be reduced to a single sentence with conjoined constituents.   Thus the structure of

> the acrobat danced and the clown danced

may be converted to that of

> the acrobat and the clown danced.

The two noun phrases have been conjoined to produce a compound noun phrase with this surface structure:

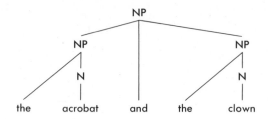

The structure of

> the acrobat sang and the acrobat danced

becomes

> the acrobat sang and danced.

Here two verb phrases have been conjoined to yield a compound verb phrase with the following surface structure:

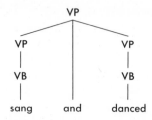

This process, called *conjunction reduction,* is possible even for sentences which share no meaning or lexical content.   The two sentences conjoined must, however, have a similar structure—this appears to be the only requirement.   So, the sentences

> Galileo scanned the skies

and

> adolescents scorned the schools

may be conjoined:

> Galileo scanned the skies and adolescents scorned the schools.

Conjunction reduction generates a single sentence containing both a compound subject and a compound verb phrase (to avoid semantic confusion, a word like "respectively" is usually added):

> Galileo and adolescents scanned the skies and scorned the schools respectively.

A sentence may contain any number of conjoined sentences:

> Galileo scanned the skies and adolescents scorned the schools and students scratched their skins and doctors scoffed at skating and surgeons scraped their scars and linguists scared off schoolmarms . . .

and so on, ad infinitum.

This means that a conjunction reduction transformation for reducing two conjoined sentences is necessary; and a different one is necessary for each number of conjoined sentences to be reduced, all the way to infinity. There is no simple rule, then, but an infinite set of conjunction reduction rules. Such a set is called a *rule schema.*

The rule schema for conjunction reduction involves

1. the conjoining of identical types of constituents, e.g., two noun phrases, only if these constituents have the same function in a sentence. Thus two noun phrases may not be conjoined if one is a subject and the other an object.
2. The conjoined constituents

NP   and   NP

become a compound NP:

That is, they will be dominated by a new NP label.
3. The original conjoined sentence labels are deleted.

You saw that the sentence

> Galileo and adolescents scanned the skies and scorned the schools, respectively

is a reduced form of the compound sentence

> Galileo scanned the skies and adolescents scorned the schools.

Conjunction reduction does not delete words. It simply conjoins constituents if they are of the same type and have the same syntactic function, and then introduces a higher label of the same kind to dominate them. But what happens when constituents are not merely the same type but contain exactly the same words referring to exactly the same entity? In earlier cases involving identity, one of the identical constituents was deleted, or perhaps converted from a noun to a personal or a reflexive pronoun. Not only identical noun phrases were deleted, but also identical verb phrases, verbals, and, as just shown, identical sentences.

With this in mind, you should be able to guess how the surface structure for

1. Ellen sang and danced

is related to

2. Ellen sang and Ellen danced.

But is

3. Ellen and Eric were brilliant

related to

4. Ellen was brilliant and Eric was brilliant

as it seems to be? The "was"-"were" alternation is not relevant here, since the conjunction reduction rules precede the agreement transformation. Conjunction reduction must precede agreement, because the former transformation will always produce a plural subject whenever the subjects of the coordinate sentences are not identical in reference.

The deep structure for sentence 1 is

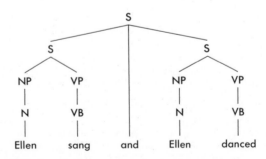

From this, conjunction reduction generates the intermediate structure

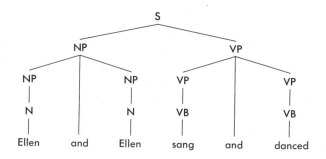

This string,

> * Ellen and Ellen sang and danced

might indeed become a grammatical one if the sentence referred to two different people named Ellen. Just add "respectively" and you have

> Ellen$_1$ and Ellen$_2$ sang and danced, respectively.

But in the string under discussion, the two words "Ellen" refer to the same person and are said to have *identical reference*. When two constituents of a compound constituent are identical to the extent that they have identical reference, an *identical conjunct*[10] *reduction transformation* reduces them to a single non-compound constituent:

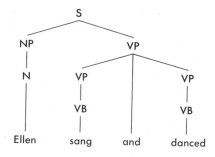

This same transformation reduces the compound verb phrase in

> * Ellen and Eric was brilliant and was brilliant

to the simple verb phrase in the surface structure of

> Ellen and Eric were brilliant.

---

[10] A "conjunct" is the name given to what is conjoined.

This notion of identity of reference requires further exploration. Suppose a structure contains the two sentences,

> this little piggy went to market
> this little piggy ate roast beef

in which different little piggies are being referred to. The compound sentence would be quite grammatical:

> this little piggy went to market and this little piggy ate roast beef.

Conjunction reduction rules could generate the rather awkward sentence

> this little piggy and this little piggy went to market and ate roast beef, respectively.

Although the forms or shapes of the subject noun phrases are identical, these noun phrases do not have identity of reference. The sentence cannot be interpreted as if the same little piggy went to market and ate roast beef. The two noun phrases have the same meaning but not the same reference, and the identical conjunct reduction transformation may not be applied. When two constituents are identical except for reference, they are described as *weakly identical*. When they are identical also in reference, they are described as *strongly identical*.

Verb phrases are also identified as strongly or weakly identical. In the basic sentence

> Ezra played cards last Saturday, and Ebenezer played cards last Saturday

the two constituents "played cards last Saturday" will be considered strongly identical if they identify the same event, "Ezra played cards with Ebenezer last Saturday," and weakly identical if they have the same meaning but do not identify the same event, "Ezra played cards with Jane last Saturday and Ebenezer played cards with Tom last Saturday." Since identical conjunct reduction must be applied to all identical verb phrases, weak or strong, the resulting surface structure is ambiguous:

> Ezra and Ebenezer played cards last Saturday.

(The word "respectively" is optionally added only under certain conditions. First, it can be added whenever conjunction reduction produces conjoined constituents which are neither weakly nor strongly identical. Second, it can be added when reduction produces noun phrases which are weakly identical. Third, it is never introduced when verb phrases are either weakly or strongly identical.)

When verb phrases in the deep structure are strongly identical, an optional transformation, *conjunction shift,* may shift the latter of the two noun phrases in the compound noun phrase, "Ebenezer" here, to the end of the sentence *and* convert "and" to "with" to yield:

Ezra played cards last Saturday with Ebenezer.

The possible difference in meaning between

5. Galileo and the adolescents laughed and cried, respectively

and

6. Galileo and the adolescents laughed and cried

is clear enough.   The first means that Galileo laughed and the adolescents cried.   Sentence 6, however, seems to be ambiguous in that it can have the same meaning as sentence 5, since the transformational introduction of "respectively" is optional, or it can mean

7. Galileo laughed and cried and the adolescents laughed and cried.[11]

You should be able to generate sentence 6 from 7 by applying the information on conjunction given earlier in this chapter.

In English there is an extremely general process which allows the incorporation of a conjoined sentence into a sentence with which it is conjoined.   Look at the compound sentence below:

John went to the store and John is lazy.

From the underlying structure of this compound sentence, it is possible to generate a grammatical sentence:

John, who is lazy, went to the store.

Here, the second conjoined sentence has been introduced inside of the first conjoined sentence.   This process involves the *non-restrictive clause transformation.*   Correspondingly, the term *non-restrictive clause* is used to refer to sentences in the surface structure which have been introduced into other sentences by this transformation.

The difference between restrictive relative clauses, which were discussed in some detail in Chapter 25, and nonrestrictive clauses should be apparent from the sentences below:

professors who enjoy poetry are idealistic
professors, who enjoy poetry, are idealistic.

---

[11] The ambiguity of 6 exists, it should be pointed out, in the dialect of the authors.   Many speakers of English will probably feel that the sentence is unambiguous, having only the meaning of the sentence below:

Galileo laughed and the adolescents cried.

These sentences differ in a number of ways. First, when spoken, they sound different. Normally, when you pronounce the second sentence, the relative clause will be set off by slight pauses. No such pauses are present in the pronunciation of the first sentence. From the point of view of deep structure, however, a second difference between the sentences is even more important. The first sentence is a single assertion about a certain subclass of professors, only those who enjoy poetry. The assertion is that such professors are idealistic. But the second makes two assertions: that *all* professors are idealistic and that *all* professors enjoy poetry. It is characteristic of non-restrictive relative clauses that they are interpreted as assertions which could stand in their own right as independent sentences without changing the meaning of the sentences in which they appear. Thus, the assertion

> professors are idealistic

has the same meaning in the compound sentence

> professors are idealistic and professors enjoy poetry

as it does in the sentence

> professors, who enjoy poetry, are idealistic.

On the other hand, if a restrictive relative clause is removed, the meaning of the sentence in which it appears will be completely changed.

Restrictive clauses are generated from a sentence embedded in a noun phrase containing another noun phrase. Non-restrictive clauses are independent conjoined sentences introduced into noun phrases by the non-restrictive clause transformation.

Grammarians have long been aware of the semantic significance of non-restrictive relative clauses, but only quite recently have they attempted to understand such constructions in transformational terms. The non-restrictive clause transformation is, in certain respects, quite a simple process. When two compound sentences exist, the transformation introduces one of these sentences into the other immediately after a noun phrase. For example, if we have the structure below:

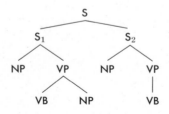

the non-restrictive clause transformation will generate

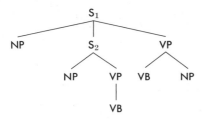

When this transformation has been performed and a non-restrictive clause contains a noun phrase identical to the noun phrase preceding it in the main sentence, one of two things is possible. The identical noun phrase in the non-restrictive clause may be converted into a pronoun. The constituent structure of the sentence

Hercules, and Hercules is not to be trifled with, will arrive soon

qualifies for the application of the pronoun transformation. This generates the structure of the sentence below:

Hercules, and he is not to be trifled with, will arrive soon.

However, the relative clause transformation, which was discussed in Chapter 25, *may be applied,* in which case the sentence

Hercules, who is not to be trifled with, will arrive soon

will also be generated.

The fact that the relative clause transformation can apply here raises a perplexing question, the answer to which is not currently known. You will recall from the restrictive relative clause chapter that the relative clause transformation operates on a structure of the following sort:

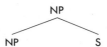

However, the pronunciation of non-restrictive relative clauses suggests that such clauses are not embedded inside of noun phrases, but rather are adjoined to noun phrases as in the following diagram, which illustrates the structure of a sentence after a non-restrictive clause has been adjoined to the subject noun phrase:

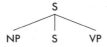

Thus, it appears that the relative clause transformation must operate on two distinct environments rather than just one. It is perhaps the case that the non-restrictive clause transformation actually does incorporate the non-restrictive clause into the noun phrase, then the relative clause transformation applies, and finally the non-restrictive clause is moved outside of the noun phrase. But this is a speculation at best, at present, and it is necessary to await the results of further grammatical research.

Non-restrictive clauses of all sorts have a parenthetical quality about them. Such clauses seem almost like afterthoughts. In part, this quality is captured by this description, which treats such clauses as sentences conjoined at the end of other sentences. Still, many questions about non-restrictive clauses remain unanswered. For example, restrictive clauses may contain relative pronouns which refer not to a particular noun phrase but to the entire preceding sentence. Compare the following sentences:

> Aeneas came late, and it bothered Anchises
> Aeneas came late, which bothered Anchises.

Presumably, these sentences originate as a compound sentence something like the one below:

> Aeneas came late and Aeneas's coming late bothered Anchises.

No grammarian has as yet been able to show the process by which the first two sentences are generated. However, it is at least fairly certain that non-restrictive embedded sentences must originate from conjoined constructions, and this is a large step forward.

SUMMARY

Sentences of the same type may be conjoined. The compound sentences thus formed may be reduced to conjoined noun phrases, verb phrases, verbals, complements, relative clauses, nouns, and even prepositions in the surface structures. This process is known as conjunction reduction and accounts for the generation, from conjoined sentences, of compound constituents other than sentences.

In deep structures, constituents which are weakly identical have the same meaning only. Constituents which are strongly identical have both the same meaning and the same reference. The identical conjunct reduction transformation reduces only strongly identical compound noun phrases, but can reduce either strongly or weakly identical compound verb phrases.

One or more sentences in a coordinate construction may be introduced inside other sentences in a compound structure by means of the non-restrictive clause transformation, which adjoins the sentence(s) in the coordinate construction to the right of noun phrases contained in these other sentences. The embedded sentences are called non-restrictive clauses and can, under certain conditions, be transformed into non-restrictive relative clauses.

EXERCISE TWENTY-NINE

1. Explain the following:

   a. agreement
   b. conjunction reduction
   c. the transformational cycle
   d. a rule schema
   e. elementary transformations

2. What is the difference between "reference" and "meaning"?

3. What is the conjunction shift transformation?

4. Draw deep structure trees for the following:

   a. Professors who enjoy poetry are idealistic.
   b. Professors, who enjoy poetry, are idealistic.
   c. Joseph happens to be a Senator.
   d. That question was asked by an obstinate reporter.

5. Show how the deep structures for 4a, 4b, and 4c become surface structures.

6. Describe those transformations having to do with identical noun phrases.

7. In a short essay, discuss how grammar provides the basis for the explanation of a central intellectual characteristic of all human beings.

8. From your knowledge of the structure of English, explain the inadequacy of of the hypothesis that a child learns his native language by imitating his elders.

EPILOGUE ═══════════

Paul M. Postal

I. LINGUISTIC NOVELTY AND THE PROBLEM OF GRAMMAR

Grammar is something that we are all apparently familiar with by the time we graduate from high school; indeed, a lot of time has been spent studying matters which are normally referred to as "grammar." The assumption behind this book is not that you have somehow done a bad job or failed to learn what was taught in your study of English "grammar" from primary school to the present. Rather, this book is based on the fact that there is a real, very complex and little known field of study rightfully called "grammar" which is only very indirectly related to what you have studied in previous years. Let us briefly contrast this new field of study with that which is usually called "grammar."

The purpose of this book has been to provide the basis for an explanation of an almost miraculous and easily overlooked fact: Any speaker of a human language, like English, French, or Chinese, can produce and understand utterances which are completely *novel* to him. "Completely novel" means that, as whole, single sentences, these utterances have never been produced or heard by the person who makes use of them, and in most cases they have not been produced or heard by anyone else either. Although there is a large number of familiar expressions which are used again and again (such as "Hello!" "How are you?" or "What time is it?"), these expressions make up only a tiny portion of normal linguistic behavior. The vast majority of utterances used from day to day are completely novel.

As an illustration of this novelty, you will observe that the sentences on this page are completely new to you; that is, you have never seen exactly these sentences before. Perhaps the easiest way to convince yourself that normal use of language involves completely novel expressions is to try to find in a book or a newspaper some sentences which you can reasonably claim to have experienced before in their entirety. A search of this sort will reveal an interesting fact: Even in a long book it is unlikely that you can find a repetition of the same sentence.

In another sense, however, all of these sentences are somehow not totally novel; that is, they are composed of parts which are completely *familiar*. The subject of familiarity will be discussed later. First, let us explore some of the implications of novelty in the normal use of language.

Why is this element of novelty in linguistic behavior so important? The reason is this: Since people typically operate with novel expressions, it must be the case that what we learn when learning a language is something more than a list of sentences. Learning Chinese, for example, is not a matter of memorizing an enormous list of Chinese sentences. The number of sentences used in normal communication in any language is so large that it would be impossible to learn all of them directly. In English, for example, the number of possible sentences consisting of twenty words or less is estimated at 10^{30}. There are about 3×10^9 seconds in a century, so you can gauge how titanically large that number of sentences is.

But finally, it is clear that even this enormous number of expressions does not exhaust those that can *in principle* be used. In reality there is no end to the number of sentences in any human language. That is, as is usually said, the number of sentences is infinite. The reason for this is that there is *no longest sentence*. So for example there is no arbitrary termination for a series of the form:

(1) a. I saw Joe and Carl
    b. I saw Joe, Carl, and my mother's brother
    c. I saw Joe, Carl, my mother's brother, and the boy whom you don't like
    d. I saw Joe, Carl, my mother's brother, the boy whom you don't like, and a horse . . . .

That is, there is no maximum number of elements which can be conjoined to form an English sentence.

An objection may come to mind at this point. It could be pointed out that in fact, because of human limitations, we can only produce and understand a finite number of utterances; namely, those which are not too long or complex. For example, no one would be able to produce or understand a sentence which was so long that its production time was eleven and a half weeks. This perfectly true observation might then lead to the view that languages must be finite in scope even if enormously large. But this view ignores a fundamental distinction, namely, that between knowledge and behavior or, more exactly, between linguistic *competence* and linguistic *performance*. It is quite true that the performance of any finite organism, humans included, must necessarily be finite; that is, any performance is limited by various physical, neural, and temporal factors inherent in all biological creatures. This does not mean, however, that the knowledge or competence is finite.

Rather, it is simply that performance limitations impose a constraint on our ability to use the infinite language we know.

A description of actual behavior must account for the finite and highly restricted character of that behavior. But this does not require the assumption that the underlying system of knowledge, or language, is finite. Quite the contrary: The finite character of performance is determined by a variety of other factors besides linguistic knowledge, that is, besides *language*. Memory limitations, for instance, severely constrain linguistic performance, for demands are made on memory in speaking and hearing. But it would be a mistake to assume that these memory limitations define the language. They only determine (in part) that portion of the language that can be used. The distinction between the language known and that portion of the language which is usable makes it possible to account for otherwise inexplicable facts. For example, it is well known that *written* performances may use longer sentences on the average than spoken performances. The reason is that with the written medium, the use of language makes fewer demands on memory, and more of the total number of sentences can be used. The following sentence is barely understandable when written, but when spoken it is beyond comprehensibility because of the excessive demands it makes on our perceptual apparatus:

(2) The rat which the cat which the dog chased ate was black.

The distinction between a language, which is an infinite system of sentences, and linguistic performance, which can use only a finite portion of those sentences, is quite analogous to the distinction between the knowledge and performance of simple mathematics. We have all learned the rules for multiplication. This system of knowledge guarantees that we can multiply any two whole numbers. But any single person, or even everyone together, can make and has made only a finite number of such computations. This does not mean that arithmetic deals only with a finite set of numbers. It is simply a consequence of memory and other grosser limitations, such as a finite life span. Quite analogously, the finite character of our linguistic performance does not mean that the language we know contains only a finite number of sentences. Since there is no longest sentence, the number of sentences is, in fact, infinite. It is not surprising, therefore, that the majority of sentences encountered or used from day to day are completely novel.

II. INFINITE KNOWLEDGE IN A FINITE ORGANISM

The fact that there is an infinite number of sentences in a language is crucial and very closely related to one of the most basic differences between the grammar you have studied in this book and "grammar" as the word is normally used. Consider these facts: Each human being is a finite organism that can learn and store within itself only a finite amount of information, even if a very large amount; still, it has been determined that each speaker of a language in some sense knows an infinite number of expressions. This appears to be a paradox or contradiction. It is neither, however, since there are kinds of finite systems which, in a clear sense, define and characterize, or, as we shall technically say, *generate*, infinite collections of objects. Rather than discuss this abstractly, let us consider an elementary example of such a system and examine how it works.

Consider an artificial "language" which is made up of strings consisting of just the two letters *a* and *b* and in which "sentences" are defined as those strings which contain a certain number of *a*'s followed by an equal number of *b*'s. In this language, (3)–(5) are well-formed sentences, but (6)–(8) are not:

(3) ab
(4) aabb
(5) aaaaabbbbb
(6) abb
(7) bbaa
(8) bbba

It is clear that this "language" will contain an infinite number of "sentences," since there is no limit to the number of *a*'s which may begin a well-formed expression. The problem, however, is to show how some finite system can represent the infinite number of sentences in the language.

Imagine a very simple machine which can carry out elementary instructions—a computing device of a very restricted kind. The machine is based on a finite system consisting of three symbols: *Sentence*, *a*, and *b*. The machine is subject to two kinds of instructions, General Instructions (GI) and Particular Instructions (PI). The Particular Instructions are:

(PI 1) Replace the symbol *Sentence* by the string of symbols *a b*.
(PI 2) Replace the symbol *Sentence* by the string of symbols *a Sentence b*.

The General Instructions are:

(GI a) The PI will be used to construct a sequence of symbols. Each string in the sequence will be formed by the application of one and only one of the PI to the preceding string.
(GI b) Each sequence will begin with the string consisting of the single symbol *Sentence*.

(GI c) The PI may be used in any order.

(GI d) Any PI may be used any number of times.

(GI e) A sequence of strings formed by the PI may be terminated after any number of uses of one of the PI providing only that the last string in the sequence is formed by the use of PI 1.

Each single operation (in accord with the GI) of the simple computer is called a *run*, and each sequence of strings produced by a run is called a *derivation*. A possible run would look like this:

(9) Line	Symbol String on Line	Origin of String
1	*Sentence*	GI b
2	*a Sentence b*	PI 2
3	*a a Sentence b b*	PI 2
4	*a a a Sentence b b b*	PI 2
5	*a a a a b b b b*	PI 1

In this run, the derivation consists of the sequence of strings *Sentence, a Sentence b, a a Sentence b b, a a a Sentence b b b,* and *a a a a b b b b*. This derivation is well formed in accordance with the Particular and the General Instructions, and a proper run through the system did, in fact, produce a well-formed sentence of the language which consists of the symbols *a* and *b* and in which a well-formed sentence is defined as a number of *a*'s followed by an equal number of *b*'s.

The number of well-formed sentences which the computer can generate is infinite, since, according to General Instruction d, any Particular Instruction can be used any number of times. Each use of PI 2 yields a derivation whose last line is one *a* and one *b* longer than the preceding line. If there is no occurrence of PI 2 in the run, the derivation will consist of only two lines: *Sentence* (per GI b) and *a b* (per PI 1 and GI e). If there is one occurrence of PI 2, a sentence consisting of four symbols (*a a b b*) will result; if, as in the sample run above, there are three occurrences of PI 2, eight symbols will result. Any proper run—that is, any run which is in accord with the General and the Particular Instructions—will by necessity produce a derivation the last line of which will be a string of a certain number of *a*'s followed by an equal number of *b*'s. In other words, the computer can not only produce an infinite number of sentences in the *a b* "language," but also, when operating properly, it will produce *only* well-formed sentences in that language.

Obviously the system containing five General Instructions and two Particular Instructions is a finite system; it can be represented in some physical apparatus (such as a computer) or can be learned by a human being. But a physical apparatus which contains this finite system is capable of operating with the infinite number of "sentences" which it describes, subject to finite performance limitations such as memory.

Similarly, a human being who "knows" this finite system is capable of using the infinite number of sentences described by the system, subject to such finite limitations as life span and memory.

There is consequently no paradox at all involved in the idea of learning a finite system which describes an infinite set of elements. Human languages are infinite sets, and human beings are finite physical objects with finite storage and learning capacities. It follows that we must assume that a human language is, in another and more interesting sense, some finite system which can describe the infinite set of sentences of that language in a way analogous to that in which our simple system describes the infinite "language" of strings "$a^n b^n$" (an indefinite number of a's followed by the same number of b's). We need a term for finite systems which describe infinite sets, and with respect to sets of sentences in human languages, the term *grammar* has come into use.

By the *grammar of English*, therefore, is meant that finite system which generates the infinite number of possible English sentences. Each of us must have such a grammar represented in us. It is the possession of this grammar which makes it possible for us to produce and understand an infinite number of sentences, the vast majority of which are completely *novel* to us. For although a particular sentence is novel to us in the sense that we have not uttered or heard it before, it is *familiar* in the sense that it is fully described by a system which we have learned and which is consequently part of us.

III. KNOWLEDGE AND BEHAVIOR

When discussing almost any aspect of human affairs, we must consider two separate, though intimately related, domains: the domain of knowledge, competence and ability, on the one hand; and, on the other, the domain of behavior, performance and action. The latter consists of observable activities and affairs which we can see and hear; the former, however, is not nearly so accessible. The distinction between these two domains can be clarified by reference to music; it is quite normal to distinguish between a certain piece of music and various performances of that music.

In linguistic affairs, although the same distinction is crucial, it is seldom made. In the discussion of the infinite character of human languages, we distinguished between knowledge-competence, on the one hand, and behavior-performance, on the other. It cannot be too strongly emphasized that grammar is a description of part of what people *know*, not of what they *do*.

The discussion can be further clarified by considering the distinction between such notions as *sentence, language, grammar* and the notions *utterance, linguistic behavior.*   *Sentence* is a notion which belongs to the world of abstract elements, analogous to *concerto* in music.   *Utterance* is a term relating to the world of behavior or performance.   Though it may at first seem a bit odd, it can be said that utterances are *performances of sentences.*   Clearly, the abstract structure of the sentence is the primary determinant of the performance.   But many other factors enter into any particular performance.   Thus the actual behavioral event is controlled by such factors as the physical structure of the particular speech apparatus involved, by the presence of food in the mouth, by the presence of noise in the environment, or by the emotional state of the speaker.   But all of these factors are irrelevant linguistically; that is, they are all irrelevant to the study of linguistic *knowledge.*

Grammar, now in a second sense as the name for a field of study, is concerned with linguistic knowledge—that is, with the primary but by no means only factor which must be taken into account in the study of linguistic performance.

Sentences and grammar, therefore, are abstract objects.   Many different kinds of abstract objects are familiar in daily life: numbers, laws, symphonies, driving regulations, jokes.   All of these objects have the negative property of not being physically located in time and space.   That is, one cannot sensibly ask "Where is the law against embezzlement?" or "Where is Mozart's 40th Symphony?" or "Where is English?"   But all of these abstract objects can be represented in physical objects or can be performed in space and time; and one can sensibly ask where the representations or performances can be found or where they took place.   There is another class of words in English which refers, sometimes ambiguously, both to the abstract object and to the physical object in or by which the abstract object is represented.   The words "book," "magazine," "newspaper," "manuscript," and "diary" are examples of this class.   When we say, "Where is my book?" or "That book is ripped," we are speaking of "book" as a physical object located in space and time.   But when we say "That book is poorly written," or "The book *Gone With The Wind* was a best-seller," we are speaking of "book" as an abstract object not located in space and time.

Languages are abstract objects, but from the point of view of ordinary acquaintance with such things, languages are unusual abstract objects in a sense already considered.   That is, languages are *infinite,* while most of the abstract objects encountered in daily life, outside of the study of mathematics, tend to be *finite.*

Sentence, therefore, is the concept which refers to the individual elements of which languages contain an infinite number.   *Grammar* is the concept which refers to the finite systems which specify and generate these infinite numbers of sentences.   Since languages are infinite abstract objects, they can be viewed in two different, but equivalent, ways. It can be said, for instance, that the English language is simply the infinite collection of English sentences, or it can be said that the English language is exactly that finite system which generates this infinite collection of sentences.

Although both sentences and grammars are abstract objects, it must be emphasized that grammar is a much more abstract notion. We can gather information rather directly about sentences by considering performances of them and by specifying our intuitive knowledge of the properties of some of the sentences of a language we know. The character of grammars is much more obscure and difficult to determine. This fact is related to a connotation which our use of the term 'linguistic knowledge' may have, a connotation which is quite undesirable. When thinking about knowledge, we may accept only something which is or can be explicit. If I know how to multiply, I can tell you how to multiply. In this sense, then, knowing English grammar would mean being able to describe it explicitly. It is evident that this is not the case. We cannot readily make explicit our knowledge of the principles of grammar. This knowledge is evidently below the level of direct awareness or access. If this were not so, one could simply write down all of the grammar of any language one knew and grammatical investigation would be easy and trivial, instead of being the difficult pursuit it is.

One might say, therefore, that linguistic knowledge is typically largely unconscious, although this term is not very clear. In fact, however, inexplicit knowledge is quite familiar and common. For example, a familiar case of unconscious knowledge, although we normally don't call it this, is that our bodies know how to digest food and must contain within them a representation of the complex biochemical operations required for this. Such an organic representation, which is analogous in many ways to the program of an electronic computer or the built-in instructions of any of the many automatic machines which exist in factories, is obviously *not* present in such physical systems as adding machines, telephone exchanges, or anti-missile computers. These, however, have represented in them various forms of knowledge not necessarily present in humans. But, unaided, one cannot make explicit these digestion principles any more than a computer can describe its program. If a biologically uneducated person is asked how digestion takes place, he can say almost nothing about it. Or again, the human eye perceives physical objects according to quite definite principles, different in part from those of many other animals. Yet again, unaided by inquiry, a person cannot directly make these principles explicit. Therefore, there is nothing unique about finding an organism or complex mechanism with implicit knowledge which is not subject to direct awareness and not capable of being made explicit directly.

In the case of language, we are from one point of view better off than in these other cases. While we do not possess direct, explicit knowledge of the underlying system of grammar as such, we do have some knowledge of sentences, either explicit, or easily made explicit with a little effort. Therefore, inquiry into the nature of grammars reasonably begins with sentences. We determine what some of the properties of these are. Only then can questions be raised about the kinds of finite systems which can describe the appropriate infinite set of sentences. Fortunately, many years of inquiry by a vast number of scholars and our basic intuitive knowledge provide us with a good deal of information about sentences.

IV. THE PROPERTIES OF SENTENCES

Human sentences, as abstract objects, are made up of certain quite distinct properties. Consider the following examples:

(10) Harry owns that house
(11) That house belongs to Harry
(12) Harry saw that house.

First of all, each of these sentences involves properties concerning knowledge of pronunciation. That is, one knows what sequence of movements must be made by the speech apparatus in order to produce utterances which will be understood as performances of the sentences. An account of this knowledge can be called a *phonetic representation*. The phonetic representation of a sentence is a sequence of *phonetic segments,* each of which is a complex of instructions for the different parts of the speech apparatus. A single phonetic segment determines the ideal behavior of the speech apparatus for a fixed period of time, roughly that needed for the production of a single "sound." Obviously (10), (11), and (12) have different, though partially similar, phonetic representations associated with them.

Secondly, each of the sentences involves properties concerning the knowledge of meaning. For instance, (10) and (11) have essentially the same meaning, which is quite different from the meaning of (12). The representation of the meaning of a sentence is called a *semantic representation.* A primary fact is that sentences consist of pairings or associations of information about meaning with information about pronunciation. We know that (10) and (11) have identical meanings paired with partially different pronunciations. But in the case of (13) and (14), below, we know that identical pronunciations are paired with different meanings:

(13) What annoyed Harry was being investigated by the committee

(14) What annoyed Harry was being investigated by the committee.

This utterance can mean either "Harry was annoyed that the committee was investigating him" or "The committee was investigating the thing that annoyed Harry."

Comparing the properties which semantic representations account for with the properties which phonetic representations account for, one observes an important contrast. Phonetic representations are relatively well understood with respect to their formal structure, the substantive constraints on them, and especially their relations to the world of observable behavior and objects. That is, phonetic representations are a system of instructions governing the movements of a physical system —the speech apparatus—and as such they are relatively easily understood. Semantic representations, on the other hand, are largely mysterious. Their relation to the observable world of objects and events is most unclear. Certain facts can, however, be ascertained. Since we know the meanings of an infinite number of expressions, which could not have been learned by rote, there must be some finite way of representing these meanings. Furthermore, meanings are analyzable into components. For example, among the words below, (15) through (17) share a semantic property which is not possessed by (18) and (19); similarly, (18) and (19) share a property not possessed by (15) through (17):

(15) boy
(16) rooster
(17) uncle
(18) woman
(19) daughter

What seems to emerge is a system of semantic primitives which represent components of meaning and which combine in various ways to form the semantic representations of sentences and their parts. Although knowledge about facts like those observed in (15) through (19) makes the study of semantic questions possible, inquiry into such matters is admittedly in its very beginning, and knowledge of these matters is very limited at present.

Finally, each sentence involves certain syntactic properties which are distinct from the meaning and the pronunciation of the sentence. That is, sentences are strings of words; these are made up of various elements; these elements are of different types, and there are various relations among them. A speaker of English knows that the expression in (20) is ambiguous:

(20) O'Hanrahan enjoys entertaining ladies.

That is, (20) has one analysis in which the relation between "entertain" and "ladies" is the same as it is in (21), and another in which it is the same as in (22), and yet a third in which it is the same as in (23):

(21) I am entertaining ladies
(22) The extremely entertaining ladies were unmarried
(23) Ladies who entertain should never be profane.

Similarly, we know that in (24) and (25) there exists an identical relation between "someone" and "who owns a Mercedes Benz." There is no such relation between these forms in (26):

(24) Someone drove away who owns a Mercedes Benz
(25) Someone who owns a Mercedes Benz drove away
(26) Someone drove away the boy who owns a Mercedes Benz.

We recognize that in structures like (27), the adjective "nice" "modifies" either "boys" alone or both "boys" and "girls," while in (28) it "modifies" only "boy":

(27) Carol met some nice boys and girls
(28) Carol met a nice boy and a girl.

We also recognize that the ambiguity of modification in (27) is related to two different possible pronunciations of the sentence: one in which there is a pause after "nice," and one in which there is a pause after "boys."

Also, our syntactic knowledge is manifested in the recognition that some strings are well formed while others are not, and to varying degrees. As speakers of English we know that (29) through (31) are natural or well-formed English sentences:

(29) Harry understands Cromwell
(30) Harry understands himself
(31) Cromwell was understood by Harry.

But neither (32) nor (33) is completely well formed:

(32) * Harry was understood by himself
(33) * himself was understood by Harry.

Notice that the deviation in (32) and (33) must be syntactic, since semantically they are perfectly all right and not even ambiguous. Furthermore, although both (32) and (33) violate some principles of English sentence formation, (33) is less grammatically correct or less well formed than (32).

In summary, we conclude that what we refer to as a sentence is actually a complex association of at least three kinds of properties: phonetic, semantic, and syntactic.

It is easy to see why sentences should have semantic and phonetic properties. Semantic properties represent the "message" or the "ideas" transmitted. They are, as it were, the very reason why languages exist. Similarly, it is understandable why phonetic properties exist, since they are concerned with correctly characterizing the modification of the physical medium needed to transmit a "message" or "idea." But the function of syntactic properties is much less clear. Unlike the semantic and phonetic properties, the syntactic properties seem to have no connection with the non-linguistic world of events and objects. This raises the general question of the relationship among the three kinds of properties.

V. THE OVER-ALL GRAMMAR

Suppose, for the moment, that one assumes *incorrectly* that the set of sentences in a language is not only finite but small enough to be learned directly. The description of such a language could consist simply of a large list of associations between semantic and phonetic representations. In other words, it could consist of a kind of sentence dictionary or *sentence lexicon.* Such a language would not have a grammar in the sense of our earlier discussion, and there would be no need for syntactic properties, since the lexicon would directly connect all semantic and phonetic information.

It has been observed, however, that human languages are not like this because they include an infinite number of semantic-phonetic associations which, by definition, cannot be listed in a lexicon. Real languages must, therefore, contain some apparatus other than a finite list of semantic-phonetic associations. That is, they must contain grammatical systems capable of generating an infinite number of structures—an apparatus analogous to the instructions of the simple illustrative "grammar" discussed in relation to the "language" consisting of a's and b's. This grammar is the chief basis for the existence of syntactic structure. Or, to put it more clearly, sentences have syntactic structure in addition to phonological and semantic characteristics, because they are not finite sets which are directly learnable, but infinite sets learnable only indirectly through internalization of some finite grammar which generates them.

Syntactic structure is basically a by-product or derivational process of a productive grammar which generates sentences rather than lists them. The existence of syntactic structure is closely linked to the fact that linguistic behavior typically involves operations with expressions which are *as wholes* novel. This is made possible only by the existence of productive grammars which associate syntactic organization with the sentences which they specify.

Once again we must distinguish between the two kinds of novelty— the novelty of utterances as wholes as opposed to that of utterances which are formed from parts which are not novel. This distinction should be clarified and related to the notion of lexicon. Although it is impossible for the description of a language to consist exclusively of an exhaustive list of phonetic-semantic associations, it is possible and, in fact, it is true that languages do contain such collections of associations. These collections link semantic and phonetic information, not for whole sentences but for certain parts of sentences. Every language has a finite lexicon containing a large number of associations of information about meaning and pronunciation and, to a lesser degree, about some syntactic properties. The dictionaries of our ordinary experience, the large books found on our shelves, can be regarded as rather gross attempts to state such associations. A lexicon will simply list all those arbitrary and unpredictable associations of facts of meaning with facts of pronunciation.

One obvious sense in which ordinary linguistic behavior does not involve novelty (or involves it only to a minor extent) is that this behavior is based on a previously known vocabulary of lexical items, each with inherent semantic and phonetic properties. This raises the question of the relation between semantic and syntactic properties.

A speaker of a language must learn a finite lexicon of semantic-phonetic associations directly. However, this speaker knows not this finite number of associations but rather an infinite number. The overall grammar must therefore provide some finite way for the possessor of a lexicon to *project* this finite knowledge of pronunciation to the infinite knowledge of the pronunciation of all sentences.

A natural framework to account for this linguistic projection, which is really the defining character of human language, would be the following. Assume that a grammar has three components, a *Syntax*, a *Semantics*, and a *Phonology*. The Syntax contains a finite set of rules of some sort plus a finite lexicon. It generates an infinite set of *Syntactic Structures*, each of which contains individual lexical items (with their inherent semantic and phonological properties) as parts. The Syntax thus embodies the 'creative power' of the grammar, that property which permits a finite system to generate an endless set.

However, the Syntax alone does not in principle account for our full knowledge of sentences. With respect to meaning, for example, the Syntax says nothing about the meaning of anything beyond the individual lexical items. It does not account for the semantic properties of whole sentences or of any of their parts "larger" than lexical items (such parts are technically called *constituents*). Observe, in particular, that there may be different syntactic structures containing identical lexical items which nonetheless have overall quite different meanings.

(34) Harry loves Lucille
(35) Lucille loves Harry

The function of the semantic part of the grammar now becomes partially clear. It must operate on each of the syntactic structures specified by the Syntax and, on the basis of the *inherent semantic properties* of their lexical items, plus the *syntactic organization of these*, assign a semantic interpretation to the sentence as a whole as well as to each of its constituents. The function of the phonological part is now also clear. It must analogously operate on each of the syntactic structures specified by the Syntax and, on the basis of the *inherent phonological properties* of their lexical items plus the *syntactic organization of these*, assign a phonetic interpretation to the sentence as a whole and to each of its constituents.

It might seem that the Phonology is really unnecessary, since the pronunciation of each sentence might be fully determined by the sequence of pronunciations of each of its successive lexical items. But in fact the pronunciation of sentences in real languages is never determined exclusively in this elementary way. Many lexical items are pronounced one way in one context, another in another (compare *pirate/piracy; oblige/obligation*). Many aspects of pronunciation (for example, English stress and intonation) are not directly associable with any particular lexical items. There is thus a rich function for the Phonology to fulfill.

It has been emphasized repeatedly that the grammar of a human language is not just a device which *directly* associates meanings and pronunciations. But from this brief description of the form of grammar, it is clear that grammar is, in the sense of this discussion, a device which *indirectly* associates semantic and phonetic representations—indirectly because the process is mediated through the infinite number of syntactic structures. Each structure generated by the Syntax is semantically interpreted by the Semantics and phonetically interpreted by the Phonology. In this way the over-all grammar does associate phonetic and semantic representations, but it does this *productively* through the mediation of the Syntax and not simply in a list. For the moment, a grammar can be represented schematically in the following manner:

(36)

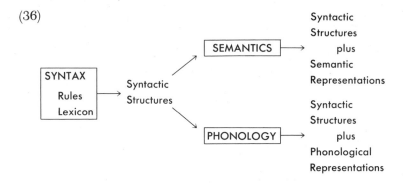

We shall presently see that even this apparently complex scheme of grammar is oversimplified in at least one crucial respect.

It can be seen from this discussion that the roles of the three components in a grammar are not equal. The Syntax is definitely primary; the Semantics and Phonology are both subsidiary. The Syntax is a system with no real *input;* it "creates" or generates an infinite number of structures. The other two components are *input-output* devices; they operate on the structures specified by the Syntax and assign further structure to them. In contrast to the creative character of the Syntax, the Semantics and Phonology are only interpretive. The Syntax is fundamental in that both of the other components operate on information provided by the Syntax. It is therefore no accident that the present book has dealt with syntactic questions, since an understanding of these is basic to any inquiry into the interpretive parts of language.

Suppose we say that that aspect of syntactic structure operated on by the Semantics for the purpose of semantic interpretation will be called *Deep Structure.* And let that aspect of syntactic structure operated on by the Phonology for the purpose of phonetic interpretation be called *Surface Structure.* Notice that thus far nothing substantive has been said since it is logically possible that the terminology is empty. That is, it is possible that the structures relevant for both types of interpretation are *identical,* a tacit assumption embodied in the diagram. This is, in effect, the assumption of almost all traditional linguistic discussion. But perhaps the fundamental revelation of the present approach to grammar, which is now referred to as *transformational,* is that this assumption is false, in fact drastically so. The structures relevant for semantic interpretation turn out to be very different indeed from those which are relevant for phonetic interpretation. Only the latter, or Surface Structures, are really similar to what we normally think of as the syntactic structures of sentences. The distinction between Deep and Surface Structures has been dealt with at length in the body of this book.

The fact that syntactic structure is bifurcated into two distinct aspects, Deep and Surface, requires modification of the diagram. One must now think of the Syntax as having two parts. One, the Base, consists of rules and a lexicon, which together generate the infinite set of Deep Structures. These are the inputs to the Semantic Component of the grammar. There is then a second or *Transformational* part of the Syntax, whose function is to associate Surface Structures with Deep Structures. That is, the Transformational subcomponent also takes Deep Structures as input. It is the output of this subcomponent, the Surface Structures, which are the input to the Phonology. The pairing of phonetic representations and semantic representations is thus even more indirect than indicated by the diagram. In reality, this pairing is mediated not through a single syntactic structure but through the association of two quite distinct forms of syntactic organization.

This outline discussion of the form of an over-all grammar has been quite general. In this book, you have been introduced to the kinds of syntactic facts which must be dealt with in English: the kinds of Deep Structures which must be assumed, the kinds of rules which generate those structures, and some of the transformations which are involved in associating the proper Surface Structures with the Deep Structures.

VI. LINGUISTIC UNIVERSALS

We have spoken several times of the process of "learning a language," insisting that this involves the internalization of some finite system of rules, rather than simply the memorization of a fixed list of linguistic expressions. But even this unusual way of speaking, more accurate as it is, involves an underlying assumption which must be questioned. The usage "learning a language" implies that the whole system must be learned from scratch. That is, it implies that the overall linguistic system which the growing child represents internally is determined *entirely by his experience*. There is, however, not the slightest reason to believe this. Quite the contrary—it is definitely not the case.

A substantial portion of the structure of any particular language is not learned, but determined by the innate linguistic organization of the human organism. This innate organization specifies the overall structure of a grammar, the kinds of rules it can contain, the kinds of elements and the possible interrelations among these. It also determines to an unknown extent part of the actual content of particular grammars, that is, the particular rules and elements these contain.

The assumption of a rich, universal (innate) linguistic structure, which is the basis for every language and the real foundation which permits first language-learning to take place, is required on many grounds. First, it accounts for the many fundamental similarities manifested by all languages, similarities which are disguised by many factors, such as our general ignorance of anything but the most superficial facts of grammar. In particular, failure to recognize the Deep Structure–Surface Structure distinction, briefly described earlier, has obscured for many the rich system of similarities underlying the superficial syntactic differences which different languages reveal. Second, the assumption of an extensive, genetically determined linguistic organization accounts for the remarkable feat of first language-learning. This takes place so uniformly, rapidly, perfectly and independently of direct instruction, intelligence, etc., as to preclude the possibility that the total output system is a full function of the arbitrary, capricious, and limited experience of particular children. It is easy to overlook the extraordinary character of the task accomplished here because of a tendency to greatly underestimate the scope, complexity, and abstractness of the system actually constructed, i.e., a human language. A better appreciation of what is involved, and of the absurdity of assuming that the result can be fully a function of experience, is obtained by reviewing briefly even what we have concluded above. A child is necessarily restricted to a relatively small, certainly finite, and arbitrarily limited linguistic experience. Thus he hears only a finite number of utterances; many of these are ill-formed; there is much noise, irrelevance, etc. Yet he rapidly constructs a linguistic system which provides him with knowledge of an infinite system of linguistic expressions, no fraction of which he has ever experienced directly. Furthermore, these linguistic expressions are not simply strings of noises, but extraordinarily complicated combinations of semantic, syntactic, and phonological properties. Phrased in this way, it becomes clearer that language learning must be guided by a rich system of unlearned, inborn constraints. Otherwise, the task would be impossible.

Of course, languages do differ in many, often substantial, ways. But this does not preclude the existence of a far-reaching system of innate linguistic principles any more than the very real differences between molecules, tables, planets, and galaxies precludes the existence of a rich set of physical laws governing the behavior of all of them. What is perhaps most interesting about languages is that they reveal in complex and little understood ways the interaction between innate biological structure and experience in the formation of complex systems of knowledge.

The question of linguistic universals, or biologically determined linguistic structure, links the study of grammar to the wider study of human and animal psychology and biology, of which it is really a special part. It shows that in studying the structure of any particular language, one is not only detailing some accidental linguistic facts in space and time, but also necessarily dealing with a defining characteristic of human nature. It is the question of linguistic universals which makes the study of grammar today something beyond the parochial, often narrow, or even pedantic pursuit which it has not infrequently been in the past. Another key difference between grammar in the sense of this book and grammar as we may have encountered it in past schooling is that the principles of English syntax presented in this volume have been developed and been carefully considered within the context of the study of linguistic universals.

VII. LANGUAGE DIFFERENCES AND PRESCRIPTIVISM

We have used the term *English grammar* to refer to an over-all system which fully describes our knowledge of the phonetic, semantic, and syntactic properties of all English sentences. This term seems to assume that *English* is a monolithic whole, a uniform language spoken by millions. But it is well known that there are vast differences in the languages of those we refer to as "speakers of English." In fact, it is almost certain that no two people really have completely identical languages. The most obvious difference in individual languages is lexicon: It is inconceivable that two people would know exactly identical sets of lexical items. Differences in phonology are also common and familiar to all of us. Nor are distinctions in syntax lacking.

These differences are not purely individual. Speakers of English, and other languages as well, fall into groups defined by associations of similarities and differences. These groups are called *dialects*. Dialects exist as a function of all forms of linguistic isolation and separation—in space, time, social class, occupation, age, etc. But the existence of dialects does not preclude the sensible use of the term *English grammar*, because it is obvious that both dialects and individual variations of our language do share a large number of underlying similarities. This is especially true of English syntax, and it may be even more true of semantics, although at present we have hardly any means to investigate the latter. By studying the deeper underlying principles of syntax, we are in a better position to appreciate how minor the differences among variants of the same language really are. Studies of phonetic differences have already revealed that dialectic variations in phonology may in fact be the function of an overlay of superficial rules on an extensive body of common phonological principles.

This aspect of the study of grammar brings us to another important difference between grammar as it has been presented in this book and the grammar we are familiar with from our previous schooling. School instruction in grammar is usually dominated by two considerations which are foreign to the subject matter and aims of this book: One is the teaching of writing and composition, a subject we will return to shortly; the other is the attempt to teach a more or less standardized dialect of English to students who often speak another dialect. A substantial portion of what is called "grammar" in schools is concerned with the minor features which distinguish different dialects. Long hours are spent rehearsing the difference between expressions such as those in (37) and (38):

(37) a. It is me
     b. It is I
(38) a. I am not going
     b. I ain't going.

But much less attention is given to the vast body of sentence formation principles common to *all* dialects of English—principles which for all speakers of English distinguish between the sequences in (39) and the sequence in (40):

(39) a. * I up to in come will should off so
     b. * I saw the boy you like him
     c. * I book John give
(40) a. I should come in
     b. I saw the boy that you like
     c. I gave John a book.

In short, much of school grammar is concerned with teaching the forms of the prestigious "standard" language to speakers of the less "standard" (often labeled "substandard") dialects of English. But the so-called "standard" language is itself a dialect or variant of English, specifically the one which is linked to literacy and to the literary tradition. This is really a kind of social engineering in which certain speakers are asked to alter certain details of their language to fit those of the more prestigious speakers. This kind of instruction is perhaps a socially defensible goal, defined more precisely and achieved more efficiently in a number of other countries. One difficulty in the United States is that the standard which is taught is not very standard and may vary considerably from place to place.

But whatever value we attach to this linguistic "engineering," it has no real linguistic interest or importance, and most of the "linguistic" justifications for it are either imaginary or completely silly. It is often claimed, for example, that various non-standard forms of speech not only involve linguistic "decay" but also prevent effective communication. This particular argument is as pompous and indefensible as it is empirically without basis.

Another aspect of school grammar, which we refer to here as *prescriptive* grammar, is its insistence that old, even now archaic, forms must continue in use and that many new formations must be excluded. A good example of this is the endless struggle to prevent the use of "like" in those places where older forms of English would have used "as." Prescriptive grammar, virtually by definition, involves resistance to the never-ending process of linguistic change. The baseless assumption behind this resistance is that we are headed for a "breakdown in communication" unless linguistic change is opposed by the guardians of the language. And this assumption, groundless though it may be, dominates much popular discussion of grammar and usage both within the schools and without, and even the most obvious evidence to the contrary does not seem to shake this false view. Does anyone wish to maintain seriously that modern French is a less adequate vehicle for communication than the Latin from which, in a certain sense, it developed, by just those processes of change which prescriptive grammar seeks to resist? Similarly, many hundreds of languages are maintained despite ongoing linguistic change without any tradition of grammatical prescriptivism, without any literary tradition, without any writing system. Prescriptive grammar tends to assume implicitly that human language is a fragile cultural invention, only with difficulty maintained in good working order. It fails to recognize that language is an innate attribute of human nature.

Prescriptive grammar is thus not very much concerned with the nature of language as such, nor with the nature of English in particular. It is interested instead in "correct English," that is, in enforcing the use of one particular dialect (that of the particular prescriptive grammarian, or at least that which he thinks is his). A final aspect of prescriptive approaches is a tendency to oppose colloquial styles of speech in favor of more formal ones (*is not* is better than *isn't*, etc.). This is linked to many things perhaps but probably most closely to a concern with the usages of the writing system which is more closely related to formal styles of speaking. There is a groundless tendency here to assume that writing has some sort of primacy over speech and to view colloquial styles as a "decay" from formal speaking, which is already taken to be a deviation from the "true language" given by writing.

Prescriptive grammar is closely linked to the curious assumption that it is necessary to teach "grammar" in schools—that is, to the assumption that the child comes to school with no knowledge of grammar. This assumption is obviously based on a very different conception of grammar from that discussed above. A five-year-old child already has a substantial grasp of most of the principles of sentence formation and interpretation. The truth of the assumption made by prescriptive grammar depends on interpreting the phrase "knowing grammar" to include the ability to discuss one's implicit linguistic knowledge, hence the teaching of concepts like the parts of speech; this interpretation of "knowing grammar" also involves knowledge of the writing system and its adequate use, and knowledge of the details of the prestigious or standard dialect.

It is important, therefore, that we do not confuse the concerns of this book with those of prescriptive grammar. When it has been said that an expression like (41) is a "well-formed English sentence" but an expression like (42) is not, it is not meant that the expression is well formed in some ideal, "standard" language:

(41) Harry wants to go
(42) * Harry wants going.

The expression in (41) is a well-formed sentence in the particular dialect being described, which is actually that of the authors. However, examples have generally been chosen which will almost certainly be valid for just about any dialect. The interest here is in the vast body of structural and syntactic principles which are common to *all* varieties of English rather than in the minor details which differentiate them. These details are what have occasioned so much argument and emotion within the framework of prescriptive grammar.

VIII. WRITING

We mentioned above that prescriptive grammar tends to view writing as the primary aspect of language, and speech, or the vocal aspect of language, as a kind of unstable deviation from writing. But this view is completely erroneous. Writing systems are without exception parasitic on language; they are attempts (often rather bad attempts) to represent certain aspects of linguistic structure, usually phonological aspects. Furthermore, writing systems are relatively new inventions, dating back only a few thousand years, compared to the much more enormous span of time which must be assumed for language. Most of the languages on earth still have no writing systems associated with them, and they exist perfectly well without writing.

It is important not to misinterpret what was just said.   We have not said that *speech* is primary; we do assert, however, that *language* is primary.   Speech, after all, is behavior or performance.   As we have seen, language is the system of knowledge which underlies this behavior. There are, however, many ways in which speech is more naturally related to language than any form of writing activity.   The vocal-auditory medium is built right into the human organism, and all normal humans can use the medium of speech for performing sentences.   But millions of humans cannot use any writing system.   Although speech is the "natural" medium for performing language, and writing is a derived or secondary technique, this fact tends to be obscured for us by the great value of writing and by the role which it plays in more complex forms of highly developed social life.

It is therefore neither by mistake nor by accident that this book has considered language as if, in effect, writing systems did not exist.   This approach recognizes that language, together with its "natural" perform-ance medium of articulate speech, is a natural consequence of the human organism.   Writing, on the other hand, is a special technique for performing the elements of language, and as such it is a clever inven-tion rather like the telephone or algebra.

IX. THE PRESENT STATE OF GRAMMATICAL STUDIES

One of the chief results of research within the framework of trans-formational grammar has been the realization that the depth, scope, complexity, and abstractness of linguistic structure have been almost always seriously underestimated.   The informality and the lack of pre-cision of most descriptions of grammar, particularly those underlying our school grammars, have produced a tendency to think of languages as much simpler and more obvious systems than they are in reality.   The usual approach in these descriptions is to pick out arbitrary example sentences and then to say various things about them or analyze them in various ways.   Such descriptions never really face the problem of determining the precise system of rules that tell one who knows the language all (and only) the facts about each example sentence.   That is, they do not deal with the problem of providing a finite grammar which generates the infinite number of sentences in a language.   But it is obviously a far simpler task to pick example sentences, even a very large number, and to say things about those particular sentences than it is to discover the exact mechanisms which generate these and all other sen-tences.   In short, traditional linguistic discussion, and school grammars in particular, do not concern themselves with the problem of construct-ing an explicit system of grammatical rules.

The approach of this book has been quite different. The attempt has been made to provide a precise and explicit account of the system of rules underlying our syntactic knowledge. But this is a very complicated task. Consequently the class of constructions dealt with is much smaller than one might have expected from the older grammars. This is not a matter of deliberate omission, but rather a result of the limitations of our explicit knowledge of the complex, abstract system of principles which forms the grammar of a human language. Within those areas covered, however, this book has provided a degree of precision and explicitness in its discussion of various sentences—a degree of precision and explicitness which traditional grammars are precluded from obtaining by their vague rules and their reliance on the reader's built-in knowledge of the language and his presumed ability to extend the comments about particular examples to an infinite number of unlisted sentences.

The ultimate goal must be to combine breadth of coverage with depth and precision of analysis. But the attainment of this goal will require the intensive research of many grammarians for a long period of time. We must recognize that language in general, and English in particular, still remain largely beyond our serious understanding despite the many years of study by generations of scholars.

This book has been an introduction to the kinds of results that can be obtained by the attempt to construct a precise, explicit grammar of a language. These results are all the more impressive when we consider the fact that they represent what has been achieved by only the very beginning of precise studies of the form and content of the grammars of human languages.

Further Reading

This bibliography is selective not comprehensive. Wherever possible we have tried to refer to published papers. Many of the unpublished ones are available through the Indiana University Linguistics Club in Bloomington, Indiana. Our selections for Chapters 18 through 29 assume some degree of sophistication on the part of the readers. These selections are also more numerous since most of the topics discussed are the more crucial ones in transformational discussion today.

Chapter 1 Language as a Scientific Subject Matter

NOAM CHOMSKY, *Aspects of the Theory of Syntax* (1965), pp. 3–9, 15–30: grammatical theory, organization, and justification.

Chapter 2 Constituent Structure

J. A. FODOR AND BEVER, T. G., "The Psychological Reality of Linguistic Segments" in L. Jakobovits and Miron, M. (eds.), *Readings in the Psychology of Language* (1967), pp. 325–332: experiment to determine whether constituent structure segments function as perceptual units.

Chapter 3 Deep Structures, Surface Structures, and Transformations

NOAM CHOMSKY, *Language and Mind* (1968), pp. 21–36: deep and surface structure, the lexicon, and the phonological component of a grammar.

Chapter 4 Transformations and Elementary Transformation Processes

NOAM CHOMSKY AND MILLER, G. A., "Introduction to the Formal Analysis of Natural Languages" in R. Luce, Bush, and Galanter (eds.), *Handbook of Mathematical Psychology*, Vol. II (1963), Section 5.2, pp. 300–306: a more technical discussion of transformational operations.

Chapter 5 Linguistic Explanation and Ordered Rules

PAUL POSTAL, "Underlying and Superficial Linguistic Structure" in J. A. Emig, Fleming, and Popp (eds.), *Language and Learning* (1966), pp. 153–175: containing among other interesting material a more detailed discussion of reflexivization.

RODERICK JACOBS, *On Transformational Grammar,* Monograph No. 1, New York State English Council (1968), pp. 45–56: discussion of a set of transformations and their explanatory role.

Chapter 6   Determining the Constituents of a Sentence

GEORGE LAKOFF AND ROSS, J. R. R., "A Criterion for Verb Phrase Constituency" in *Mathematical Linguistics and Automatic Translation,* NSF-17 (1966), Part II, pp. 1–11: a clear and interesting treatment of the problem in determining the constituent role of adverbs.

Chapter 7   Noun Phrase Constituents

PETER ROSENBAUM, *The Grammar of English Predicate Complement Constructions* (1967), pp. 9–14: Rosenbaum applies a number of tests to demonstrate that certain kinds of embedded sentences are in the noun phrase.

Chapter 8   Verb Phrase Constituents

OTTO JESPERSEN, *Essentials of English Grammar* (1964), pp. 113–119: a scholarly traditional approach to some constituents of the verb phrase.   Many of the properties of verbs discussed here have not yet been satisfactorily accounted for by transformational grammarians.

Chapter 9   Features, Lexical Items, and Deep Structures

GEORGE LAKOFF, *On the Nature of Syntactic Irregularity,* NSF-16, Computational Laboratory, Harvard University (1965), Appendix A, pp. 1–26: a more detailed analysis of the arguments for treating verbs and adjectives as members of a single lexical category differing only by a syntactic feature.

Chapter 10   Constituent Functions

NOAM CHOMSKY, *Aspects of the Theory of Syntax* (1965), pp. 63–64, 68–74: a more formal treatment of functional notions such as subject and object.

Chapter 11   Articles, Suffixes, and Segment Transformations

Chapter 12   Pronouns and Articles

PAUL M. POSTAL, "On So-called Pronouns in English" in Roderick A. Jacobs and Rosenbaum, P. S., *Readings in English Transformational Grammar* (1970), pp. 56–82: a difficult but very important analysis that underlies the one included in the present book.

Chapter 13   Verbals and Particles

F. R. PALMER, *A Linguistic Study of the English Verb* (1965), Chapter 10: covers some of the same ground as the present chapter, but from a non-transformational viewpoint.

Chapter 14   Aspect—Perfect and Progressive

NOAM CHOMSKY, *Syntactic Structures* (1957), Section 5.3, pp. 38–40: the classic transformational treatment compactly accounting for all the major restrictions on the potential make-up of the auxiliary.

Chapter 15   The Auxiliary

JOHN R. ROSS, "Auxiliaries as Main Verbs," unpublished paper, M.I.T.   Also in *Linguistic Institute Packet of Papers,* University of Illinois, Summer, 1968: this paper represents more recent developments in transformational syntax, suggesting that what is treated here as the deep structure verb phrase is in fact an embedded sentence governed by a main verb (which is in the present analysis, an auxiliary).   "On Declarative Sentences" in Jacobs and Rosenbaum, *Readings,* pp. 222–272: more general but very relevant discusssion.

Chapter 16   Agreement

G. O. CURME, "Number and Person" in *Parts of Speech and Accidence* (1935), pp. 237–239: a treatment by a traditionalist of subject-verb agreement.

Chapter 17   Prepositions

A. L. BECKER AND ARMS, D. C., "Prepositions as Predicates" in R. Binnick et al. (eds.), *Papers from the Fifth Regional Meeting of the Chicago Linguistic Society* (1969), pp. 1–11: a claim that verbs and prepositions may be surface realizations of the same abstract semantic categories.

Chapter 18   Prepositions, Indirect Objects, and the Cross-Over Principle

C. L. FILLMORE, "A Proposal Concerning English Prepositions," unpublished paper, Ohio State University (1966): this paper makes a number of extremely interesting suggestions concerning the nature and role of prepositions.   Arising in part from this, the author proposes a case-oriented framework for grammar, one that has since proven quite fruitful (see, for example, Fillmore's "The Grammar of Hitting and Breaking" in Jacobs and Rosenbaum, *Readings*).

PAUL POSTAL, *Crossover Phenomena: A Study in the Grammar of Coreference,* unpublished monograph, IBM: Yorktown Heights, New York: a brilliant but difficult analysis of some of the most puzzling aspects of syntax.

Chapter 19   Questions

J. KATZ AND POSTAL, P., *An Integrated Theory of Linguistic Descriptions* (1964), pp. 84–117: a detailed analysis explicating the Q and WH constituents.

R. LANGACKER, "An Analysis of English Questions," unpublished paper, University of California, San Diego, (1970): an important paper containing both a critical survey of previous work on interrogatives and also some useful proposals for deriving questions from conjoined embedded sentences governed by an abstract performative verb.

Chapters 20–24   Sentence Embedding

Underlying these chapters is:

PETER ROSENBAUM, *The Grammar of English Predicate Complement Constructions* (1967): there have been some extremely interesting criticisms, modifications, and counter-proposals since this book was written.   They include:

F. BOWERS, "English Complex Sentence Formation," *Journal of Linguistics,* Vol. 4, No. 1, pp. 83–88.

PAUL KIPARSKY AND KIPARSKY, C., "Fact" in *Recent Advances in Linguistics,* M. Bierwisch and Heidolph (eds.), forthcoming.

G. LAKOFF, "Deep Surface Grammar," unpublished paper, Indiana University Linguistics Club (1968), pp. 13–28.

T. LANGENDOEN, "The Syntax of the English Expletive 'it'," Georgetown University Monograph Series on Language and Linguistics, No. 19 (1966), pp. 207–216.

R. P. STOCKWELL; SCHACHTER, PAUL; AND PARTEE, BARBARA HALL, *Integration of Transformational Theories on English Syntax*, Vol. II, ESD-TR-68-419, University of California, Los Angeles (1968), pp. 530–557.

Chapter 25   Relative Clauses

S. ANNEAR, "Relative Clauses and Conjunctions," in *Working Papers in Linguistics*, Report No. 1, Ohio State University (1967): the writer presents evidence for the claim that relative clauses are derived from conjoined sentences.

E. BACH, "Nouns and Nounphrases" in Bach and Harms (eds.), *Universals in Linguistic Theory* (1967): a proposal for deriving surface nouns from relative clauses.

J. DEAN, "Determiners and Relative Clauses," unpublished paper, M.I.T. (1967).

S-Y. KURODA, "English Relativization and Certain Related Problems," *Language* 44 (1968), pp. 244–266.

P. POSTAL, "Crazy Notes on Restrictive Relatives and Other Matters," unpublished paper, I.B.M.: Yorktown Heights, N.Y. (1967).

C. SMITH, "Determiners and Relative Clauses in a Generative Grammar of English," *Language* 4 (1964), pp. 37–52.

Chapter 26   Pronouns and Case

R. JACKENDOFF, "An Interpretive Theory of Pronouns and Reflexives," Indiana University Linguistics Club (1968): an analysis within a theoretically very different transformational framework which denies the necessity of transformational apparatus to account for pronominalization.

G. LAKOFF, "Pronominalization, Negation and the Analysis of Adverbs" in Jacobs and Rosenbaum, *Readings*, pp. 145–165.

———, "Pronouns and Reference," unpublished paper, Indiana University Linguistics Club (1968).

R. LANGACKER, "Pronominalization and the Chain of Command" in D. Reibel and Schane (eds.), *Modern Studies in English* (1969).

J. McCAWLEY, "Where Do Noun Phrases Come From" in Jacobs and Rosenbaum, *Readings*.

P. POSTAL, "On So-called Pronoun in English" in Jacobs and Rosenbaum, *Readings*.

J. Ross, "On the Cyclic Nature of English Pronominalization" in *Festschrift for Roman Jakobson* (1968).

Chapter 27   Simplicity and the Search for Deep Structures

NOAM CHOMSKY, "Remarks on Nominalization" in Jacobs and Rosenbaum, *Readings*, pp. 184–221: a difficult but very important paper marking a shift from standard transformational theory to a "lexicalist" or "interpretive semantics" transformational theory with which many major transformational grammarians disagree.

B. Fraser, "Some Remarks on the Action Nominalization in English" in Jacobs and Rosenbaum, *Readings,* pp. 83–98.

A. Hale, "Conditions on English Comparative Clause Pairings" in Jacobs and Rosenbaum, *Readings,* pp. 30–55.

R. Jacobs, "Recent Developments in Transformational Grammar," *The English Record* (1969), Vol. XIX, 4.

———, "Syntax and Meaning," *The English Record* (1970), Vol. XX, 3.

R. B. Lees, *The Grammar of English Nominalizations* (1960): this is the pioneer work on the subject.

———, "On Very Deep Grammatical Structure," in Jacobs and Rosenbaum, *Readings,* pp. 134–142.

Chapter 28   The Cyclic Principle

Noam Chomsky, *Language and Mind* (1968), pp. 36–40: discussion of the cycle in both phonology and syntax.

J. Kimball, "Cyclic and Non-Cyclic Grammars," unpublished paper, M.I.T. (1968): a fairly technical, well thought out paper claiming that the cyclic principle is unnecessary.

R. Lakoff, "Deep-Surface Grammar," unpublished paper, Indiana University Linguistics Club (1968), Section 2, "The Cycle," pp. 29–53: a very skillful and detailed paper which accepts the cyclic principle as necessary.

Chapter 29   Conjunction and Non-Restrictive Clauses

R. Dougherty, "Coordinate Conjunction," unpublished paper, M.I.T. (1967).

L. Gleitman, "Coordinating Conjunctions in English," *Language* 41 (1965), pp. 260–293.

R. Lakoff and Peters, S., "Phrasal Conjunction and Symmetric Predicates" in NSF-17, Computational Laboratory, Harvard University (1966): a very useful paper.

S. Peters, "Coordinate Constructions in English," Ph.D. dissertation, M.I.T. (1968).

Index

Accusative case, 220

Action-nonaction verbals, 63

Active sentence, 23, 224

Adjectival shift transformation, *see* Adjective transformation

Adjective ⟨–V⟩, 63

Adjective transformation, 204–205, 212; applied, 207

Adjunction, 26

Adverbial clause, "time-place" test for, 210

Adverbials, past time, 121

Adverb preposing transformation, 210

Abstract auxiliary, 124

Affix segment, 83; replaced by "en," 117; replaced by "ing," 110, 117; replaced by "s," 89, 133

Affix transformation, 110; applied, 111, 112, 115, 117

Agreement, 74, 130–35, 168; without auxiliary in surface structure, 132; determined by surface subject, 75; of verbal with surface subject, 130

Agreement transformation, 104–105

Alice in Wonderland, 81n.

Ambiguity of sentences, 5–6; in nominalization, 228

Anaphoric pronoun, 218

Animateness, 59

Articles, 44; as features of nouns, 85; list of, 85

Article segment, replaced by "I," 96; replaced by "the," "which," 202; replaced by "these," 89

Article transformation, 84, 86, 95; applied, 104, 208; double application of, 201; in WH questions, 157

Artificial language, 270–72

Aspect, 108–118; perfect and progressive properties, 108

Auxiliary, 40–41, 120–28; as abstract entity, 124; in declarative and interrogative sentences, 41; in deep structure, 41, 127; domination of progressive segment, 112; interrogative transformation test for, 40; as a modal, 128; as a non-modal, 127; replaced by "does," 127; syntactic evidence for, 37; transformed from copula, 124

Auxiliary agreement transformation, 131

Auxiliary constituent, *see* Auxiliary
Auxiliary incorporation transformation, 124; applied, 131, 152–53
Auxiliary segment, 121

"Be . . . ing," 109
Braces, meaning of, 50

Case transformation, 221
Chomsky, Noam, 4, 8*n.*
Classification difficulties, v
Clause complementizer, 164, 185
Cleft sentence test, 40*n.*, 165; applied, 136, 180, 184, 192, 210; applied unsuccessfully, 185
Cleft sentence transformation, 39–40; unworkable situations for, 40
Comparative, 232–33
Competence, 268
Complementizer deletion transformation, 169
Complementizers, 164–69; list of, 164
Complementizer transformation, 164; applied, 185
Compound noun phrase, 254
Compound noun phrase tree diagram, 255
Compound sentences, 253–59
Compound verb phrase, 254
Conjunction reduction, 254
Conjunction reduction transformation, 255
Conjunction of sentences, 163, 253–59
Conjunction shift transformation, 259
Conjunctive sentences, 253–58
Constituent domination, 71
Constituents, classification of, 37; copula, 101; definition of, 11; identification of, 37; position in deep structure, 71; question, 122, 151; tests for determining types of, 37; verb particle, 103
Contraction transformation, 21, 26
Coordinate construction, 262
Copula, becoming an auxiliary, 124; "be" constituent, 101; as neither progressive nor perfect, 113
Copula segment, required by adjectives, 112
Copula transformation, 101–102, 108; applied, 111, 123, 124, 188
Cross-over principle, 147–48
Cyclic principle, 235–48

Declarative sentence, 19; auxiliary in, 41; related to yes–no question, 150
Deep structure, 17–19, 21, 225, 281; auxiliary in, 41; basic constituents in, 37
Deep structure subject, 71–72
Deep subject of the sentence, 74
Demonstrative adjectives, *see* Demonstrative articles
Definite article, 44, 86–87

Deletion, 26
Demonstrative articles, 44–45, 87; as listed in lexicon, 88
Descartes, vi, 8
Dialect, described, 284; idiosyncrasies, 168, 175; using "ones," 98
Disjunctive sentences, 253
"Does," 127
Double object constructions, 147, *see also* Indirect object

Elementary transformations, 26
Embedded sentence, 45, 49, 192–93; in noun phrases, 45, 192; in verb phrases, 55, 193
Embedded questions, 179–82; *see also* Indirect questions
English grammar, defined, 284
Extraposition, 171–77
Extraposition transformation, 151, 172–75; applied, 172, 174, 177, 243–44

Features, 60–63; *see also* Word properties; influence on word choice, 62–63
Form of a sentence, *see* Surface structure
"For . . . to" complementizer, 164

Genitive, 231–32
Gerundive complementizer, 164
Gerundive noun phrase complement, 166
Grammar, 224–25, 272–73, 278–82; components of, 279–82; current research in, 288; intuitive knowledge of, 3

"Have," in auxiliary position, 153; as verbal in deep structure, 128
Head noun, 164, 172
Head noun phrase, 203–04

Identical conjunct reduction transformation, 257
Identical phrase deletion transformation, 193–94
Identical noun phrase deletion transformation, 27, 55; applied, 166, 167, 196–97
Identical reference, 257
Identical verb phrase deletion transformation, 27, 41, 233
Identity of reference, 258
Imperative sentences, 31
Imperative transformation, 32–33
Indefinite article, 44, 85
Indirect object, 54, 143
Indirect object inversion transformation, 54, 145, 148
Indirect questions, 158, 179–82; *see also* Embedded questions
Infinitive complementizer, 164, 185, 190
Infinitive noun phrase complement, 166

"I" in noun phrases, 186–87

Intermediate structure, 21

Interrogative pronouns, confused with relative pronouns, 208–209; containing ⟨+WH⟩, 154

Interrogative sentence, 19; *see also* Question sentence auxiliary in, 41; non-embedded, embedded compared, 179–80

Interrogative transformation, 19–21, 101, 122–23, 181; affect on auxiliary in questions, 155–56; applied, 125, 127, 153; as test for auxiliary, 40; as test for noun phrase, 38

Intransitive adjective, 65

Intransitive verbal, 52

Intransitive verb phrase complement constructions, 194

Irregular verb forms, 134

"It," in deep structure, 173; distinguished from "what," "one," 153; as head noun, 174

"It" deletion transformation, 174; applied, 176

"It" replacement transformation, 184–85, 187–90, 195; applied, 236–37, 238–39

Language acquisition, vi, 28

Lees, R. B., 227*n*.

Lexical entry, elements of, 60

Lexicon, 59–62; sample entries, 61–62

Linguistic universals, v–vii, 282–84; adjunction, substitution, deletion, 28

Main sentence, 77

Manner adverbials, 228–31

Manner adverbial transformation, 229

Mass nouns, 61; *see also* Noun features

Meaning of a sentence, *see* Deep structure

Modals, 41, 120–21; in question sentences, 152; syntactic tense of, 121

Multiple embedding, 235

Negation constituent, 125; *see also* Negative

Negative (NEG), 125–26; replaced by "not," 126

Negative adjunction transformation, 126

Negative placement transformation, 125

Negation transformation, 20–21

Nominalization, 53, 225–28; analysis of, 227; as revealing prepositions, 136–37

Nominalization transformation, 226

Nominative case, 220

Nominative pronouns, 96–97

Non-restrictive clause, 259–61; compared to restrictive, 260

Non-restrictive clause transformation, 259

Non-restrictive relative clause transformation, 262

Noun constituent, missing from noun phrase complement, 172

Noun features, 60–66, 81–87, 92, 209; method of specification, 81

Noun phrase (NP), 24, 38–40; association with prepositions in deep structure, 136; compared to sentence, 226; as constituent of verb phrase, 147; containing embedded sentence, 192; containing relative clause, 47; immediately dominated by S, 71; inverted within a verb phrase, 147; moved by question transformation, 140; as object of verb phrase, 74; passive test for, 38; preposition feature of, 148; relativizing of, 49; two within verb phrase, 143

Noun phrase complement, 49, 76, 164–69; cleft sentence test for, 165; "it" in deep structure of, 173; in subject noun phrases, 184; tree diagram for, 199

Noun segment, containing ⟨+WH⟩, 153; replaced by "which," 201

Noun segment deletion transformation, 95–96

Noun suffix transformation, 83–84, 89, 133

Number, as noun feature, 82

NP, *see* Noun phrase

"One," 87; following personal pronouns, 97–98; as pronoun, 206; in Southern dialect, 98

Ordering of transformations, 105, 175; for agreement, 134

Parentheses, meaning of, 42

Particles, distinct from prepositions, 106; as features of verbs, 139

Particle movement transformation, 105–106

Particle segment, 104

Particle segment transformation, 104

Particle transformation, 139; *see also* Particle segment transformation

Passive test, 38; applied, 192

Passive transformation, 23–26, 194, 224; applied, 73, 146–47, 171, 176–77, 197; definition of, 24; as test for noun phrase, 45

Passive sentence, 23

Perfect aspect, 108; in deep structure, 118; illustrated, 118

Performance, 268

Perfect segment, replaced by "be," "have-has," 117

Perfect segment transformation, 114; applied, 123

Perfect transformation, *see* Perfect segment transformation

Personal pronouns, as articles in surface structure, 93–94; as article segment, 98; in deep structure, 93–94; as definite article, 98; distinct from nouns, 94; list of, 220; as noun segment, 98; number features of, 92; person features of, 92

Person features, 130

Phonetic representation in sentences, 275

Phonetic segment, 275

Phonology, 279–82; interpretive character of, 281

Phrase structure rules, 44–48, 52–57; for basic sentences, 57; for noun phrases, 45–46, 48, 57; recursive sequence, 46–47; for verb phrases, 53–54, 56–57

Planck, Max, 3, 8

PL constituents, 82–83

Prepositions, 53, 102, 136–41; analysis of, compared to particle analysis, 139; association with noun phrases in deep structure, 136; in deep structure, 137; different from verb particles, 102; as features on noun segments, 138–39; introduced by transformation, 141; in noun phrases, 53; origin of, 137–38; as revealed by nominalization, 136–37

Preposition deletion transformation, 54

Prepositional phrase, 140–41; moved by question transformation, 141

Preposition transformation, 144

Predicate nominative, 113

Prescriptive grammar, 286–87

Progressive aspect, 64, 108; "be . . . ing" sequence, 109; in deep structure, 118

Progressive segment, 110–12; replaced by "are," 110

Progressive segment transformation, 109; applied, 111, 123, 152–53

Progressive transformation, *see* Progressive segment transformation

Pronominalization, 208, 219–20; with identical noun phrases, 220

Pronoun deletion transformation, 182

Pronouns, 92–98, 217–22; in deep structures, 220; features of, 92–93, 154–55, 220; as indirect objects, 145; introduced by transformation, 217

Pronoun transformation, 206–207; applied, 218

Question constituent, 20, 122–24, 151; deletion of, 123

Question deletion transformations, 152–53, 181; applied, 125, 179

Questions, 150–58

Question sentence, *see also* Interrogative sentence; embedded as noun phrase complement, 182

Recursive sequence of rules, 46–47

Reflexivization, 189

Reflexive pronoun, 30, 186–89; form explained, 187

Reflexive sentences, 30–33, 84

Reflexive transformation, 31–32, 63; applied, 237

Reflexivization rule, 241

Relative clause, 199–211; as function of embedded sentence, 75; generated from deep structure, 202; genitive constructions, 231; as noun phrase, 49; in noun phrases, 47; origin of, 200; as subject noun phrase, 199–201; surface structure variation, 203; with transitive verbal, 200; tree diagram for, 199, 211

Relative clause reduction transformation, 204, 212; applied, 205

Relative clause transformation, 49, 200–202, 211

Relative pronouns, 201–209; confused with interrogative pronouns, 208–209; deletion prohibited, 204; "when," 209; "where," "which," 201–202; "who," "that," 202

Relative pronoun deletion transformation, 203–204, 211

Restrictive relative clause, 259

Rule schema for conjunction reduction, 255

S (Sentence), as relative clause, 76–77; as noun phrase complement, 76–77; as verb phrase complement, 76–77

Second lexical pass, 84, 157

Segment, 66

Segment structure rules, 66–67

Segment transformation, 84; article transformation, 86, 95; noun suffix transformation, 90

Selectional restrictions, of adverbs, adjectives, 229; nouns, 60

Semantic interpretation of sentences, 71

Semantics, 279–82; interpretive character of, 281

Sentence, 10–15, 272–78; compared to noun phrase, 226; compared to utterance, 272–74; definition of, 10; semantic representation of, 275

Sentence recursion, 163

SG constituent, 82–83

"'s . . . ing" complementizer, 164

Strongly identical constituents, 258

Substitution, 26

Substitution test, 13

Surface subject, 75–76; agreement with verbal, 130; determines agreement, 75

Surface structure, 17–19, 281; as form of communication, 18–19; role of, 17

Synonymy, 23
Synonymy of sentences, 6–7; examples, 195
Syntactic functions of S, 76–77
Syntactic structure, 279
Syntactic tense, 121
Syntax, 279–82; interpretative character of, 281; two parts of, 282

"That," as a complementizer, 164; indicating embedded sentence, 45
"There," local vs. existential interpretation, 85
Time-place deletion transformation, 209–10, 212
Time-place test, 210
Transformation, 19–33, 243–47; definition of, 23; cyclic application of, 243–47; general properties of, 26; as meaning-preserving process, 74; ordering relations, 30, 32–33
Transformational cycle, 236–48
Transformational ordering, 111
Transformations, adjective, 204–205, 212; adverb preposing, 210; affix, 110; agreement, 104–105; article, 84, 86, 95; auxiliary agreement, 131, 135; auxiliary incorporation, 124; case, 221; cleft sentence, 39; complementizer, 164; complementizer deletion, 169; conjunction reduction, 255; conjunction shift, 259; contraction, 21, 26; copula, 101–102, 108; elementary, 26; extraposition, 151, 172–75; identical conjunct reduction, 257; identical phrase deletion, 193–94; identical noun phrase deletion, 27, 55, 196–97; identical verb phrase deletion, 27, 41, 233; imperative, 32–33; indirect object inversion, 54, 145, 148; interrogative, 19–21, 101, 122–23, 181; "it" deletion, 174; "it" replacement, 184–85, 187–90, 195; manner adverbial, 229; negative adjunction, 126; negative placement, 125; negation, 20–21; nominalization, 226; non-restrictive clause, 259; non-restrictive relative clause, 262; noun segment deletion, 95–96; noun suffix, 83–84, 89, 133; particle segment, 104; particle movement, 105–106; passive, 23–26, 194, 224; perfect segment, 114; preposition, 144; preposition deletion, 54; progressive segment, 109; pronoun, 206–207; pronoun deletion, 182; question deletion, 152–53, 181; reflexive, 31–32, 63; relative clause, 49, 200–202, 211; relative clause reduction, 204, 212; relative pronoun deletion, 203–204, 211; time-place deletion, 209–10, 212; verb agreement, 135; verbal

agreement, 132; verb suffix, 133–35; WH question, 156
Transitive adjectives, 65
Transitive verbals, 200
Transitive verb phrase complement construction, 194, 196
Tree diagram for major sentence constituents, 44
Tree-pruning, 205
Triangle, meaning of, 75

Verb $\langle +V \rangle$, 63; as feature of verbal, 63
Verb affix, 133
Verb agreement transformation, 135
Verbal agreement transformation, 132; prevented by complementizers, 168
Verbal constituent (VB), 48, 52
Verbal features, 109–117
Verbals, action-nonaction, 63–64; agreement with surface subject, 130; dependent on noun features, 139; features of, 108–118; lexical entries for, 64–65
Verbal segment, replaced by "paint," 117; replaced by "study," 110
Verbal selection process, imposed by pronouns, 93
Verb features, 102–103, 139
Verb particles, 102–103; constituents in deep structure, 103
Verb phrase (VP), 27, 41–42; embedded sentences in, 55, 193; with surface structure variation, 100; syntactic evidence for, 37; with two noun phrases, 143
Verb phrase complement, 192–98; immediate domination by verb phrase, 193; transformations required, 197; tree diagram for, 199
Verb suffix transformation, 133–35
VP, *see* Verb phrase

Weakly identical constituents, 258
Weak pronominalization, 219
"When," as relative pronoun, 209
"Where," as relative pronoun, 209
"Which," as relative pronoun, 201
"Who," as replacement for WH segment, 181
WH question, 150; embedded as noun phrase complement, 181–82
WH question transformation, 156; applied, 179, 181
Writing, 287–88
Word properties, 59; *see also* Features

Yes-no questions, 150
"You" understood, 31–33